Second and Foreign Language Learning Through Classroom Interaction

Second and Foreign Language Learning Through Classroom Interaction

Edited by

Joan Kelly Hall

and

Lorrie Stoops Verplaetse

2000

LAWRENCE ERLBAUM ASSOCIATES, PUBLISHERS
Mahwah, New Jersey   London

Lawrence Erlbaum Associates, Inc., Publishers
10 Industrial Avenue
Mahwah, NJ 07430

Cover design by Kathryn Houghtaling Lacey

Library of Congress Cataloging-in-Publication Data

Second and foreign language through classroom interaction /
edited by Joan Kelly Hall and Lorrie Stoops Verplaetse.
        p. cm.

Includes bibliographical references and index.
ISBN 0-8058-3513-X (cloth : alk. paper)
ISBN 0-8058-3514-8 (pbk. : alk. paper)
1. Language and languages—Study and teaching.
    2. Interaction analysis in education.   I. Hall, Joan Kelly.
    II. Verplaetse, Lorrie Stoops.
P53.447 .D48   2000
418'.0071—dc21   99-087596
                                                        CIP

Books published by Lawrence Erlbaum Associates are printed
on acid-free paper, and their bindings are chosen for strength
and durability.

Printed in the United States of America
10 9 8 7 6 5 4 3

Contents

Preface

This collection of studies is born out of a number of discussions conducted by the editors and several of the chapter contributors during the 1997 meeting of the American Association of Applied Linguistics (AAAL) in Orlando, Florida and the Annual Roundtable Meeting on Sociocultural Theory and Second Language Acquisition (SLA) held the same year in Las Vegas, Nevada. During those discussions we recognized the abundance of studies focusing on the importance of interaction to second-language acquisition and the growing number of studies that defined particular language teacher behaviors, particularly studies that identified behaviors that were prohibitive to student interaction. Missing, however, was a breadth of studies that provided positive models of teachers' language behavior, behavior that supported and even promoted student interaction. Also missing was a body of research that demonstrated empirically a relation between learner interaction and development of a particular aspect of second or foreign language.

In these same conversations we increasingly found ourselves in the company of SLA researchers who were looking to sociocultural theory as a framework to explain and to explore aspects of additional language development. Again, missing from the literature at that point was a collection of studies that analyzed positive models of classroom interaction in second- and foreign-language classrooms from a sociocultural perspective.

In response to the aforementioned needs we developed a colloquium for the 1998 AAAL conference in Seattle, Washington, entitled: *The construction of learning through interactive practices in classrooms with linguistically diverse students*. The colloquium, which included three papers later developed into chapters for this collection, those by Boyd and Maloof (chap. 8), McCormick and Donato (chap. 9), and Verplaetse (chap. 11), became the cornerstone for this volume. The additional chapters were solicited from colleagues who were engaged in related research on classroom interaction and additional language learning.

Acknowledgments

Having completed our work, we would like to extend an invitation to the readers of this collection. Through our own experiences in the collaborative construction of this book we have confirmed that meaningful learning does indeed come from interaction. Therefore, we invite you to use the topics taken up in the various chapters of this book to initiate discussions—discussions with the editors, the chapter authors, and among each other. It is our hope that these studies, the myriad conversations they generate, and subsequent research on interaction and additional language learning engendered from the findings presented here will lead us to deeper understanding of the intrinsic links between the discursive environments we create in our second and foreign language classrooms and the developmental consequences they give rise to. Such understanding can only help us continue to shape our classroom interactional practices in ways that foster the development of effectual communities of additional language learners and users.

The ongoing development of this collection has been a perfect example of socially constructed knowledge. So many people have been involved in its creation, and we are indebted to each and every one. We would like to acknowledge and thank, first of all, the chapter contributors, not only for their valued contribution, but for the timely, detailed manner in which they collaborated with us. Second, this collection would not exist if it were not for the teachers who allowed us in their classrooms for the purpose of research. It takes a courageous person to open up his or her classroom to the scrutiny of research; we are deeply indebted to each. Thanks also go to Carol A. Klee and Mary Schmida whose responses to the initial draft of the volume helped us more clearly articulate its direction. Finally, we thank Lori Hawver,

April Montana, and Naomi Silverman from Lawrence Erlbaum Associates for their time and expertise in helping us complete this book.

In addition, we each have our own collection of folks to whom we are grateful. From Lorrie: I have listed specific acknowledgments at the end of my chapter. But at this time, I would like to especially thank Salisbury State University's Kathleen Schafer for the many hours she provided helping me format and edit manuscripts. Also, I wish to thank Bob and Marilyn Stoops, who gave me, at an early age, a deep respect for learning and the discipline required to work through a task as arduous as this, and my son, Christopher Verplaetse, who has supported this work in so many ways from patiently accepting my emotional distance when I found myself wrapped up in writing to engaging in critical discussions with regards to the research findings. Finally, I wish to express gratitude for their inspiration to Mr. Phil Laesch, my high school Latin teacher, and to "Granny" Hana Grebler, sole English teacher to two generations of Czech villagers, both of whom understood the importance of and practiced interactive language learning long before it was fashionable to do so.

From Joan: I am fortunate to have had many colleagues and graduate students over these last several years whose enjoyment in trying continually to raise the intellectual ante of our conversations has nourished mine. They ask provocative questions, examine complicated issues, and in their activities, are willing to cross disciplinary borders and explore other theoretical territories in search of deeper understandings of that which seems so familiar. Interest in and the energy needed to complete this project are a direct outgrowth of these conversations. To all of them, I am deeply grateful. To my family, Bill, Kate, and Kelly, I extend heartfelt thanks for being the main inspiration in my life. Their unflagging support for this project, no matter how tedious it—and I—have been sometimes, coupled with their keen sense of humor have helped to keep me focused on what is most important.

1

Second and Foreign Language Learning Through Classroom Interaction

Joan Kelly Hall
Lorrie Stoops Verplaetse

In the field of second language acquisition (SLA), interaction has long been considered important in language learning. However, much of this research has been based on a traditional psycholinguistic perspective of language and learning. In this view, language is assumed to be a discrete set of linguistic systems external to the learner, whereas learning is viewed as the process of assimilating the structural components of these systems into preexisting mental structures. Although the specific goals of research carried out from this perspective may vary from finding the most effective way of facilitating the assimilation of new systemic knowledge to discovering and constructing the ideal linguistic system, it is generally agreed that language learning and language use are two distinct phenomena (Firth & Wagner, 1997, 1998; Gass, 1998; Hall, 1993, 1995, 1997).

By and large, the authors of the studies presented in this volume on classroom interaction and language learning began their explorations into second and foreign language learning from this more traditional perspective. However, in the investigations they report on here, they cross disciplinary borders and draw on theoretical insights and empirical evidence found in areas outside of what has generally been considered the main purview of the SLA field. Their findings join our interests in reconceptualizing second and foreign language learning using a broader, sociocultu-

1

ral perspective of language and learning with practical concerns for nurturing classroom communities of successful second and foreign language learners. In addition to helping build a foundation for the development of a more comprehensive model of second and foreign language learning, we believe that what we learn from these studies will help us in the creation of a set of principles for identifying and sustaining classroom interactional practices that foster additional language development. In what follows, we first provide a brief review of the findings on interaction and additional language learning that have emerged from the more traditional strands of research in SLA and discuss the assumptions about language and learning on which these studies are based. We then provide an overview of the theoretical assumptions on language and learning on which the studies presented here are based. Concluding the chapter is an overview of each of the 12 studies comprising the volume.

INTERACTION AND SLA: AN HISTORICAL PERSPECTIVE

Interaction as an Outgrowth of Foreigner Talk Literature

Research on interaction and second language learning grew out of early studies on foreigner talk (FT). Once it was determined that native speakers do indeed modify their input when talking with non-native speakers (NNSs; Ferguson, 1975) in a manner similar to the way caretakers alter their talk to babies (BT), the FT research expanded from simply describing the linguistic features of FT to exploring FT's role in interaction. Given the achievement differences between first and second languages, Freed (1980) sought to determine the differences between BT and FT and found that although both were syntactically similar, they differed functionally. The primary function of FT was to convey information, whereas the function of BT was to elicit interaction.

Shortly thereafter, Long's (1981) study of modifications in native speaker (NS) input to NNSs made a distinction between linguistic modifications and interactive modifications, claiming that the interactive modifications were facilitative and necessary for second language acquisition. In this study, he credited the NS input with the following interactive modifications "presumably intended to facilitate comprehension and participation by the NNS" (p. 263):

1. Topics are treated simply and briefly as compared to NS talk to NSs (NT).
2. Topics are dropped unexpectedly and shifted to accommodate miscommunications by the NNS.
3. Topics initiated in FT are signaled by additional stress, left dislocation, intrasentential pauses, question forms as topic initiators, and frames (i.e., "ok," "well").

Long (1981) further credited FT with the following techniques "to sustain conversation and to lighten other aspects of the NNS's interactional burden" (p. 264):

1. NSs engage in cooperative dialogue by supplying information to the NNS's utterances to help the latter express an idea.
2. NSs answer their own questions and ask rhetorical questions.
3. NSs frequently use an interrogative style, thereby requiring answers and, hence, sustaining the conversation.
4. NSs use many and frequent clarification devices to avoid conversation problems and to repair miscommunications.

Long (1981) claimed that these modifications are necessary and facilitative to SLA, arguing that "current knowledge suggests they [the interactive modifications] are found in all cases of the successful acquisition of a full version of SL" (p. 275). His claim was supported by other studies (Arthur, Weiner, Culver, Lee, & Thomas, 1980; Hatch, 1983).

Although Long's arguments are convincing, he made no distinction between different aspects of SLA that may be differentially affected by these modifications. Nor did he account for the fact that such FT modifications are also present in cases of unsuccessful SLA; that is, these modifications are found in nearly all cases of NS interactions with beginning NNSs. Moreover, although such modifications may well be necessary for comprehension and hence facilitative in early stages of SLA, and although they may be intended to facilitate participation by the NNS, their full impact on the NNS's opportunities for interaction has not been satisfactorily analyzed. In fact, in a recent study, Verplaetse (1993) found NS modifications to have patently detrimental effects on NNS participation in conversations, thus challenging the general premise that NS modifications are primarily beneficial to NNSs. She suggested that at some developmental point in the second language learner's acquisition process, certain

NS modifications become a hindrance to the NNS's opportunities for production.

Importance of NNS's Role in Interaction

A second group of SLA researchers followed this interest in interaction and second language learning, focusing on the importance of the NNS's role in interaction. Research such as that by Scarcella and Higa (1982), Gass and Varonis (1985), Pica, Doughty, and Young (1986), and Pica (1988) echoed the importance of interaction in SLA, focusing in particular on the NNS's role in the negotiation of meaning. These studies acknowledged that comprehensible input is necessary for SLA, but they claimed that it is the NNS's work in the negotiation of meaning that increases and ensures that the input is maximally comprehensible. Thus the NNS's role in the process of negotiating meaning became crucial to the acquisition process.

Importance of Output in Interaction

In the early to mid-1980s the research on interaction had been focused primarily on the learner's input. Beginning in the mid-1980s, however, investigatory concerns were enlarged to include the importance of the learner's output in interaction. According to Swain (1985), output provided three functions: noticing, hypothesis testing, and reflection. During the time that a learner is required to process input only, he or she may not need to attend to all features of language to comprehend the content. However, at the point when he or she must produce output, the learner may first notice that a gap of linguistic knowledge exists between what he or she wants to convey and his or her ability to convey it. When the learner attempts production, using what linguistic knowledge is currently available in his or her interlanguage, the learner tests out hypotheses about the organization of the language system. Finally, through the learner's output and the interlocutor's response to that output, the learner can reflect on and ultimately modify his or her language use. In a more recent study, Swain (1995) provided empirical evidence to support her claim concerning the role of output in SLA.

Role of Interaction in the Classroom Event. Because so much of language learning occurs in the classroom, SLA researchers have also focused on the role of interaction in the classroom event. One primary concern has been with the role that teacher talk plays in SLA. Krashen's (1980, 1989) theoretical work on comprehensible input has perhaps given most attention to this talk. According to Krashen, meaningful teacher talk is central to the process of language learning. Although in his own work Krashen provided little empirical evidence for this claim, it motivated much interest among others.[1] For example, there has been quite a bit of work attempting to define the features of teacher talk considered crucial to its role in making the message comprehensible. These investigations have included the examination of such features as the degree of syntactic complexity, the rate of speech, and the length of utterance. Discourse features of teacher talk such as feedback, error correction, and use of questions have also been examined for the roles they play in making talk comprehensible.[2] Because second language learning also occurs in the content classroom, additional studies have described and compared the nature of teacher talk to native speaking and NNS students in content classrooms (Early, 1985; Green, 1992; Schinke-Llano, 1983; Slaughter & Bennett, 1982; Verplaetse, 1998).

In a related direction, there has been interest in investigating input enhancement and form-focused instructional talk. Of specific concern has been the examination of the roles these special genres of teacher talk play in the raising of students' consciousness about the syntactic aspects of the target language and their subsequent learning of these forms. In a summary of this research, Schmidt (1994) concluded that such teacher talk helps to explicitly focus the learners' attention on the syntactic forms in question, and thus facilitates their development of the knowledge and use of these forms in the second or foreign language.

Finally, there has been research concerned with the description of task conditions from which negotiated speech—morphosyntactically simplified speech that has been claimed to facilitate second language acquisition—emerges (Crookes & Gass, 1993a, 1993b).[3] The data category of interest here is talk produced between NS–NNS and NNS–NNS pairs in particular classroom activities, which is examined for indications of speech modifications such as clarification requests and comprehension checks. For the most part, the interest has been in examining the conditions influencing the emergence of such speech, such as one-way versus two-way information flow, and collaborative versus competitive goals, and

[1]See Braidi (1995) for a review of research on input and SLA.
[2]See Chaudron (1988) for a review of the research on features and roles of teacher talk.
[3]See Pica (1994) for a review of this research.

less so in the impact such negotiation has had on second language learning in general.

To summarize, over the last 20 years or so, the role of interaction in second language learning has been examined from different angles, moving from early FT studies to the study of the role of the NNS in interaction and on to the study of teacher- and task-based talk in the foreign and second language classroom. Although these studies on interaction and SLA have taken somewhat different routes in investigating language development, most share some fundamental assumptions about the nature of language and learning that differ from those on which the studies in this volume are based. Perhaps most striking is the way that additional language learning has been operationalized: as distinct increases in the comprehension or use of correct grammar. There has been little consideration of other areas considered essential to competent language use such as discourse or sociolinguistic competence. Likewise, although there has been some acknowledgment of the socially constructed nature of language learning, few studies have been placed in the larger social context of real communicative interaction.

Voicing some concern with this narrow construction of language and learning, researchers in the field of SLA have begun to look into other fields for theoretical and methodological insights into language and the process of language learning that might help them conceptualize a broader and at the same time more detailed understanding of additional language learning (Block, 1996; Firth & Wagner, 1997, 1998; Hall, 1995, 1997; Lantolf, 1995; Lantolf & Appel, 1994). Although the studies presented in this volume vary in terms of the specific bodies of knowledge they draw on to generate their research questions, they share several assumptions about the sociocultural nature of language and learning. We outline some of these premises in the next section.

SOCIOCULTURAL PRINCIPLES OF LANGUAGE AND LEARNING

A sociocultural perspective of language and learning is based on theoretical speculations and empirical investigations on the nature and development of psychological character that have taken place in the United States over the last few decades from a variety of disciplines. Findings from a wide range of studies on first language acquisition, for example, provide strong evidence of an intrinsic link between language activities and language development (e.g., Allen & Shatz, 1983; Berman & Slobin, 1994;

Hopper & Thompson, 1993; Levy & Nelson, 1994; Ninio & Snow, 1996; Ochs, 1988; Pine, 1994a, 1994b; Shatz & McCloskey, 1984; Snow, 1989; Snow, Cancino, de Temple, & Schley, 1991; Tomasello, Conti-Ramsden, & Ewert, 1990). Findings from this research have revealed that the source of children's language development is located in their speech and other significant sociocultural activities. More specifically, it has been shown that the language they learn depends on their repeated participation in these activities with other more competent participants. Over time, and with help from more expert participants, the novice participants develop expectations about the communicative value of the linguistic resources constituting these activities and, in doing so, create prototypes for action. These prototypes become the building blocks on which the children's subsequent communicative development is based. With time and experience they learn to anticipate a variety of linguistic actions and to choose the appropriate elements needed in the formulation of a response. The different constellations of linguistic resources comprising their speech activities and the various means by which children appropriate them form differently configured language learning conditions, which, in turn, give rise to distinct developmental outcomes.

Findings from research in cultural psychology also provide evidence that our development is intimately tied to the activities in which we engage (e.g., Bronfenbrenner, 1993; Fischer, Bullock, Rotenberg, & Raya, 1993; Light & Butterworth, 1993; Lucariello & Nelson, 1987; Resnick, Levine, & Teasley, 1991; Rogoff & Lave, 1984). The findings show that our cognitive development is shaped through extensive and varied practice and experience in activities that display regular patterns of resources. It is suggested that the conventionality and frequency of use of these resources increase the likelihood that what is significant in the activities will be noticed. The building of context-specific patterns of expectations allows us to recognize problem patterns and respond to them with practiced solution procedures. This, in turn, increases our chances of controlling and learning the skills needed for competent engagement (D'Andrade, 1992; Stone & Forman, 1988).

Based on these findings, it has been argued that such psychological processes as thinking and memory originate in and are fundamentally shaped by the varied arrangements of our activities' resources (Flavell, Miller, & Miller, 1993). They are defined then, not in terms of inherent formal properties, but in terms of clusters of context-sensitive principles that are linked to and thus constrained by particular groupings of pragmatically important goals and relations to these goals (Girotto & Light,

1993; Roux & Gilly, 1993). These constellations form the base of our reasoning processes and we approach and work our way through tasks with them. That is, we use them both as tools to think about what we and others are doing in an activity and as building blocks for the development of more complex and creative behavior (D'Andrade, 1992; Flavell et al., 1993).

Existing alongside this multidisciplinary research is a body of theoretical work, the major tenets of which form an explanatory web for many of these findings. Vygotsky's (1978, 1981, 1986) theory of learning, first proposed more than 50 years ago, is probably the most well known. One of his major contributions was to link both the nature and development of psychological character to its sociohistorically formed environments. More recent theoretical formulations on the substance of knowledge and its development have built on, and in some cases modified and extended this earlier work (e.g., A. A. Leontiev, 1981; A. N. Leontiev, 1981; Tulviste, 1991; Wertsch, 1991, 1994; Wertsch & Tulviste, 1992).

Several premises of this perspective are of special significance to second and foreign language learning. The first has to do with development. According to this perspective, the individual mind is created in the pursuit of action in our material and social worlds. Constituting these worlds is a varied mix of goal-directed intellectual and practical activities. Through our repeated and extended engagement in these activities with others who are more knowledgeable or expert, we transform the specific means for realizing these activities into individual abilities. It is the eventual self-regulation of the specific means for realizing our activities that characterizes psychological growth.

In this perspective, learning and development are linked. As A. A. Leontiev (1981) noted, the inherited biological characteristics of language constitute only the necessary preconditions for the capacity and ability to learn. The fundamental core of what gets learned and the shape it takes are defined by the environment, constituted by the myriad activities available to us and our particular ways of participating in them. These dynamic environments shape at the same time both the conditions for and the consequences of our individual development. Key components of this process include the specific contexts of human action and the particular opportunities provided to or created by novice participants to use the means and to develop relationships with the more expert participants in these contexts.

A second important premise has to do with the means by which involvement in our learning environments is realized. According to this perspective, our participation and subsequent development are mediated by the symbolic tools and resources constitutive of these environments (Wertsch, 1991, 1994; Wertsch & Bivens, 1992). These tools and resources with which we both internalize and (re)create cultural values include communicative, computational, and other meaning-making resources. The ways in which we use these tools to realize our activities with others do not simply enhance our individual development. Rather, they fundamentally shape and transform it. In activities that are realized primarily through interpersonal interactions, the communicative means we use together with others to engage in them provide the most extensive tools for developing shared attention, working with others, and intervening in our own mental processes (Smagorinsky & Coppock, 1994). The specific means used in these interactions define both the content and direction of our individually formed communicative competence (A. N. Leontiev, 1981). In this perspective then language plays multiple roles. It is the means by which our history is generalized and handed down, a condition for our individual appropriation of our experiences, the means by which we pursue our goals in our experiences, and its form of existence in our consciousness (A. N. Leontiev, 1981).

A third premise has to do with how we undertake the investigation of learning. According to this perspective, the study of individual development is the study of the processes by which mind and external worlds are linked. It begins with the analysis of the concrete historical conditions surrounding the individual and entails the study of the actual processes of interaction between individuals and their learning environments to understand the specific changes that occur, the conditions that bring about these changes, and the developmental consequences that result (A. N. Leontiev, 1981; Wertsch, 1994).

The Role of Classroom Discourse

From this perspective on language and learning, classrooms—and more particularly the activities comprising classrooms—are considered important sites of development. Because many classroom activities are created through classroom discourse—the oral interaction that occurs between teachers and students and among students—its role is especially consequential to the creation of learning environments and ultimately to the shaping of individual learners' development.

Substantial research on activities created through classroom discourse in first language classrooms links student involvement in them to their communicative and conceptual development (Baker, 1992; Bowers &

Flinders, 1990; Cazden, 1988; Eder, 1982; Gutierrez, 1994, 1995; Smagorin-sky & Fly, 1993; Wells, 1993, 1996). Findings from this research reveal that differences in interactional activities across classrooms and within the same classroom and same activities in terms of the learning opportunities made available to individual students are consequential to individual development. Because teachers are considered to be the experts in their classrooms, their role in structuring and managing these intellectual and practical contexts in which the students learn has been shown to be espe-cially consequential. Through their communicative actions in their interac-tional activities, teachers shape the learners' developmental paths in the following ways. First, they make salient to the learners certain properties of the world constituted within their classrooms, providing models of what they consider appropriate communicative actions and ways to go about acquiring those actions as they do. Second, they mediate both the quantity and quality of opportunities the students will have to participate in and learn from the activities. In doing so, they make visible their own attitudes toward the activities and toward the students' involvement in them. This, in turn, shapes the degree of individual learning that will occur. Third, in and through their interactions with learners, teachers make apparent the stan-dards against which students' performances are measured.

Given the significant role of classroom discourse in learning, and given that oral communication is both the medium of learning and an object of pedagogical attention in the second and foreign language classrooms, the role of classroom discourse in additional language learning is especially important. It is in their interactions with each other that teachers and stu-dents work together to create the intellectual and practical activities that shape both the form and content of the target language as well as the processes and outcomes of individual development. Given this signifi-cance, if our aim is to facilitate learners' development in the target lan-guage in our classroom activities, the question becomes: What practices constituted in our classroom discourse engender such development? It is this question that the studies presented here address.

OVERVIEW OF THIS VOLUME

This edited collection presents 12 studies that describe in microanalytic detail particular activities constructed in the interaction of a variety of classroom contexts ranging from primary grades to university levels, and in a variety of languages, including English, French, Japanese, German, Hebrew, and Dutch, that promote the learning of an additional language. In addition to focusing on a variety of language learning settings and a variety of target languages, the studies are distinguished in three ways. First, consonant with a sociocultural perspective on learning, these studies assume that language learning is not a strictly individual, cognitive act, equivalent across learners and situations. Rather, it is presumed to be a fundamentally social enterprise, jointly constructed and intrinsically linked to learners' repeated and regular participation in their classroom activities. Because development is tied to learners' participation in their classroom activities, and because these activities are realized primarily through classroom interaction, the focus of learning in these studies is on the interactional environments in which learners are involved. Also of interest are the kinds of assistance that are provided to the learners in using and interpreting the uses of the linguistic and other resources constituting the interactional activities, and their individual responses to their involvement.

A second distinguishing feature has to do with the objects of investigation. Rather than viewing language as discrete grammar points, as has been the case in much traditional work on SLA, these studies assume language to be fundamentally communicative, defined by and organized around the linguistic means used by individuals to engage in activities particular to their sociocultural worlds. Considered to be inherent aspects of the discursive environments created in classroom interaction, the objects of investigation include such skills and knowledge as interactional patterns of academic discourse, topical content and lexical meanings, linguistic resources for building solidarity among peers and sustaining the affective dimensions of learning, and particular strategies by which students can regulate their own learning and provide assistance in learning to their peers. The authors argue that these resources are essential to learners' development both as learners and users of the target language and thus must be given both theoretical and empirical attention in the study of additional language development.

A third distinguishing feature is methodological. Because language learning is assumed to be situated within, indeed shaped by, sociohistorically framed and locally defined interactional contexts, these investigations do not rely on traditional experimental methods for collecting and analyzing data. Rather they involve primarily the use of ethnographic and discourse analytic methods. All the studies entail careful observation of the contexts of language learning and rely on audiotaped or videotaped data collected from actual classroom contexts as well as field notes compiled during the tapings as the primary source of data. Thus, these analyses are firmly grounded in the actual processes of interaction occurring between individuals and their particular learning environments.

The volume is divided into two parts. Part I contains six chapters documenting foreign language learning as it occurs in language classrooms. Part II also contains six chapters. Here, however, the focus of the research is on second language learning as it occurs in both content classrooms, where the second language learners' needs to interact in the new language are immediate and consequential, and language classrooms. The decision for this distinction was based on the following considerations. Although second and foreign language development share considerable procedural similarities, they differ in two main aspects: (a) the amount of exposure to input and opportunities for output, and (b) the learner's probable motivation to engage in the additional language learning event. Exposure to and opportunities for target language interaction are restricted most often to the classroom in the foreign language learning event. The second language learner, however, may be immersed in the target language and culture, and thus be provided greater opportunities for using the target language. Regarding motivation, the foreign language learner's interest may range from the minimal need to meet a course requirement to the sincere desire to become fluent in the foreign language. However, the foreign language learner's motivation does not include the immediacy or the survival nature of that of the second language learner. For the second language learner, the need for language learning occurs not only in the safe confines of the language classroom, but in every life situation that brings the learner into a social interaction in the target culture. Because of these differences, and because this collection of studies focuses on the role of interaction in different classroom settings, we decided to group them accordingly.

Part I

In chapter 2, Kinginger examines how involvement with French peers via computer-mediated communication encourages university learners of French to appropriate a particular form of the language, the use of the *tu* form, for the expression of solidarity. She takes a developmental approach in the investigation, documenting the relation between the learners' understandings of the social meanings of this language form and the qualities of assisted performance and consciousness raising provided by native-speaking peers in e-mail and video-conference exchanges. She concludes that it is not the technology itself that is beneficial to learners. Rather, it is the social context in which participants seek to establish interpersonal relationships with others who interest them that facilitates the learners' development of everyday communicative skills and abilities.

Ohta (chap. 3) also examines the learning processes of university language learners, who, in this case, are learning Japanese. Her focus is on the processes by which individual learners appropriate the classroom interaction as a tool of thought. Looking at private speech data (i.e., learners' self-addressed utterances), Ohta shows that learners are indeed actively pursuing learning even when they are not the direct focus of the teacher's interactional attention. By repeating or recasting utterances heard in the interaction between the teacher and other students, individual learners are able to create their own learning opportunities. Such opportunities, she argues, are as consequential to the language development of these learners as more direct, teacher-fronted opportunities are.

Sullivan (chap. 4) focuses on creating and sustaining contexts of language learning in interpersonal relationships. Her data come from a university-level English as a foreign language (EFL) classroom in Vietnam. The focus is on the discourse of one teacher as he incorporates storytelling and wordplay into his teaching. She argues that these play performances fully engage the classroom members in such a way as to challenge them to broaden their vocabulary and their ways of thinking about the meanings of words in interaction. In addition, through the performances, class members make their perspectives known, show support for each other, and in other ways help to sustain their interpersonal relationships. From this perspective, Sullivan argues, these playful excursions serve as preparation for conversation outside the classroom as they represent "real life" and thus are important components of the language learning process.

Consolo's focus (chap. 5) is also on an EFL classroom. The larger context is Brazil. In a study of private language schools and university EFL classrooms serving students aged 13 to 44, Consolo analyzes the talk of nine EFL teachers to determine if NSs and NNSs differ in their ability to generate student classroom talk. He finds in his quantitative analysis that there is little significant difference, and suggests that the lack of difference may be due to the similar patterns of classroom discourse that are practiced by each of the teachers and driven by the textbooks. He did find, however, a trend in two of the NNS teachers' classes for greater teacher–student interaction and more student contributions. Through a qualitative analysis, Consolo explores the nature of these two teachers' talk to determine just what makes these two teachers' classrooms more interactive.

In chapter 6, Duff presents data from three contexts, a high school EFL content-based classroom in Hungary, and two university foreign language classrooms—one studying German and another Hebrew—in the United States. The focus of this chapter is on the presentation of a broader, more socially contextualized perspective on the role of repetition in foreign language learning. In her analysis Duff focuses on the types of constructions that are repeated, by whom, and in what contexts. She also examines the implications of the repeated language forms for learning, for effecting solidarity among the members of the class, and for helping them to construct knowledge together through their use of a foreign language. She concludes by arguing for the need for teachers and researchers to continue to examine closely the multiple roles, characteristics, and consequences of repetition in foreign language classroom discourse.

Like the study by Ohta, the study by Takahashi, Austin, and Morimoto (chap. 7) is concerned with the learning of Japanese as a foreign language. The context for their study, however, is an elementary classroom and their focus is on the development of young learners' abilities as language learners. Using data collected at three points during a 2.5-year period, they show that as the students progress in their learning, they become more active in their own learning and more adept at providing mutual assistance. The findings exemplify how instructional conversations are eventually internalized by the students and used by them in creative ways to regulate their own learning and each other's learning.

Part II

The studies in Part II examine classroom interaction and second language learning. The first three chapters focus on university-level English as a second language (ESL) classrooms. Boyd and Maloof, in chapter 8, examine language learning in a college-level English language and culture course, asking what types of intertextual links are proposed by the students and how the teacher builds on those links. Through the microanalysis of one 90-minute class, they find that student-proposed intertextual links are acknowledged through the teacher roles of affirmer, questioner, and clarifier. In these roles, the teacher incorporates the student-proposed intertextual links in her discourse, thereby transforming them into teaching tools.

In chapter 9, McCormick and Donato study a semester-long integrated skills ESL class, examining the scaffolding functions of the ESL teacher's questions and exploring the relation between the teacher's use of questions to scaffold language learning and her expressed goals for student comprehension, comprehensibility, and participation. This investigation of the function of teacher questions enables us to better understand how questions operate as tools during coconstruction of language learning within the context of teacher–student interaction. Pedagogical implications include the need to underscore to teachers the important role goals play in teaching. A second implication is to take a closer look at the characteristics of effective questions, specifically to consider the qualities of an effective question as it relates to the goal of action.

In chapter 10 Boxer and Cortés-Conde look at two university ESL content-based classrooms taught by two different instructors, exploring the issues of classroom identity, the development of relational identities, and the forming of community within the classroom. Although both teachers described their role as facilitator, and both expressed the goal to generate community within the classroom, one of the two was considerably more successful in promoting student interaction and student relational identity. For both teachers, however, Boxer and Cortés-Conde highlight moments where the teacher talk lends itself to greater student interaction. At these moments, the teachers often fostered group discussions by asking students about their own cultural norms. When teachers took on the role of information brokers, students resumed the role of passive learners. The authors argue that open dialogue is crucial to fostering pragmatic and sociocultural competence, and that teachers can create this open dialogue and a place of comfort and still encourage pragmatic awareness.

The final three chapters of this section investigate second language learning in content-based courses. Verplaetse (chap. 11) describes the interaction patterns of one highly dialogic middle school science teacher in the United States. Using both quantitative and qualitative data, she illustrates the effectiveness of two particular patterns in encouraging interaction for all students: the "wondering aloud" of cognitively rich questions about the topic and his use of paraphrase in the feedback move of the Initiation-Response-Feedback (I-R-F) sequence. Such wonderings, she argues, model academic questions for students to hear and subsequently appropriate for their own uses. Likewise, the paraphrasing provides nonjudgmental acceptance of students' utterances at the same time that it makes them public and available to others to consider and expand on. In addition to these patterns, she found that the teacher used two interactive strategies specifically to facilitate the participation of the English language learners in the classroom interaction. Verplaetse concludes that the patterns used by this teacher provide students with ample opportunities to hear and practice extended academic discourse.

Damhuis (chap. 12) reports on a teacher training project underway in the Netherlands for early elementary students learning Dutch as a second language and immersed in mainstream content classrooms. One goal of the project, entitled "Small Circle With Teacher," is to create opportunities for linguistic minority children to engage in rich interaction at high cognitive levels. During the small circle events, the teacher changes her role from the traditional knowledge source to coach; her task is to sustain thought process-es through specific types of questioning, by accepting all ideas and contri-butions from the children as valuable, and by following the student's train of thought rather than imposing the adult, knowledgeable view. This prelimi-nary study analyzes the talk of the children in the small groups aged 4 and 5 and finds that even at this early age, youngsters are capable of extended talk and talk that exhibits high cognitive levels of thinking in the target language.

Hajer (chap. 13) also studies the talk of mainstreamed linguistic minority students in the Netherlands, learning Dutch as a second language. However, this time the students are at the middle school level. Hajer looks at the same group of students as they move from one subject to another, taught by dif-ferent teachers, and analyzes the language of the teachers to determine what kinds of teacher talk promote greater interaction. A quantitative analysis finds the geography teacher and biology teacher to be the most interactive and further determines that during seated work the students have more inter-action opportunities than during teacher-fronted times of explaining infor-mation or going over seated work. It is also during seated work that students produced the most intense interactions; that is, those interactions containing the greatest number of moves. Hajer further reveals important links between the cognitive levels of discussion and the interactive climate of the discus-sions, thus encouraging classroom teachers to place cognitive and linguistic demands on their linguistic minority students. Finally, Hajer proposes that content teachers' linguistic behavior might be considered along a continuum ranging from academic language avoiding to language sensitive.

Finally, Hall, in chapter 14, provides a synthesis of the findings from each of the studies and in doing so, attempts to lay out a set of implica-tions for identifying and sustaining classroom interactional practices that foster additional language development. The chapter concludes with a dis-cussion of the theoretical and practical implications for second and for-eign language learning.

REFERENCES

Allen, R., & Shatz, M. (1983). "What says meow?" The role of context and linguistic expe-
    rience in very young children's responses to what-questions. *Journal of Child Lan-
    guage, 10*, 321–335.
Arthur, B., Weiner, R., Culver, M., Lee, Y. J., & Thomas, D. (1980). The register of imper-
    sonal discourse to foreigners: Verbal adjustments to foreign accent. In D. Larsen-Free-

man (Ed.), *Discourse analysis in second language research* (pp. 111–137). Rowley, MA: Newbury House.

Baker, C. (1992). Description and analysis in classroom talk and interaction. *Journal of Classroom Interaction, 27*(2), 9–14.

Berman, R., & Slobin, D. (1994). *Relating events in narratives: A crosslinguistic developmental study.* Hillsdale, NJ: Lawrence Erlbaum Associates.

Block, D. (1996). Not so fast: Some thoughts on theory culling, relativism, accepted findings and the heart and soul of SLA. *Applied Linguistics, 17*(1), 63–83.

Bowers, C. A., & Flinders, D. (1990). *Responsive teaching: An ecological approach to classroom patterns of language, culture, and thought.* New York: Teachers College Press.

Braidi, S. (1995). Reconsidering the role of interaction and input in second language acquisition. *Language Learning, 45*(1), 141–175.

Bronfenbrenner, U. (1993). The ecology of cognitive development: Research models and fugitive findings. In R. Wozniak & K. Fischer (Eds.), *Development in context: Acting and thinking in specific environments* (pp. 3–44). Hillsdale, NJ: Lawrence Erlbaum Associates.

Cazden, C. (1988). *Classroom discourse.* Portsmouth, NH: Heinemann.

Chaudron, C. (1988). *Second language classrooms: Research on teaching and learning.* Cambridge, UK: Cambridge University Press.

Crookes, G., & Gass, S. (Eds.). (1993a). *Tasks and language learning: Integrating theory and practice.* Clevedon, UK: Multilingual Matters.

Crookes, G., & Gass, S. (Eds.). (1993b). *Tasks in a pedagogical context: Integrating theory and practice.* Clevedon, UK: Multilingual Matters.

D'Andrade, R. (1992). Cognitive anthropology. In T. Schwartz, G. White, & C. Lutz (Eds.), *New directions in psychological anthropology* (pp. 47–58). Cambridge, UK: Cambridge University Press.

Early, M. (1985). *Input and interaction in content classrooms: Foreigner talk and teacher talk in classroom discourse.* Unpublished doctoral dissertation, University of California at Los Angeles.

Eder, D. (1982). The impact of management and turn-allocation activities on student performance. *Discourse Processes, 5*, 147–159.

Ferguson, C. (1975). Toward a characterization of English foreigner talk. *Anthropological Linguistics, 17*(1), 1–14.

Firth, A., & Wagner, J. (1997). On discourse, communication and (some) fundamental concepts in SLA research. *The Modern Language Journal, 81*(3), 285–312.

Firth, A., & Wagner, J. (1998). SLA property: No trespassing! *The Modern Language Journal, 82*(1), 91–94.

Fischer, K., Bullock, D., Rotenberg, E., & Raya, P. (1993). The dynamics of competence: How context contributes directly to skill. In R. Wozniak & K. Fischer (Eds.), *Development in context: Acting and thinking in specific environments* (pp. 93–117). Hillsdale, NJ: Lawrence Erlbaum Associates.

Flavell, J., Miller, P., & Miller, S. (1993). *Cognitive development* (3rd ed.). Englewood Cliffs, NJ: Prentice-Hall.

Freed, B. (1980). Talking to foreigners versus talking to children: Similarities and differences. In R. Scarcella & S. Krashen (Eds.), *Research in second language acquisition* (pp. 19–28). Rowley, MA: Newbury House.

Gass, S. (1998). Apples and oranges: Or, why apples are not oranges and don't need to be. A response to Firth and Wagner. *The Modern Language Journal, 82*(1), 83–90.

Gass, S. M., & Varonis, E. M. (1985). Variation in native speaker speech modification to non-native speakers. *Studies in Second Language Acquisition, 7*, 37–58.

Girotto, V., & Light, P. (1993). The pragmatic bases of children's reasoning. In P. Light & G. Butterworth (Eds.), *Context and cognition: Ways of learning and knowing* (pp. 134–156). Hillsdale, NJ: Lawrence Erlbaum Associates.

Green, M. (1992). *The role of teacher language in the education of mainstreamed second language learners of English.* Unpublished doctoral dissertation, Boston University.

Gutierrez, K. (1994). How talk, context, and script shape contexts for learning: A cross-case comparison of journal sharing. *Linguistics and Education, 5*, 335–365.

Gutierrez, K. (1995). Unpackaging academic discourse. *Discourse Processes, 19*, 21–37.

Hall, J. K. (1993). The role of oral practices in the accomplishment of our everyday lives: The sociocultural dimension of interaction with implications for the learning of another language. *Applied Linguistics, 14*(2), 145–166.

Hall, J. K. (1995). (Re)creating our world with words: A sociohistorical perspective of face-to-face interaction. *Applied Linguistics, 16*(2), 206–232.

Hall, J. K. (1997). A consideration of SLA as a theory of practice. *The Modern Language Journal, 81*(3), 301–306.

Hatch, E. M. (1983). *Psycholinguistics, a second language perspective.* Cambridge, MA: Newbury House.

Hopper, P., & Thompson, S. (1993). Language universals, discourse pragmatics and semantics. *Language Sciences, 15*(4), 357–376.

Krashen, S. (1980). *Second language acquisition and second language learning.* Oxford, UK: Pergamon.

Krashen, S. (1989). *Language acquisition and language education.* New York: Prentice-Hall.

Lantolf, J., with Pavlenko, A. (1995). Sociocultural theory and second language acquisition. *Annual Review of Applied Linguistics, 15*, 108–124.

Lantolf, J. P., & Appel, G. (Eds.). (1994). *Vygotskyan approaches to second language research.* Norwood, NJ: Ablex.

Leontiev, A. A. (1981). *Psychology and the language learning process.* Oxford, UK: Pergamon.

Leontiev, A. N. (1981). *Problems of the development of the mind.* Moscow: Progress.

Levy, E., & Nelson, K. (1994). Words in discourse: A dialectical approach to the acquisition of meaning and use. *Journal of Child Language, 21*, 367–389.

Light, P., & Butterworth, G. (Eds.). (1993). *Context and cognition: Ways of learning and knowing.* Hillsdale, NJ: Lawrence Erlbaum Associates.

Long, M. (1981). Input, interaction, and second language acquisition. In H. Winitz (Ed.), *Native language and foreign language acquisition* (pp. 259–278). New York: Annals of the New York Academy of Sciences.

Lucariello, J., & Nelson, K. (1987). Remembering and planning talk between mothers and children. *Discourse Processes, 10*, 219–235.

Ninio, A., & Snow, C. (1996). *Pragmatic development.* Boulder, CO: Westview.

Ochs, E. (1988). *Culture and language development: Language acquisition and language socialization in a Samoan village.* Cambridge, UK: Cambridge University Press.

Pica, T. (1988). Interlanguage adjustments as an outcome of NS–NNS negotiated interaction. *Language Learning, 38*(1), 45–73.

Pica, T. (1994). Research on negotiation: What does it reveal about second-language learning conditions, processes and outcomes? *Language Learning, 44*(3), 493–527.

Pica, T., Doughty, C., & Young, R. (1986). Making input comprehensible: Do interactional modifications help? *I.T.L. Review of Applied Linguistics, 72*, 1–25.

Pine, J. (1994a). Environmental correlates of variation in lexical style: Interactional style and the structure of input. *Applied Psycholinguistics, 15*, 355–370.

Pine, J. (1994b). The language of primary caregivers. In C. Gallaway & B. Richards (Eds.), *Input and interaction in language acquisition* (pp. 15–37). Cambridge, UK: Cambridge University Press.

Resnick, L., Levine, J., & Teasley, S. (Eds.). (1991). *Perspectives on socially shared cognition*. Washington, DC: American Psychological Association.

Rogoff, B., & Lave, J. (Eds.). (1984). *Everyday cognition: Its development in social contexts*. Cambridge, MA: Harvard University Press.

Roux, J.-P., & Gilly, M. (1993). Social significance of tasks, routines, and pragmatic schemas in distribution activities. *European Journal of Social Psychology, 23*, 355–371.

Scarcella, R., & Higa, C. (1982). Input and age differences in second language acquisition. In S. Krashen, R. Scarcella, & M. Long (Eds.), *Child–adult differences in second language acquisition* (pp. 175–201). Rowley, MA: Newbury House.

Schinke-Llano, L. (1983). Foreigner talk in content classrooms. In H. W. Seliger & M. H. Long (Eds.), *Classroomoriented research in second language acquisition* (pp. 146–168). Rowley, MA: Newbury House.

Schmidt, R. (1994). Deconstructing consciousness in search of useful definitions for applied linguistics. *AILA Review, 11*, 11–26.

Shatz, M., & McCloskey, L. (1984). Answering appropriately: A developmental perspective on conversational knowledge. In S. Kuczaj (Ed.), *Discourse development: Progress in cognitive development research* (pp. 19–36). New York: Springer-Verlag.

Slaughter, H. B., & Bennett, A. T. (1982). *Methods of analyzing samples of elicited discourse in English and Spanish for determining student language proficiency* (Final report to the Inter-America Research Associates and the National Institute of Education).

Smagorinsky, P., & Coppock, J. (1994). Cultural tools and the classroom context: An exploration of an alternative response to literature. *Written Communication, 11*, 283–310.

Smagorinsky, P., & Fly, P. (1993). The social environment of the classroom: A Vygotskyan perspective on small group process. *Communication Education, 42*(2), 159–171.

Snow, C. (1989). Understanding social interaction and language acquisition: Sentences are not enough. In M. Bornstein & J. Bruner (Eds.), *Interaction in human development* (pp. 83–103). Hillsdale, NJ: Lawrence Erlbaum Associates.

Snow, C., Cancino, H., de Temple, J., & Schley, S. (1991). Giving formal definitions: A linguistic or metalinguistic skill? In E. Bialystok (Ed.), *Language processing in bilingual children* (pp. 90–112). Cambridge, UK: Cambridge University Press.

Stone, A., & Forman, E. (1988). Cognitive development in language-learning disabled adolescents: A study of problem-solving performance in an isolation-of-variables task. *Learning Disabilities Research, 3*(2), 107–114.

Swain, M. (1985). Communicative competence: Some roles of comprehensible input and comprehensible output in its development. In S. Gass & C. Madden (Eds.), *Input in second language acquisition* (pp. 235–257). Rowley, MA: Newbury House.

Swain, M. (1995, March). *Collaborative dialogue: Its contribution to second language learning*. Paper presented at the American Association of Applied Linguistics Conference, Long Beach, CA.

Tomasello, M., Conti-Ramsden, G., & Ewert, B. (1990). Young children's conversations with their mothers and fathers: Differences in breakdown and repair. *Journal of Child Language, 17*, 115–130.

Tulviste, P. (1991). *The cultural-historical development of thinking*. New York: Nova Science.

Verplaetse, L. (1993, April). *Modifications in native speaker input: A hindrance to L2 production*. Paper presented at the American Association of Applied Linguistics Conference, Atlanta, GA.

Verplaetse, L. (1998). How content teachers interact with English language learners. *TESOL Journal, 7*(5), 24–29.

Vygotsky, L. S. (1978). *Mind in society: The development of higher psychological processes*. Cambridge, MA: Harvard University Press.

Vygotsky, L. S. (1981). The genesis of higher mental functions. In J. Wertsch, (Ed.), *The concept of activity in social psychology* (pp. 144–188). Armonk, NY: M. E. Sharpe.

Vygotsky, L. S. (1986). *Thought and language*. Cambridge, MA: MIT Press.

Wells, G. (1993). Reevaluating the IRF sequence: A proposal for the articulation of theories of activity and discourse for the analysis of teaching and learning in the classroom. *Linguistics and Education, 5*, 1–17.

Wells, G. (1996). Using the tool-kit of discourse in the activity of learning and teaching. *Mind, Culture, and Activity, 3*(2), 1–22.

Wertsch, J. (1991). *Voices of the mind*. Cambridge, MA: Harvard University Press.

Wertsch, J. (1994). The primacy of mediated action in sociocultural studies. *Mind, Culture, and Activity, 1*(4), 202–208.

Wertsch, J., & Bivens, J. (1992). The social origins of individual mental functioning: Alternatives and perspectives. *Quarterly Newsletter of the Laboratory of Comparative Human Cognition, 14*(2), 35–44.

Wertsch, J., & Tulviste, P. (1992). L. S. Vygotsky and contemporary developmental psychology. *Developmental Psychology, 28*(4), 548–557.

Classroom Interaction and Foreign Language Learning

2

Learning the Pragmatics of Solidarity in the Networked Foreign Language Classroom

Celeste Kinginger

Computer-mediated communication has significant potential to broaden classroom discourse options (Kramsch, 1985) by introducing learners to social contexts and relationships heretofore uncommon in classroom interaction. This study examines one such radical change, as college-age learners of French as a foreign language establish relationships, via e-mail, videoconferencing, and collaborative work, with native-speaking French peers. A new kind of social relationship, involving both the experience and the expression of solidarity, may be expected to engender changes in the learners' sociolinguistic competence, which had previously been constrained in its development by the limitations on social variation in foreign language classrooms (Hall, 1995; Kasper, 1982; Ohta, 1994).

This study examines how involvement with French peers encourages learners to appropriate forms of the language that are adequate for the expression of solidarity, especially the mutual use of the *tu* form of address in student–student conversations. The long-distance relationships formed by students offer contexts for language socialization, with support for conscious awareness of, and assisted performance in the appropriate uses of the second-person pronoun (*tu* vs. *vous*). This distinction is difficult for English-speaking classroom learners of French to maintain both because of the limitations on social variation in classrooms and because of the inherent ambiguity of the distinction. Knowledge of the rules governing address form usage in French is inadequate to guide their use by learners in actual social situations: The choice of address form is characterized by inherent sociopragmatic ambiguity whereby the same linguistic behavior may be interpreted as following either from perceived status differences or from desire to index social distance. Therefore, learners need to experience how changes in social context influence the gradient levels of appropriacy in address form use. I show that social relationships enabled by electronic networking do indeed offer a context for disambiguation and mastery of the *tu–vous* distinction as it relates to the expression of solidarity and that the medium for this development was social interaction with peers.

TU VERSUS *VOUS*: FACE SYSTEMS AND THE SOCIOPRAGMATIC AMBIGUITY OF ADDRESS FORMS

The study of politeness is concerned with the presentation of self in communication, and with the concept of interactional *face*, or the necessary balance between involvement (also known as solidarity or positive politeness) and independence (also known as deference or negative politeness; Brown & Levinson, 1987). *Involvement* is defined as being "concerned with the person's right and need to be considered a normal, contributing, or supporting member of society" (Scollon & Scollon, 1995, p. 36), whereas "independence shows that a person may act with some degree of autonomy and that he or she respects the rights of others to their own autonomy and freedom of movement or choice" (p. 37). The concept of face is fundamentally paradoxical. Yet, according to this theory, in every communication situation, involvement and independence must be anticipated and negotiated by and for every participant.

In Scollon and Scollon's (1995) description, the negotiation of face depends on *face systems*. These in turn depend on participants' interpretation of three defining situational factors: power, social distance, and weight of imposition. *Power* refers to the distance between social status of participants in a hierarchical structure, whereas *distance* concerns the closeness of interpersonal relationships. *Weight of imposition* depends on the topic under discussion (e.g., routine business vs. making a special request). Because weight of imposition in each particular conversation is context specific and dependent on the topic, Scollon and Scollon constructed their model of three basic face systems using only the dimensions of power and distance:

1. Deference (–power, + distance) is a balanced system in which participants are considered to be equals or near equals but treat each other at a distance. This system is exemplified by the relationship

that obtains between professional colleagues who do not know one another well.

2. Solidarity (–power, –distance) is the system that operates among friends or close colleagues; the participants see themselves in some ways as socially equal and close.

3. Hierarchical systems (+ power, +/–distance) are in place when "the participants recognize and respect the social differences that place one in a superordinate position and the other in a subordinate position" (p. 45).

In contrast to the other systems, the significance of one dimension, power, subsumes that of the other, social distance: A power differential creates social distance. Also, a hierarchical face system requires participants to call on different strategies depending on their status: The participant in the superordinate position will exercise some involvement strategies to bridge the gap created by social distance. Such strategies include the claim of common points of view, the assumption or assertion of reciprocity, and the use of informal address. The participant of lower status will use strategies of independence to demonstrate respect. These strategies include, for example, minimizing threat, apologizing, giving the hearer options not to participate, and using formal address.

In many European languages, the realization of face systems constructed through the dimensions of power and distance is closely related to choice of second-person pronoun. For learners of French and other European languages whose first language is English, learning the pragmatics of address forms can be particularly problematic. In French, either *tu* (singular, informal) or *vous* (plural or singular, formal), with appropriate verb usage to accompany the selected pronoun, serves in the place of the English second-person pronoun, *you*. One initial problem is achieving the realization that choice of address form significantly shapes the social context. In the early stages of learning French the relevance of this distinction is opaque for many native English learners, as evidenced by their tendency to shift from one pronoun to the other in the same context, and even, at times, within the same utterance. The distinction is learned primarily by rote memorization rather than being based on social understanding.

Having begun to appreciate the significance of the *tu–vous* distinction, learners then need to understand what effects are achieved by this choice. Specifically, they need to comprehend the complex relation between choice of address form and strategies of involvement and independence within the range of face systems as they are negotiated in particular social contexts. As described in the seminal works on the pragmatics of second-person pronouns in European languages (or T and V pronouns; Brown & Gilman, 1960/1970; Gilman & Brown, 1958; Lambert & Tucker, 1976), the *V pronoun* (as in French *vous*) can convey differential power, social distance, or both. Within hierarchical face systems, speakers use V to index respect when addressing persons of relatively high status. V is also used as a strategy of independence, to express deference, for example when addressing persons whose status equals one's own, but to whom one does not feel particularly close. The *T pronoun* (e.g., French *tu*) conveys solidarity, intimacy, or status or age inferiority on the part of the addressee relative to the speaker, or some combination of these. Speakers use T as an involvement strategy, to address children, animals, close friends and, often, fellow workers or students. According to Burt (1995):

> What is crucial here is the fact that while the V form has a positive interpretation in terms of status, it implies social distance—a possible negative; similarly, while the T form can convey warmth or intimacy, it can also convey an uncomfortable status difference between participants, with the recipient of T in a lower status position. (p. 54)

To recall, at issue is determining not the correctness, but the appropriacy of pronoun choice in a given social context. Burt (1995) described the sociopragmatic ambiguity of pronoun choice in terms of the confluence of two pragmatic maxims modeled after those of Grice (1975) and Myers-Scotton (1993). The Myers-Scotton markedness model, originally developed to account for code choice in a multilingual society, assumes that linguistic forms are linked to social rights and obligations and that certain forms are considered marked or unmarked for certain situations. Speakers select particular forms in accordance with the negotiation principle: "Choose the form of your conversational contribution such that it symbolizes the set of rights and obligations which you wish to be in force between speaker and addressee in the current exchange" (Scotton, 1983, p. 116, cited in Burt, 1995, p. 51). When applied to the choice of second-person pronoun in Burt's interpretation, this system of markedness yields the following two maxims related to speaker negotiation of social distance and status:

- Social distance: Choose the marked form of the second-person pronoun (or other form of address) when you wish to change the *social distance* between you and the interlocutor.

- Status: Choose the marked form of the second-person pronoun (or other form of address) when you wish to change the *status relationship* between you and the interlocutor.

Sociopragmatic ambiguity arises because two maxims guide the speaker to make the same linguistic choice: The choice of second-person pronoun is a case of *maxim confluence* because the same linguistic behavior can be interpreted as following from either of the preceding maxims. For example, in a working relationship involving a face system of deference, if ego opts to switch from V to T in conversation with alter, this change can be interpreted as indexing increased solidarity, as desire for intimacy, or as a change to a hierarchical face system, with the implication that alter's social status is lowered. If alter then continues to address ego as V, this implies either acceptance of a hierarchical status difference in the relationship or a desire to avoid solidarity or intimacy with ego.

CONSCIOUSNESS, ASSISTED PERFORMANCE, AND LEGITIMATE PERIPHERAL PARTICIPATION IN THE ACQUISITION OF PRAGMATIC COMPETENCE

For Schmidt (1993), one of the central questions surrounding the acquisition of pragmatic competence is the role of consciousness as a mediational link between competence and performance. Citing evidence to suggest that pragmatic competence is not, or not always, accessible to conscious reflection in skilled performance, Schmidt argued that we still do not know about the "possible role that awareness of crucial features of language rules, however incomplete and transitory, may play in the establishment of such knowledge" (p. 23). For Schmidt, the crucial event, transforming input to intake, is the learner's noticing and attending to the relevant features of the language.

In support of his argument for the importance of "noticing," Schmidt (1993) cited evidence from studies of first language acquisition of pragmatic competence. These studies suggest universal validity to the observation that "when it comes to speaking politely, adults do not leave it to the child to construct the rules on his or her own. Here, they take an active, even energetic part in directly instructing their children in the use of various politeness devices" (p. 36). Schmidt therefore argued that the widely accepted analogy linking language learning to input processing cannot obtain in the case of pragmatic competence:

Simple exposure to sociolinguistically appropriate input is unlikely to be sufficient for second language acquisition of pragmatic and discoursal knowledge because the linguistic realizations of pragmatic functions are sometimes opaque to language learners and because the relevant contextual factors to be noticed are likely to be defined differently or may be non-salient to the learner. Second language learners may fail to experience the crucial noticings for years. The fact that this does not seem to happen in first language learning is attributable not to any sort of pragmatics acquisition device, but to the efforts that parents and caregivers make in order to teach communicative competence to children, using a variety of strategies. (Schmidt, 1993, p. 36)

A greater acknowledged role for consciousness would seem to suggest a need to reevaluate assumptions about the role played by social interactions in all contexts of learning. Schmidt (1993) nonetheless held that, in contrast to first language learning, for acquisition of sociolinguistic competence in an additional language, the relevant data are difficult to obtain, requiring opportunities to "catch learners in the actual process of learning rather than simply performing their current competence" (p. 29).

Catching learners in the actual process of learning is precisely what Vygotsky (1978) claimed for his genetic approach to the study of development. A major foundational aspect of his theoretical framework (Wertsch, 1985), the essence of this claim is that development can only be understood by specifying the origins and transformations it has undergone. Development is to be understood as a process that can best be observed when it is underway (or disturbed). Vygotsky's own research applies to various genetic domains, focusing mainly on ontogenesis, but also extending to the domains of phylogenesis and social history. A microgenetic analysis is the observation of skill acquisition during a learning event. In the analysis of learner–learner discourse, according to Donato (1994), "a microgenetic analysis allows us to observe directly how students help each other during the overt planning of L2 utterances, and the outcome of these multiple forces of help as they come into contact, and interact, with each other" (p. 42)

In combination with another major theme in Vygotsky's (1981) writing, that mental functioning has its origins in social activity, the genetic view of development yields the general genetic law of cultural development:

Any function in the child's cultural development appears twice, or on two planes. First it appears on the social plane, and then on the psychological plane. First it appears between people as an interpsychological category, and then within the child as an intrapsychological category. (p. 163)

The emphasis in Vygotsky's writing on the development of mental functioning within social interaction, and its genetic analysis, is mirrored in studies of first and second *language socialization*. According to Ochs (1986), this term refers to both socialization via language and socialization to use language. The acquisition of language is fundamentally embedded in the process of socialization. Social interactions are the sociocultural contexts within which childrens' participation leads to performance competence and cognitive skill.

The studies in Ochs and Schieffelin (1979) and Schieffelin and Ochs (1986) demonstrate that in acquiring pragmatic competence, children's interactions with more mature members of society are characterized by explicit prompting and assisted performance. Although the forms of assistance vary across cultural contexts, "what has been consistently observed across cultures . . . is the practice of caregivers providing explicit instruction in what to say and how to speak in a range of recurrent activities and events" (Ochs, 1986, p. 5). In a large-scale study of the acquisition of politeness, for example, Snow, Perlmann, Gleason, and Hooshyar (1990) demonstrated that, overwhelmingly, children were explicitly told what forms to use in particular situations, and correlations between forms and the dimensions of politeness were made salient in the interaction. Caregivers' interactions with children include a variety of scaffolding practices by which they continually reinterpret children's utterances by exemplary action, resituating them within culturally appropriate contexts. It is important to note that socialization to polite behavior is also achieved via legitimate peripheral participation (Lave & Wenger, 1991), whereby learners are parties to social action, able to observe and later to emulate the activity of more skilled or mature participants.

"Languages have constructions at all levels of grammar and discourse that signal information concerning how interactants see their own and others' social position and roles. As children acquire language, they are acquiring knowledge of this vital aspect of social order" (Ochs, 1986, pp. 6–7). Awareness of social status and role is among the cognitive outcomes of using language for particular purposes in different activities. Clearly, language acquisition entails acquiring the social meaning of linguistic structures.

ACQUIRING THE PRAGMATICS OF SOLIDARITY
IN THE FOREIGN LANGUAGE CLASSROOM

In contrast to the immersion setting, where children tend to overgeneralize the use of *tu* (Lyster, 1994, 1996; Swain & Lapkin, 1990), anecdotal evidence suggests that in foreign language classrooms, adult and late-adolescent learners are exposed primarily to the use of *vous* and are explicitly counseled to concentrate on the learning and use of *vous*. This is in part due to concerns for the social success of learners on the part of French teachers, who observe that it is more likely for a foreigner to commit a gaffe by addressing a stranger as *tu* than as *vous*. Another factor is the face system of the traditional American classroom: Students address the teacher as *vous* due to the hierarchical nature of the relationship, according to which the teacher is owed expressions of respect. Typically, although there are many exceptions, teachers in turn address their individual adult students as *vous* out of respect for their status as adults.

The use of *tu* is therefore potentially restricted to the context of student–student interactions. However, these interactions are subject to complex variations that make them unreliable as a context for acquiring appropriate use of the *tu* form to express solidarity. For example, if the learners have not yet acquired a sense of the social meaning of the *tu–vous* distinction, they may use these forms in free variation. If they have understood some aspects of the distinction, they are still operating on assumptions about the social meaning of *tu–vous* that are different from those of native speakers.

The evidence that is available to learners in pedagogical materials can also prove unreliable. For example, in the first-year French textbook that was used by the participants in this study (Amon, Muyskens, & Omaggio-Hadley, 1995) we find the following explanation of *tu* and *vous*:

> *Tu* and **vous**. There are two ways to say *you* in French: ***Tu*** is used when speaking to a friend, fellow student, relative, child or pet; **vous** is used when speaking to a person you don't know well or when addressing an older person, someone in authority, or anyone with whom you wish to maintain a certain formality. The plural of both ***tu*** and **vous** is **vous**. The context will indicate whether *vous* refers to one person or more than one.

> Michelle, *tu* parles espagnol?   *Michelle, do you speak Spanish?*
> Maman! Papa! Où êtes-*vous*?   *Mom! Dad! Where are you?*
> *Vous* parlez bien français, Madame   *You speak French well, Madame.*
> Pardon, Messieurs (Mesdames,   *Excuse me gentlemen (ladies), do*
> (Mesdemoiselles) est-ce   *you speak English?*
> que *vous* parlez anglais? (p. 41)

This explanation, although otherwise remarkable for its succinct clarity, restricts its explication of social context to the role such context plays in determining the number of addressees. Despite the suggestive power of the examples, it does not explain that power and social distance can also determine the choice of pronoun, except in the case of hierarchical face systems. In terms of the type of classroom relationship enabled by computer-mediated communication, the virtual friendship, the rules stated here are in direct contradiction with each other: The "fellow student" is to be addressed as *tu*, but the "person you don't know well" is to be called *vous*.

The use of address forms, as we have seen, is inherently ambiguous. It is difficult to separate the rules for their use from the particulars of the social context. As in all other social settings, classrooms are populated by people who orient toward their own and each other's power and social distance in communicative interaction.

The particular case of the French versus the American classroom offers a striking contrast in expectations for the nature of social relationships. Both French and American sociologists have commented on the fact that students in the two countries orient differently to status and social distance in the classroom. According to Carroll (1988), whereas American students seek approval from authority figures as individuals in competition with each other, French students tend to develop a notion of the school class as a collective in-group and a source of power in opposition to administrative structures of authority. As Wylie and Brière (1995) argued, "Apprendre à se défendre" (learning to defend oneself) is a characteristic of group social life in France. The primary vehicle for socialization into this view is a collective school group that both defends the individual and also stands prepared for collective resistance to the demands of authority figures.

Taken together, these observations suggest that the foreign language classroom learning environment alone provides little evidence allowing American learners to understand the *tu–vous* distinction as it relates to the expression of solidarity. As a context for language socialization, the classroom's face system tends to favor the overgeneralization of *vous* for addressing individuals. In the pedagogical materials provided to the learners in this study, the *tu–vous* distinction remains ambiguous, especially as it relates to the expression of solidarity. Above all, American learners do not share the expectations of French learners in terms of the social organization of the classroom: They do not understand that by virtue of the participants' status as fellow students, their French partners will be inclined to judge that the relationship is one of solidarity, calling for the use of reciprocal *tu* as the unmarked form of address:

Depuis les années 1960, le passage au tutoiement se fait beaucoup plus vite et plus fréquemment qu'avant, surtout parmi les adolescents et jeunes adultes. On tutoie non seulement les membres de sa famille et ses amis, mais très souvent aussi ses collaborateurs et collaboratrices professionnels d'un rang équivalent. . . . Le tutoiement traduit une certaine égalité et une certaine familiarité (qui peut être purement professionnel). Il n'implique pas nécessairement l'amitié au niveau personnel.

[Since the 1960s, people, especially adolescents and young adults, switch to *tu* more quickly and more frequently. One uses *tu* not only with family members and friends, but very often also with professional colleagues of equivalent rank. . . . The use of *tu* implies a certain equality and a certain familiarity (which can be purely professional). It does not necessarily suggest personal friendship.] (Wylie & Brière, 1995, p. 99)

THE STUDY

Setting

The data for this study were collected in the context of a tele-collaborative learning experiment linking an English class at a graduate school of telecommunications engineering in France with a French class at a regional state university in the midwestern United States. The classes were linked with the express purpose of improving communicative competence and intercultural awareness through a series of parallel tasks on French and American cultural differences, with discussion of the tasks to take place via electronic mail exchange and real-time, whole-class videoconferencing (Kinginger, 1998; Kinginger, Gourvès-Hayward, & Simpson, 1999).

Most of the 14 students in the American French class were of local origin and had little access to the French language outside of their academic course work. Only one student had traveled to France, for a short tour during her high school years. Almost all of the students worked part time in addition to being in school. The course was open to students at the level of the fifth semester or beyond. The focus of the course was French and American intercultural communication, with practice in writing and speaking. For the majority of these students, this course provided the first contact with native-speaking French peers.

Many of the 10 participants in the English class in France had already lived or traveled in an English-speaking country. The aim of their course was to encourage cross-cultural awareness, through both self-analysis and contact with a different culture, in preparation for careers requiring knowledge of the global marketplace.

As the course began, each of the students was assigned a keypal in the partner class, or, in the case of four American students, a keypal in another English class at the same French school. The students were instructed to use their access to a native-speaking peer to discuss questions that might arise in their readings and analyses of parallel texts (film remakes and children's literature). In practice, however, students used e-mail primarily for informal socializing. Their choice meant that it was incumbent on them to establish a relationship in the initial phase of the project.

Analysis

The database for this study consists of approximately 350 e-mail messages voluntarily forwarded to the instructor by the American students as evidence of participation in the e-mail exchange. The messages were collected and archived throughout the semester during which the course took place. To facilitate analysis, all of the e-mail messages were printed at the end of the semester and arranged chronologically to reflect the exchanges between particular pairs of students. The object of the analysis was to observe and document the qualities of particular e-mail exchanges as they unfolded over time and as they provided a medium for language learning and socialization. The analysis focused particularly on the microgenesis of the American learners' understanding and use of the *tu* form for the expression of solidarity, and on the qualities of assisted performance and consciousness raising provided by native-speaking peers.

Findings

The quality of the e-mail exchanges showed a great deal of variation as a language learning medium for individual students. This variation was due to differing levels of interest in this aspect of the project, the variable success of the initial contact between keypals, and the choice of code, which in some cases was largely restricted to English. The following analysis focuses first on the initial e-mail contacts and then on the e-mail exchanged between three pairs of students (Lilian and Robert, Susan and Pierre, and Mandy and Martin) who corresponded at length and in French.

Initial Contacts. Although e-mail was interpreted by the participants as an informal medium, in almost every case, during the initial phase of the project, the American learners addressed their keypals as *vous*, thus demonstrating that the use of *vous* was at that point the unmarked address form for these learners in this context. For example,[1] in Mark's initial e-

---

[1]The examples are reproduced exactly as they appeared in the original e-mail messages. Readers familiar with the French language will note the absence of diacritical marks in the examples. Although the use of accents was supported by most of the e-mail packages used by the participants, the process of inserting accents in e-mail messages was most often deemed too cumbersome by the study participants, who opted instead to write without accents.

mail to François, the *vous* form of address is used throughout (instances of *tu* and *vous* are marked T or V):

Example 1: Tuesday, February 11, 1997

> Salut! Je m'appelle Mark, et je suis un membre de la classe aux Etats-Unis qui fera de la communication avec la votre (V). (Je m'excuse en avance qu'il n'y a pas des accents dans ce message—les ordinateurs ici ne les utilisent pas, malheureusement). . . .

> Je sais bien que *vous* etes (V) en train de faire les examens. C'est bien. Ecrivez-moi (V) quand *vous* avez le temps. Un reponse n'est pas important que vos (V) e*tu*des. Je sais que nous aurons le temps pour bavarder quand *vous* retournez (V) de vos (V) vacances. Bon chance, et bonnes vacances!

> Hi! My name is Mark, and I am a member of the class in the United States that will communicate with yours. (I apologize in advance for the lack of accents in this message. The computers here don't use them, unfortunately). . . .

> I know that you are now taking exams. That's okay. Write to me when you have the time. A reply is not important as your studies. I know we will have the time to chat when you come back from your vacation. Good luck and enjoy your vacation!

In Melissa's first response to her keypal, Marguerite, the same use of *vous* is observed:

Example 2: Tuesday, February 4, 1997

> Bonjour Marguerite. C'est tres bien *vous* (V) rencontrer. J'espere que *vous* me comprenez (V). Votre (V) anglais est tres bon! J'ai compris toutes les choses que *vous* avez (V) ecrit!

> Qu'est-ce que *vous* faites (V) pour les loisirs a la Bretagne? Ecrivez-moi (V) et nous pouvons parler plus.

> Hello Marguerite. It is good to meet you. I hope you understand me. Your English is very good. I understood all the things that you wrote.

> What do you do in your spare time in Brittany? Write to me and we can talk more.

Lilian and Robert.   Lilian's first e-mail was sent to a student in the French class, Martin, who had already established a relationship with another student in the American class, Mandy. Using the same strategy as the other American students in initial contacts, Lilian addressed Martin as *vous*:

Example 3: Tuesday, January 28, 1997

Martin,

Bonjour. Je m'appelle Lilian. J'habite aux Etats-Unis. J'ai vu votre (V) web-page. J'ai pense que votre (V) message etait tres humourous. J'etudie le Fran-cais . . . j'etudie les communications aussi. J'ai besoin de beaucoup de pratique en Francais. J'espere que *vous* m'ecrivez (V) quelquefois.

Martin,

Hello. My name is Lilian. I live in the United States. I saw your webpage. I thought your message was very humorous. I study French . . . I study commu-nications too. I need a lot of practice in French. I hope you will write to me sometime.

In response to this message, Martin wrote that he was already in corre-spondence with another student:

Example 4: Tuesday, January 28, 1997

Salut Lilian,

J'ai recu ton (T) mail. Je ne m'y attendais pas, car je suis deja en relation avec une autre eleve de ton ecole, et que je pensais qu'une repartition judicieuse avait ete operee.

Je ne suis pas un fan d'ordinateurs ni d'Internet, aussi, et ne m'en veux pas (T), je souhaiterais me limiter a une correspondance unique. Cela m'est prof-itable, mais je ne desire pas y consacrer trop de temps.

Desole. Au revoir.

Martin

Hi Lilian,

I received your mail. I wasn't expecting it because I am already in contact with another student from your school, and I thought that a fair distribution had been established.

I am not a fan of computers, nor of the Internet, and please don't be angry with me. I prefer to limit myself to one correspondence. I am profiting by this, but do not wish to devote excessive time to it.

Sorry. Goodbye.

Martin

Martin's reply is written in highly formal French (*je souhaiterais me limiter, je ne desire pas y consacrer trop de temps*) suggesting that he was using formality as a distancing strategy due to the potentially face-threatening nature of his message (i.e., that he did not want to correspond with Lilian). Despite the nature of the message and the formality of the language used to write it, however, Martin nonetheless addressed Lilian as *tu* in response to her use of *vous*. The use of *tu* in this context suggests that *tu* was the unmarked form for Martin in this context of solidarity among students, even if there is no friendship or indeed any possibility of establishing a friendship.

Lilian went on to establish contact with another French student, Robert, and it was in the context of this relationship that she received explicit, immediate commentary on her use of *vous*. On Monday, January 27, 1997, Lilian sent her first reply to Robert, in the following message:

Example 5: Monday, January 27, 1997

Bonjour Robert,

J'ai pense que je voudrais envoyer un courrier electronique. J'ai aime votre (V) message hier. Je voudrais envoyer courrier electronique avec *vous* (V). Je besoin de pratique ma francais. Mais, quelquefois, je voudrai ecriver en anglais pour *vous* (V). D'accord. Je suis fatiguee aujourd'hui. Il fait froid. C'est lundi. Je deteste lundi.

Hello Robert,

I think that I would like to send an electronic mail. I liked your message yesterday. I need to practice my French. But, sometimes, I will like to write in English for you. Okay. I am tired today. It is cold. It's Monday. I hate Monday.

In response to Lilian's message, Robert wrote the following:

Example 6: Tuesday, January 28, 1997

Salut Lilian,

Je n'ai pas envie d'ecrire en anglais, aujourd'hui. Je vais donc ecrire en francais. Je vais essayer d'utiliser un francais simple.

J'ai 21 ans, aussi, donc *TU* (T) dois (T) me dire "*TU*." Je sais qu'en anglais, c'est la meme chose, "*TU*" et "*VOUS*" (you), mais en francais. il y a une difference. Et je prefere qu'on me dit "*TU*."

Voila.

Tu ecris (T) pour pratiquer ton (T) francais. Veux-*tu* (T) que je corrige tes (T) fautes? C'est facile: je recopie ton (T) texte en francais parfait, et *tu* pourras (T) voir ou *tu* fais (T) des fautes. Dis-moi (T) si *tu* veux (T) que je fasse comme ca.

Hi Lilian,

I don't feel like writing in English, today. So I am going to write in French. I am going to try to use simple French.

I am 21 years old, too, so YOU (T) must say YOU (T) to me. I know that in English it's the same thing, YOU (T) and YOU (V), but in French there is a difference. And I prefer to be called YOU (T).

There.

You are writing to practice your French. Do you want me to correct your mistakes? It's easy: I copy your text in perfect French, and you can see where you make mistakes. Tell me if you want me to do that.

In this reply, Robert brings Lilian's use of the address form to her attention and corrects her use of *vous*, pointing out that age is a relevant aspect of the context determining appropriate choice of *tu*. Additionally, he characterizes the use of *tu* as a personal preference, thus saving Lilian's face by accepting part of the dilemma as his own.

Lilian's next message to Robert was written primarily in English, but she explicitly takes note of Robert's previous commentary on her use of address forms:

Example 7: Thursday, January 30, 1997

I will try and remember to use the "*tu*" form when I write to you. It is easier sometimes for me to use *vous* though because we address our teacher with the *vous* form.

In his reply to this message, Robert's commentary on the *tu* form continues, this time with remarks on the ease of pronunciation of the verb forms associated with the informal second-person pronoun.

Example 8: Tuesday, February 4, 1997

Pour la prononciation, c'est facile: c'est presque toujours comme pour la troisieme personne. *tu* as, il a, *tu* dis, il dit, *tu* fais, il fait, *tu* bouges, il bouge, *tu* . . . facile.

For pronunciation, it's easy: it's almost always the same as the third person: you have, he has, you say, he says, you do, he does, you move, he moves, you . . . easy.

In a subsequent message, Lilian wrote to Robert in French, using the *tu* form of address appropriately.

Example 9: Tuesday, February 18, 1997

Robert,

Desole. J'ai un examen en francais dernier semaine. Je pense que je n'ai pas bien fait. Le sujet etait l'histoire de France. J'ai apprendu (?) de Charlemagne et Louis XII et Francois 1. Il etait difficile pour moi . . .

J'ai besoin d'ecrire un papier maintenant. Je voudrais envoyer une copie pour toi. (T)

J'ai regarde le film "Sabrina" hier et il y avait beaucoup de places en France. Paris. As-*tu* (T) regarde ce film?

Robert,

Sorry. I have an exam in French last week. I think I didn't do well. The subject was the history of France. I learned about Charlemagne and Louis XII and Francois I. It was difficult for me . . . I have to write a paper now. I would like to send a copy for you.

I watched the film "Sabrina" last night and there were a lot of places in France. Paris. Have you seen that film?

In all of the messages that Lilian wrote to Robert in French for the remainder of the semester, and in his responses to her, the *tu* form of address is used. This change in her choice of pronoun demonstrates that Lilian became aware of at least some aspects of the social value of the *tu* form through participation and assisted performance in the social context of e-mail correspondence.

Susan and Pierre.   Another student in the American class, Susan, wrote a message of greeting to the professors of the French class that was forwarded to her keypal, Pierre. Pierre then wrote directly to her in English:

Example 10: Thursday, January 23, 1997

I am Pierre and I am your new French "mailfriend." I received your letter yesterday and now I am writing to you to introduce myself a little bit.

I have been studying English for ten years and this year Vanessa and Alison are my English teachers. Attending lessons is quite boring, but talking with someone else in English I am quite fond of it. As you may certainly know I am in Engineering school. You wrote to me that you are studying French and German but what are your major, your minor?

In reply, Susan wrote a message directly to Pierre in which she addressed him as *vous* throughout.

Example 11: Wednesday, January 22, 1997

Merci, Pierre, pour votre (V) lettre!

Oui, dites-moi (V), s'il *vous* (V) plait, de votres (V) voyages aux Etats-Unis. Je me suis interesse beaucoup de quoi *vous* avez (V) vu et pense. Je me specialise en le francais et l'allemand, les deux. Je n'ai pas de "minor." . . .

Je n'ai pense pas que *vous* avez recevu (V) ma lettre, parce qu'elle m'a renvoye avec le message "User Unknown." Comment est-ce que *vous* avez (V) decide qui seraient un "mailfriend" avec qui? Je sais que *vous* voudriez (V) exercer votre (V) anglais, mais voudriez-*vous* (V) me commenter votres (V) lettres? Mon pere est un professeur d'anglais au lycee, donc si *vous* avez (V) des questions . . .

J'ai beaucoup de devoirs ce soir, et votre (V) lettre etait une surprise.

Thank you, Pierre, for your letter!

Yes, tell me, please, about your trips to the United States. I am very interested in what you saw and thought. I am majoring in both French and German. I don't have a "minor."

I didn't think you have received my letter, because it came back with the message "User Unknown." How did you decide who would be mailfriends with whom? I know you would like to practice your English, but would you like me to comment on your letters? My father is a high school English teacher, so if you have questions . . .

I have a lot of homework this evening, and your letter was a surprise.

There followed a regular correspondence through the months of February and March, during which Susan continued to write in French using the *vous* form, and Pierre replied in English, without comment on her use of *vous*. Nonetheless, a turning point in Susan's awareness of address form use coincided with the two classes' participation in a live, real-time video-conference during which the students asked and answered questions about the course materials. The conference was taped, transcribed, and commented on during two of the regular sessions for the American class, and the teacher pointed out the use of the *tu* form for addressing individual students both within the French class and in utterances addressed to individual American students by the French participants. Following the videoconference, Susan began to address her keypal as *tu*: Immediately following the conference, she wrote a message from which the following example is selected.

Example 12: Monday, March 24, 1997

> Le video-conference etait si merveilleux et amusement, j'ai desire de te (T) telephoner et continuer la conversation. Je voudrais avoir un video-conference chanque semaine—donc nous deviendrions plus personnel et casuel. *Tu* etais (T) tres amusant avec ton (T) T shirt. Nous avons un nouveau Hooters ici, mais je n'irai pas la, probablement, a cause de je suis trop feministe.

> The videoconference was so marvelous and amusing, I wanted to call you and continue the conversation. I would like to have a videoconference every week—so we would become more personal and casual. You were very funny with your T shirt. We have a new Hooters here but I won't go there, probably, because I am too feminist.

Although she did not receive direct comment from Pierre concerning her use of *vous*, and most of Pierre's writing to her was in English, in all her messages to Pierre following the videoconference, Susan continued appropriately to use the *tu* form of address. A switch from *vous* to *tu* would be part of the normal course of events in the context of a developing friendship. However, Susan's case also suggests a role of legitimate peripheral participation (Lave & Wenger, 1991) and for consciousness-raising efforts by the teacher in the acquisition of appropriate address form usage. Participation in the videoconference and the subsequent analysis of the event provided Susan with ample opportunities to observe the appropriate use of *tu* for address among students. Her continued correspondence with Pierre then allowed her to use that form in the context of a relationship of solidarity.

Mandy and Martin. A third and final case is that of Mandy, who developed a strong relationship with her keypal, Martin, through extensive e-mail correspondence in English and French. Like most of the other French students, Martin wrote almost entirely in English. Lacking confidence in her French, Mandy wrote lengthy messages in English with portions written in

French, usually at the beginning of the messages. As the semester progressed, and her friendship with Martin developed, the proportion of French in Mandy's e-mail increased. Unlike her classmates, Mandy had no initial difficulty with the use of the *tu* form of address in her e-mail.

Example 13: Wednesday, February 5, 1997

> Je suis tres desolee entendre que *tu* as (T) les examens maintenant. Ce n'est pas bon. Je n'aime pas les examens. Ma classe de francais regarde les films maintenant—les memes films en francais et anglais. Par exemple—Neuf Mois et Nine Months. Tres interessant!

> I am very sorry to hear that you have exams now. That is not good. I don't like exams. My French class is watching the movies now—the same movies in French and English. For example—Neuf Mois and Nine Months. Very interesting!

However, Mandy may have perceived the videoconferences as a more formal setting than the e-mail exchange; in her "face-to-face" conversation with Martin during a conference taking place near the end of the semester, she planned her question to him to include the use of the *vous* form of address.

Example 14: Wednesday, April 8, 1997

> 1. Mandy: est-ce que *vous* trouvez (V) une différence entre le sens de l'humour français et américain, par exemple dans les films ou les livres?

> Do you find a difference between the French and the American sense of humor, for example in the films or the books?

> 2. Martin: (smiles and waves) à propos des plaisanteries que *tu* (T) (others laugh) que *tu* ne comprends pas (T), j'aimerais que *tu* précises (T) en fait euh. Quels types de plaisanteries *tu* ne comprends pas (T)?

> Concerning the jokes that you (others laugh) that you don't understand, I would like you to be more precise, in fact. What type of jokes don't you understand?

> 3. Mandy: Ooh uh la langue?

> Ooh uh the language?

> 4. Martin: C'est à cause du français?

> It's because of the French?

> 5. Mandy: Oui.

> Yes.

Following the videoconference, in addition to commentary and instruction on language forms given by the teacher based on the videotape, Mandy, like Lilian, received explicit feedback from her keypal about her use of address forms. The following example is excerpted from the beginning of Martin's e-mail of April 27.

Example 15: Sunday, April 27, 1997

. . . when people know each other as we do, they usually use "*tu*" in their sentences. (Young children use it for everybody, because they learn only later that they have to say "*vous*" for grown-ups like their teachers for example.)

Martin's reaction to Mandy's use of *vous* during the conference was sufficiently strong to prompt this comment, which focuses on the familiarity the two correspondents had developed over the course of the semester. Mandy thanked him in a subsequent e-mail for his attention to her French, and there are no further instances of inappropriate use of *vous* in her use of French with Martin thereafter.

SUMMARY AND DISCUSSION

As Breen (1996) noted, significant movement toward reaching the broader goals of communicative language teaching will require constructing the learner not only as a strategic acquirer and processor of input, but also as a discursive practitioner, with attendant focus on language learning as social practice. This reconceptualization of the learner is especially useful in the study of developing pragmatic competence, where issues of grammatical accuracy are very often superceded by problems of consciousness and appropriacy of linguistic forms in particular social contexts. The inherent sociopragmatic ambiguity of second-person address forms, for example, means that reference to the actual context of their use is required to understand their social meaning. It follows that learners who have access to a range of social contexts will also, in principle, have access to awareness of these forms and to their appropriate uses.

To demonstrate precisely how this access impacts learning requires that researchers aim to study not only the products of development, but also the processes by which development is supported (or hindered) within particular settings. Consequently, one of the aims of this study was to demonstrate an approach to the study of developing pragmatic competence that attends to the context and practices of language socialization. The study took place in an interactive setting, a "classroom," that was undergoing a radical change in the qualities of learner language use through the participation of a partner class in France and a set of new communications technologies, including e-mail and videoconferencing. Using a microgenetic and developmental approach, it became possible to document the sensitive and ongoing relation between the learners' understanding of particular language forms, including their social meaning, and the qualities of assisted performance and consciousness raising provided by native-speaking peers. In a manner that closely mirrored the documented practices of children's caregivers, native-speaking keypals provided both explicit instruction and direct assistance to their partners to help them in understanding how and why the social context of solidarity is constructed in French. It was also suggested that observation of language use by others, both local classmates and native-speaking peers, constituted a case of legitimate peripheral participation (Lave & Wenger, 1991) whereby the learners in this study gained access to the construction of solidarity in French.

Most of the participants in this study had no previous experience of relationships of solidarity or intimacy in French. The development of their new virtual friendships via e-mail therefore offered an opportunity to study the developmental consequences of participation in a new social context. Specifically, in each of the three cases already outlined, although in different ways, the American learner's participation in the tele-collaborative course provided a context for socialization into appropriate use of mutual *tu* in addressing a fellow student.

In two cases (Lilian and Mandy), the learner's experience bears a marked resemblance to that of children learning to interact appropriately in their first language: They were given direct and explicit instructions on what to say and how, and the relevant social factors (e.g., age, familiarity) were made salient by their partners. Lilian began the semester with little experience in the use of *tu* and limited appreciation of the ways in which address form contributes to the construction of social context in French. Through participation and direct, explicit assistance provided by her partner, she became aware of the social value of the *tu* form and began to use it consistently in this context.

For Mandy, who began the semester using *tu* appropriately in e-mail, difficulty arose with a change in participation format, from e-mail to the videoconference. Mandy was also given explicit assistance by Martin to clarify that the use of *tu* depends on the qualities of personal relationships.

Susan initially overgeneralized the use of *vous* in e-mail to her partner, but as the semester progressed, her relationship with Pierre as well as the general contact with spoken French among peers provided a context for observation, peripheral participation, and use of the *tu* form. By the end of the semester she had demonstrated her mastery of this concept in a series of lengthy e-mail messages.

Thus, in each of the cases explored, the context of a virtual friendship served to disambiguate the *tu–vous* distinction and supported the learner in developing her awareness and use of the linguistic dimensions of solidarity in French.

In drawing the implications of discursive approaches to research and teaching, Breen (1996) noted that "A key issue for language pedagogy is how it may facilitate the disembedding of language learning from the prevailing discourse of lessons" (p. 101). The communication resources afforded by new technologies are often hailed as tools that will ultimately assist the profession in digging itself out of its own limited pedagogic routines, to enhance the relevance and authenticity of classroom language learning. Dramatic increases in access to resources and people provide the basis for many optimistic claims about the benefits of computer-mediated communication in the foreign language classroom (Grandjean-Levy, 1997; Knight, 1994; Lunde, 1990). Networked communication is believed to offer access to a broad range of people and interactive practices, rearranging the power hierarchy of the traditional classroom in radical, transformative ways. Access implies choice, and the profession now must strive to make informed choices from the many options available for interactive classroom work. In arguing for a developmental analysis of learning via new technologies, I make the case in this chapter that professionals in language education need to know more about the social processes enabled by the new communications tools and how these processes interact with language learning.

This developmental analysis of learners' experiences suggests that telecommunications technology may indeed broaden classroom discourse options, enabling assisted participation and learning in a range of interactive practices involving variations in status and social distance. However, it is not the technology itself that is beneficial to learners, but rather the vagaries, perils, and delights of making sense in the company of other human beings who interest them. In other words, one potential of the networked classroom is to bring institutional learning more in harmony with real life, leading perhaps to the development of everyday communicative skills and abilities. To the extent that the profession is sincere in its appreciation of these abilities, and able to incorporate them successfully into its conception of academic language learning, we may hope that the benefits of networked social life will extend into the classroom.

REFERENCES

Amon, E., Muyskens, J. A., & Omaggio-Hadley, A. (1995). *Vis-à-vis: Beginning French.* New York: McGraw-Hill.

Breen, M. P. (1996). Constructions of the learner in second language research. In J. E. Alatis, C. A. Straehle, M. Ronkin, & B. Gallenberger (Eds.), *Linguistics, language acquisition and language variation: Current trends and future prospects* (pp. 84–107). Washington, DC: Georgetown University Press.

Brown, P., & Levinson, S. (1987). *Politeness: Some universals in language usage.* New York: Cambridge University Press.

Brown, R., & Gilman, A. (1970). The pronouns of power and solidarity. In R. Brown (Ed.), *Psycholinguistics* (pp. 302–335). New York: The Free Press. (Original work published 1960)

Burt, S. M. (1995). Where does sociopragmatic ambiguity come from? *Pragmatics and Language Learning, 6,* 47–57.

Carroll, R. (1988). *Cultural misunderstandings: The French/American experience* (C. Volk, Trans.). Chicago: University of Chicago Press.

Donato, R. (1994). Collective scaffolding in second language learning. In J. P. Lantolf & G. Appel (Eds.), *Vygotskian approaches to second language research* (pp. 33–56). Norwood, NJ: Ablex.

Gilman, A., & Brown, R. (1958). Who says "*tu*" to whom. *Etc., XV,* 169–174.

Grandjean-Levy, A. (1997). Caught in the net. *The French Review, 69,* 825–833.

Grice, H. P. (1975). Logic and conversation. In P. Cole & J. Morgan (Eds.), *Syntax and semantics 3: Speech acts* (pp. 41–58). New York: Academic Press.

Hall, J. K. (1995). "Aw, man, where we goin'": Classroom interaction and the development of L2 interactional competence. *Issues in Applied Linguistics, 6,* 37–62.

Kasper, G. (1982). Teaching-induced aspects of interlanguage discourse. *Studies in Second Language Acquisition, 4,* 99–113.

Kinginger, C. (1998). Videoconferencing as access to spoken French. *Modern Language Journal, 82,* 502–513.

Kinginger, C., Gourvès-Hayward, A., & Simpson, V. (1999). A tele-collaborative course on French/American intercultural communication. *French Review, 72,* 853–866

Knight, S. (1994). Making authentic cultural and linguistic connections. *Hispania, 77,* 288–294.

Kramsch, C. (1985). Classroom interaction and discourse options. *Studies in Second Language Acquisition, 7,* 169–183.

Lambert, W., & Tucker, R. G. (1976). *Tu, vous, usted: A social psychological study of address forms.* Rowley, MA: Newbury House.

Lave, J., & Wenger, E. (1991). *Situated learning: Legitimate peripheral participation.* New York: Cambridge University Press.

Lunde, K. R. (1990). Using electronic mail as a medium for foreign language study and instruction. *CALICO Journal, 7,* 68–78.

Lyster, R. (1994). The effect of functional-analytic teaching on aspects of French immersion students' sociolinguistic competence. *Applied Linguistics, 15,* 263–287.

Lyster, R. (1996). Question forms, conditionals, and second-person pronouns used by adolescent native speakers across two levels of formality in written and spoken French. *Modern Language Journal, 80,* 165–182.

Myers-Scotton, C. (1993). *Social motivations for codeswitching*. Oxford, UK: Oxford University Press.

Ochs, E. (1986). Introduction. In B. Schieffelin & E. Ochs (Eds.), *Language socialization across cultures* (pp. 1–13). New York: Cambridge University Press.

Ochs, E., & Schieffelin, B. (1979). *Developmental pragmatics*. New York: Academic Press.

Ohta, A. S. (1994). Socializing the expression of affect: An overview of affective particle use in the Japanese as a foreign language classroom. *Issues in Applied Linguistics, 5*, 303–326.

Schieffelin, B., & Ochs, E. (1986). *Language socialization across cultures*. New York: Cambridge University Press.

Schmidt, R. (1993). Consciousness, learning and interlanguage pragmatics. In G. Kasper & S. Blum-Kulka (Eds.), *Interlanguage pragmatics* (pp. 21–42). New York: Oxford University Press.

Scollon, R., & Scollon, S. W. (1995). *Intercultural communication: A discourse approach*. Oxford, UK: Blackwell.

Scotton, C. M. (1983). The negotiation of identities in conversation: A theory of markedness and code choice. *International Journal of the Sociology of Language, 44*, 115–136.

Snow, C. E., Perlmann, R. Y., Gleason, J. B., & Hooshyar, N. (1990). Developmental perspectives on politeness: Sources of children's knowledge. *Journal of Pragmatics, 14*, 289–305.

Swain, M., & Lapkin, S. (1990). Aspects of the sociolinguistic performance of early and late French immersion students. In R. Scarcella, E. A. Andersen, & S. D. Krashen (Eds.), *Developing communicative competence in a second language* (pp. 41–54). Rowley, MA: Newbury House.

Vygotsky, L. S. (1978). *Mind in society*. Cambridge, MA: Harvard University Press.

Vygotsky, L. S. (1981). The genesis of higher mental functions. In J. V. Wertsch (Ed.), *The concept of activity in Soviet psychology* (pp. 144–188). New York: M. E. Sharpe.

Wertsch, J. V. (1985). *Vygotsky and the social formation of mind*. Cambridge, MA: Harvard University Press.

Wylie, L., & Brière, J.-F. (1995). *Les français* (2nd ed.). Englewood Cliffs, NJ: Prentice-Hall.

3

Rethinking Recasts: A Learner-Centered Examination of Corrective Feedback in the Japanese Language Classroom

Amy Snyder Ohta

This chapter looks at the question of how learners respond when corrective feedback takes place in Japanese foreign language classrooms.[1] Studies of corrective feedback in second language classrooms have traditionally focused on the teacher–student exchange. Correcting errors is, after all, something that language teachers do. Researchers interested in teacher use of corrective feedback have questioned the effectiveness of the classroom correction of student errors. At one time, language learning was viewed as development of stimulus–response "habits," and all errors were to be stamped out, with the idea that they could be prevented. In Japanese language teaching today, proponents of rigorous error correction work with the intent of preventing fossilization.[2] The necessity felt by some of correcting every error, however, lies in contrast with the results of studies of developmental sequences. These studies have found that learners follow predictable developmental paths, with nontarget-like forms along the way occurring as part of developmental stages that must be passed through on

---

[1]An earlier version of this chapter was presented as Ohta (1999a).

[2]Roberts' (1995) study of corrective feedback described a class conducted using such an approach.

the way to acquiring the ability to use particular forms in target-like ways. For example, work on the development of negation in Japanese has shown that nontarget-like forms are part of a predictable developmental sequence on the way to acquisition of appropriate negation strategies (Kanagy, 1994, in press). However, variable success by learners in acquiring the target language has led researchers to consider how form-focused instruction or consciousness-raising activities might alter the path of second language acquisition (SLA; Doughty & Williams, 1998; Fotos, 1993). Corrective feedback is one way of focusing learner attention on second language (L2) grammatical form (Koyanagi, Moroishi, Muranoi, Ota, & Shibata, 1994; Lightbown & Spada, 1990).

To understand the function of corrective feedback in classroom SLA processes, L2 researchers have analyzed interaction between teachers and learners. One goal of this research has been to determine which methods might be most successful in helping students to increase accuracy of production. Researchers working in the interactionist tradition of SLA research hypothesize that language acquisition proceeds through negotiation of L2 form and meaning, both because interactional modifications make input more comprehensible (Long, 1983) and because production of interactional modifications may promote development of the learner's interlanguage (Pica, 1988; Swain, 1985, 1993). From this perspective, corrective feedback may be viewed as a type of negotiation that may prompt the interactional modifications hypothesized to lead to SLA. When there is "uptake" of corrective feedback—when the learner who was corrected produces an oral response to the feedback in the next turn—the learner's language production may be modified, a process thought to promote acquisition (Lyster, 1998; Lyster & Ranta, 1997). Uptake is hypothesized to be critical to the impact of corrective feedback on acquisition processes, because interactional modifications only occur if there is uptake. Lyster, Ranta, and Chaudron followed this line of thought, suggesting that techniques that are successful at pinpointing errors and generating learner reformulation are potentially more effective in promoting language learning than other techniques. Although such claims of effectiveness properly refer only to the degree that a particular technique is successful in generating an oral response or reformulation, use of a theoretical framework that emphasizes the role of interactional modifications strongly suggests a connection with effectiveness in promoting SLA (Chaudron, 1986; Lyster, 1998; Lyster & Ranta, 1997). This chapter reconsiders the salience and potential effectiveness of recasts by considering a source of classroom data that has not, as yet, been considered: private speech data. Private speech, learners' self-addressed utterances, provides a window into the mental activities of learners. These data reveal learners to be mentally active in attending to and analyzing recasts. Because private speech reveals mental activity, the findings suggest that even when private speech does not occur, recasts present salient contrasts to learners that they are able to process and utilize in their inner speech or thought.

THE EFFECTIVENESS OF RECASTS: L2 RESEARCH

Recasts are broadly defined as responses to learners that provide expansion or implicit correction. They are widely used with language learners of first and foreign languages in naturalistic and classroom settings. Different researchers have used a range of different terminology to identify different types of recasts. For example, Chaudron's (1977) "repetition with change" and "expansion" are both types of recasts. L2 researchers have strongly suggested that, based on the infrequency of student responses, recasts are less effective than other methods of corrective feedback. Not all corrective feedback techniques are equal when it comes to generating uptake. Lyster and Ranta (1997) found that recasts resulted in uptake much less frequently than did other feedback types, as shown in Table 3.1.

Chaudron (1977) was concerned about learners' tendencies not to orally respond to recasts, saying that "in many cases the teacher assumes that his correct model is automatically perceived, and he neglects to insure its 'intake' by the learner with new elicitative acts" (p. 43). The implication here is that teachers should not assume that recasts are salient, but should follow up recasts with additional moves that prompt a learner to orally respond. Chaudron also expressed concern that recasts may lack precision in isolating the nature of the learner's error. More recently, Pica, Holliday, Lewis, and Morgenthaler (1989) noted that recasts do not promote reformulation of the ill-formed utterance. The work of Lyster (1998) and Lyster and Ranta (1997) underscores these concerns. Not only do recasts fail in gaining an oral response, but even if the learner does repeat the recast,

TABLE 3.1
Uptake Following Teacher Feedback (Data From Lyster & Ranta, 1997, p. 54)

Feedback Type	Recast	Explicit Correction	Repetition	Metalinguistic Feedback	Clarification Request
Uptake	31%	50%	78%	86%	88%

because recasts provide a correct reformulation the learner is not pushed to draw on his or her own resources in producing a corrected utterance. Within the interactionist view, repetition may be considered less significant in terms of linguistic development than the sort of reformulation that occurs when learners are pushed to rely on their own resources, as when corrective feedback pinpoints a problem but does not provide the right form. This is the rationale underlying researcher recommendations that teachers should use explicit feedback techniques that force the learner to reflect back on the error and reformulate.

Such suggestions to teachers may be premature. First, L2 research has only worked to understand how recasts impact the addressee, who is one of many members of the classroom community. Whether and how classroom recasts impact other learners in the classroom has not been investigated. Second, L2 researchers are not all in agreement about what addressee responses to corrective feedback mean. For example, Doughty (1993) analyzed 6 hours of classes conducted by the same French teacher and determined that the teacher's use of recasts was predictable, not ambiguous. Contrary to concerns expressed by other researchers cited earlier, Doughty concluded that learner responses to the teacher's recasts suggest that the contrast between learner errors and teacher recasts was noticed. Recent L2 experimental research has also suggested that recasts may be effective (Mackey & Philp, 1998; Oliver, 1995; Philp, 1999).

RECASTS AND FIRST LANGUAGE ACQUISITION

In contrast to the conclusions of L2 classroom research, a range of first language (L1) acquisition research has shown maternal use of recasts to be related to measures of child language development (Baker & Nelson, 1984; Moerk, 1992; Nelson, 1989; Scherer & Olswang, 1984). Rather than measuring the effectiveness of recasts by the presence or absence of uptake, L1 acquisition researchers investigate the impact of recasts on the child's language development over time. Use of recasts by mothers has been found to result in toddlers with larger vocabularies who produce longer utterances (Uzgiris, Broome, & Kruper, 1989), and faster growing language skill (Nelson, Denninger, Bonvillian, Kaplan, & Baker, 1983). In a study that more specifically examined the relation of recasts with growth in L1 syntax, language disorders specialists Camarata, Nelson, and Camarata (1994) found recasting therapy to be effective in leading to the acquisition of targeted forms by children with language impairments. The children in the study only repeated 2.3% of the target forms contained in the recasts during therapy sessions. Neither lack of uptake nor the lack of opportunity for reformulation was a telling predictor of whether or not recasts were effective in promoting language acquisition. Recent L2 experimental studies suggest that Camarata et al.'s findings may relate to adult SLA processes as well, showing that English as a second language learners who were experimental participants both noticed (Philp, 1999) and made use of recasts (Mackey & Philp, 1998). These studies agree with the child L1 acquisition findings that repetition or reformulation is not necessary for recasts to have an effect.

This work is at odds with claims of classroom researchers that recasts are ineffective in promoting L2 development. Lyster (1998) argued that most recasts used in communicatively oriented immersion content classrooms are unlikely to be noticed by learners, because teachers also repeat and recast utterances that do not contain errors. To Lyster, this ambiguity potentially reduces the salience of recasts that follow ill-formed utterances. Child language researchers disagree, even though, just as in L2 classroom interaction, adult caregivers recast both well-formed and ill-formed utterances and also engage frequently in noncorrective repetition. L1 researchers, however, do not consider caregiver behavior to be ambiguous, as recasts occur most frequently following utterances containing errors (Demetras, Post, & Snow, 1987).

L1 researchers attribute the effectiveness of recasts to their salience. What seems to be critical is not whether or not the child repeats the recasts, but the fact that recasts are semantically contingent on the child's own utterance. Before recasts are even possible, when children are preverbal, researchers report that contingent responses have an effect; infants whose mothers imitate the sounds they make are more vocally experimental than other infants (Masur, 1989). Moreover, recasts include not only the redundant component, but also something new—a contrast with the child's own utterance in, for example, phonology, grammatical form, or information presented. Moerk (1992) found simple recasts that present one contrast to be powerful in explaining the development of Eve, the young child he studied. Meltzoff and Gopnik (1989) found expansion to be particularly engaging, stating that "duplication coupled with expansion and recasting" appears "to be maximally interesting and useful for the children," at the same time serving "as a frame and motivation for further exchange" (p. 37). The effectiveness of recasts results from the salience inherent in reformulations that follow the learner's own interest. In addition, because the limited capacity of attention puts constraints on processing, semantic redundancy relieves a measure of the effort needed to understand the recast, promoting salience of the contrast between the recast and the child's own utterance. VanPatten (1989) stated that "simultaneous processing of meaning and form . . . can only occur if comprehension as a skill is automatized, thus releasing attention for a focus on form" (p. 409). With recasts, because meaning is held constant, the learner's focus is naturally drawn to the contrast between the learner's own utterance and the recast. The redundancy of recasts results in a reduced semantic load, freeing processing capacity for the reformulation (Camarata et al., 1994). For adult learners who are trying to express their own meanings with mixed success, continued semantic focus on the learner's utterance would also promote learner attention to the recast, which often constitutes a new and improved version of the learner's own utterance. For learners struggling to express themselves, recasts should be particularly salient.

These disparate views of recasts as effective or ineffective in promoting language acquisition result from the collection and analysis of different types of data. The L2 research examines teacher–student interaction, with student voices collected as a group. In contrast, the L1 research tracks children longitudinally, looking at connections between a particular child's social interactive environment and considering individual language production outcomes over time. L1 experimental studies, in the same way, look at how a particular social environment created in the experiment impacts the language production of a particular child down the road. This study takes a further look at corrective feedback in the L2 classroom setting, examining how recasts impact learners by examining a new kind of data: the private speech of individual learners.

CLUES FROM PRIVATE SPEECH DATA

Vygotskian psycholinguistic theory provides the L2 researcher with a theoretical framework appropriate for development of a sociocognitive view of SLA. In contrast to the interactionist view, which prioritizes examination of input and output, a sociocognitive view of SLA considers language acquisition as a process whereby the language of social interaction is gradually appropriated by the individual as a tool of thought. Reception and production are not discrete processes, but interpenetrate one another. SLA involves learning a new way to think and interact (Leontiev, 1981). In this view, language development and cognitive development are mutually constitutive and proceed through a process of dynamic internalization. Private speech, oral language addressed by the student to himself or herself, is part of this dynamic internalization process. Private speech is called "private" not because of any inherently personal content, but because private speech utterances are produced for the self and are not adapted to an audience. Although private speech is most evident among children (Vygotsky, 1978, 1987), adults also produce private speech when learning new skills (John-Steiner, 1992), including the learning of another language (Lantolf, 1997; McCafferty, 1992, 1994a, 1994b; Ohta, 1999a, in press).

Private speech emerges through the sociocognitive processes of language learning. When children are acquiring their first language, language is available to them in social interaction. As children appropriate this social dialogue they develop the capacity for independent thought. Cognitive processes are social in origin, with the realities of social interaction forming the structures of cognition. As social speech is internalized for individual cognitive purposes, it becomes abbreviated. Private speech is part of this internalization process, being itself a transitional form between social speech and inner speech. At this transitional stage, children may become unable to function in problem-solving situations if not allowed to verbalize orally (Vygotsky, 1987). For adults, who have completed this internalization process, private speech is usually no longer a necessary component of cognitive activity, but may reemerge during times of cognitive stress, as found by John-Steiner (1992). In addition, the process of learning a new language brings with it a whole new internalization process, with private speech again serving as a cognitive tool (Ohta, in press). For the second language learner, private speech functions as a tool for the internalization of the L2, and as a productive, hypothesis-testing device whereby learners think aloud as they work to solve L2 problems. In addition, I have found that private speech provides individual learners with avenues of participation in L2 classroom activities even when they are not being directly addressed by the teacher (Ohta, in press). Through the use of private speech, learners participate by taking their own private turns, making the interaction immediately relevant to themselves as learners.

Private speech has long been a productive source of data for L1 researchers, with growing attention from researchers interested in the SLA of children (Saville-Troike, 1988) and adults (Lantolf, 1997; Lantolf & Frawley, 1985; McCafferty, 1992, 1994a, 1994b). Adult private speech provides the SLA researcher with a source of cognitive processing data that has tended to be overlooked. Audio and video recordings of classroom interaction, for example, generally mike students as a group rather than as individuals, losing the individual record of interaction. Because SLA, whether it occurs in a naturalistic or classroom setting, is a sociocognitive process that involves one learner in interaction with his or her social world, this individual record is an important one.

THIS STUDY

This study, like previous L2 studies, investigates how learners respond to recasts. However, this study does not define learner responses in terms of uptake as defined by next-turn oral responses directed to the teacher. Instead, through the individual miking of students, the relation between private speech and recasts is probed. This study asks what private speech data tell us about both the salience of recasts and the process of corrective feedback in classroom language learning. Specifically, private speech is examined for insights into (a) the salience of contrasts presented in recasts, (b) the impact of recasts on other members of the class who are not the individual to whom the feedback is addressed, and (c) whether and how learners are able to make use of utterances that contrast with their own ill-formed utterances.

The Data

In this study, seven university-level learners, four enrolled in first-year Japanese and three enrolled in second-year Japanese, were followed through an academic year. These learners' classes were audio and video recorded three to five times per quarter. Both first- and second-year Japanese courses were multisection courses, so the targeted learners experienced instruction from different teachers throughout the year, and were usually enrolled in different sections. Audio recording was conducted with small tape recorders and individual microphones clipped to each learner's collar or the front of his or her shirt. Individual microphones were sensitive enough to reliably collect both the learner's individual voice and the voices of the teacher and other students. Each class was also carefully observed on data collection days, with detailed field notes kept on the time, instructional events, and what was written on the blackboard during the events. Copies of materials used in class such as overhead transparencies and handouts were also collected, with the time and manner of their use recorded in the field notes. The audio recordings for about five classes for each learner, spaced throughout the year, were transcribed in detail, resulting in a corpus of 34 hours of classroom instruction. Each transcript was produced collaboratively by the researcher and research assistants using the methodology of conversation analysis, with a high level of attention paid to overlap and pauses. In transcribing private speech, different levels of volume of learner utterances were also noted.

In these classes, the language of instruction was Japanese, with rare use of English by teachers, and broadly followed an eclectic, communicatively oriented approach. In first-year Japanese, the textbook incorporated a grammatical syllabus that was overlaid by a topical one. Most activities were designed to promote the understanding and use of grammar and vocabulary, with particular topics providing broader coherence to classroom activity. In the second-year class, there was less topical coherence for textbook chapters. The grammatical syllabus of the text was broadly utilized, with topics for language practice selected that would prove useful in providing grammar practice. Lessons included communicative tasks such as interview tasks and information gap tasks, along with role playing, communicative and structural drill, and reading and writing activities. In all of these classrooms, a strong focus on form was maintained throughout teaching and learning activities, with explicit grammar lectures once a week, and instructional activities and peer learning tasks designed to target particular grammatical structures and vocabulary.

Methodology of Analysis

For this study, episodes containing private speech were the focus of analysis. Private speech utterances were identified using a fairly narrow definition of private speech: reduced volume, lack of adaptation to an interlocutor, and lack of response from an interlocutor (Ohta, in press). All seven of the learners produced private speech, but four of the learners produced private speech with moderate to high frequency (14–54 times per class.) Three of these learners were first-year learners (Candace, Kuoming, and Sara) and one was a second-year learner (Bryce). These four learners also responded to recasts and contrasting utterances in their private speech, and these data form the core of this investigation.

Analysis utilized a qualitative, discourse-analytic approach. Private speech was examined for the insight it might provide into how corrective feedback, particularly recasts, impacted the learners. Through an iterative process of analysis, research questions were formed in more specific terms, and the data reexamined as questions were formulated. The question of how recasts impacted learners in general was always kept in mind, with specific reference to the three points outlined earlier: (a) information about the potential salience of recasts, (b) how recasts impact both addressees and those who are not specifically addressed, and (c) whether and how learners make use of utterances that contrast with their own ill-formed utterances.

Through the iterative process of qualitative analysis, it became apparent that traditional definitions of corrective feedback did not capture what functioned as corrective from the learners' perspective. From the learners' perspective, corrective feedback consisted not only of what has been traditionally examined—teacher responses that treat addressee errors. Corrective feedback was also found to include utterances that were corrective in nature, whether produced in response to a targeted learner's utterance or not. Analysis proceeded by examining learner private speech utterances, taking note of what preceded them, and whether or not private speech was responsive in any way to corrective feedback. In addition, if the private utterance was ill formed, analysis proceeded to identify whether or not learners were afforded information through the interactive process that might allow them to notice their own error. During the process of analyzing the data, it was found that occasionally utterances that had not been coded as private speech, such as learner utterances produced at normal volume as part of a collection of individual responses that resulted when the teacher addressed a question to the class as a whole (choral responses), were relevant to corrective feedback sequences. Although the volume of these utterances was not reduced, they did constitute private turns (van Lier, 1988) and were functionally utterances for the self. Thus, regardless of volume, utterances in private turns were examined to determine their relation to corrective feedback. These utterances are evident in the transcript as they are not marked as having reduced volume. In reporting the results of this analysis, I specifically address what these individual learner contributions tell us about the role of corrective feedback, particularly recasts, in the Japanese foreign language classroom.

In considering the relation between private speech and corrective feedback, following Bell (1984), learners were considered as conversational participants not only when they were the addressees of corrective feedback, but also when they were in the role of auditor. *Auditors* are persons who are not being addressed, but whose participation in the particular group is licensed. Auditors may become addressees at any time. In the classes examined here, the targeted students were at times addressees, but were quite often auditors. By analyzing these students' participation, both when addressees and when auditors, we can better understand how recasts impact the learners.

Results

Analysis of private speech provides insight into the mental activity that learners engage in with respect to corrective feedback. Learners produced private speech most often when they were not individual addressees, but when they were auditors. Other private turns occurred when learners were addressed as members of the class as a whole. In discussing the results, I first provide examples of private speech responses to teacher recasts that were produced by auditors. Second, I show how a learner-centered analysis of data shows corrective feedback to incorporate a range of utterances not normally considered as corrective in nature. The results show that activity by learners in their own private turns creates the opportunity for them to produce utterances that, if ill formed, may incidentally contrast with those of others. When this occurs, contrasting utterances of other students or the teacher function as incidental recasts. Incidental recasts function as recasts from the learner's perspective, whether or not they were intended as corrective by those who uttered them, and even though they are not individually addressed to the learner. Learner responses to these incidental recasts provide evidence of the salience of the contrasts. Results show that what functions as corrective feedback from the learner's perspective is quite different from what an analyst might identify as an instance of corrective feedback based on traditional methods of analyzing classroom discourse.

Auditor Responses to Recasts. Lack of an oral response from the student who is corrected by the teacher has been taken as a sign of potential ineffectiveness of corrective feedback, but private speech data show that learners produce very subtle oral responses that would not be captured by a microphone some distance away. In fact, auditors, those not directly addressed by the teacher, are actively involved in utilizing the corrective feedback addressed to others, responses that provide evidence for the salience of recasts. This active involvement is evident in private speech, but is actually a much broader phenomenon, as adult learners are also well able to capitalize on their inner voices in active, silent responses. Learners, in fact, vary dramatically in the extent to which they produce audible private speech.

My data clearly show how actively auditors involve themselves in utilizing episodes of corrective feedback. In Excerpt 1, Kuo-ming repeated a recast directed to a fellow classmate. The classmate used the wrong tense of the verb *suru* 'do' to describe hurting his leg. The key expression is as shown:

a. Ashi ni kega o   suru
   Leg DAT injury ACC do
   "To hurt one's leg" or "(I) will hurt my leg."

The citation form of the verb *suru* 'do' is the nonpast form, and results in a historical present or future interpretation, depending on the context. To indicate that one has injured one's leg, the past tense of *suru*, *shita* 'did' must be used. In Japanese, the morpheme *–ta* indicates completative aspect. In Excerpt 1, Kuo-ming uses the nonpast *suru* instead of the completative *shita*. The relevant verbs are underlined in the Japanese. Here, underlining does not indicate any emphasis when uttered, but assists the reader in identifying the verbs relevant to the analysis. Small caps indicate that a particular word was uttered with emphasis.

Excerpt 1, Kuo-ming, May 22[3]

1. T: Hai ja rokuban. Kore wa doo desu ka? Eh:to ja:: S9-san to S10-san.
          Yes number six. How about this? Okay uh:: S9 and S10.

2. S9:   Doo <u>shita</u> n desu ka?
          What happened to you?

---

[3]The following transcription conventions and abbreviations are used in this chapter:

DAT	Dative marker
ACC	Accusative marker
AN	Adjectival noun
ADJ	Adjective
cop	Copula
neg	Negative marker
° °	Reduced volume—soft voice
° ° ° °	Reduced volume—whispered
° ° ° ° ° °	Reduced volume—very soft whisper, with consonant sounds articulated and certain vowel sounds difficult to determine
[	Overlap with similarly bracketed portion in neighboring turn
→	Indicated line of excerpt
___	Portion of special note to the current analysis is underlined
CAPS	Small caps show the speaker's emphasis
?	Rising intonation
,	Slight rise in intonation
.	Falling intonation
(( ))	Transcriber's comments
:	Elongation of a syllable
(.)	Brief pause
(..)	Slightly longer pause
-	False start
^	Glottal stop
T:	The teacher in the particular excerpt; the identity of T may differ across excerpts
S1:, S2:	Unidentified student

3. S10:   Uh ashi ni uh kega o <u>suru</u> n desu.

          Uh I hurt ((nonpast, "will hurt")) my leg.

4. T: Ashi ni kega o [(.) <u>shita</u> n desu

          I hurt ((past tense)) my leg

→   5. Km: [ashi ni^ <u>shita</u> n (.) aah!

                              Hurt ((past tense)) (.) aah!

6. T: ( ) ashi ni kega o <u>shita</u> n desu. Ne? Ashi ni kega o SHITA

          ( ) I hurt ((past tense)) my leg. Right? I HURT ((past tense)) my leg.

→   7. Km: [<u>shita</u> n   [de::su.

            <u>hurt</u> ((past tense))

8. T: [Past tense o tsukatte kudasai. [Ii desu ka? Ashi ni kega o <u>shita</u> n desu.

          Please use past tense.   Okay? I hurt ((past tense)) my leg.

→   9. Km: [°kega o <u>shita</u> n°

            °hurt ((past tense)) my leg°

10. T: [Hai ja nanaban Kayla-san to Sam-san.

          Okay well number seven, Kayla and Sam

Here, although the teacher's correction is directed to another student (S10) who does not overtly respond to the teacher, Kuo-ming notices the contrast between her recast using *shita* 'did' and the student's response, which used *suru* 'do.' He begins to repeat after the teacher's answer, and says "aah!" in Line 5 as he notices the discrepancy. He continues to focus on the word *shita* in Lines 7 and 9, reducing volume to a whisper, as he works to make the form his own, as the teacher expands on her recast by explicitly reminding S10 and the class to use the past tense with this expression. Candace, another first-year student, also repeats recasts that are directed to others, as shown in the next three excerpts. In Excerpt 2 the teacher is helping the students learn how to negate adjectival nouns. Kim, the student called on by the teacher, answers using the wrong negative form. Negation is made more difficult because in Japanese there are two types of adjectivals. Adjectival nouns behave much like nouns, and are negated as nouns are, and adjectives are verbals that inflect in a verblike way. These different negation patterns are shown in Table 3.2.

In Excerpt 2, Kim, who is called on by the teacher, uses the wrong form to negate the adjectival noun *hima* 'having free time.' The teacher recasts Kim's malformation in Line 3, Kim repeats the recast in Line 4, and Candace repeats the recast in private speech in Line 5.

TABLE 3.2
Adjectival Negation in Japanese

	Affirmative Form	Informal Negative Form	Formal Negative Form
Adjectival noun (AN)	hima (having free time)	hima ja nai AN neg	hima ja arimasen AN neg (formal)
Adjective (ADJ)	chiisa-i (small) adj-nonpast	chiisa-ku nai ADJ neg	Chiisa-ku arimasen ADJ neg (formal)

Excerpt 2, Candace, January 24

  1. T: kon shumatsu hima desu ka? Kim san
         This weekend are you free? Kim

  2. K: Um (..) iie (.) um (.) uh:: (.) hima- (.) hima: (.) <u>hima nai</u>,
         Um (..) no (.) um (.) uh:: (.) not (.) not (.) not free ((ERROR—"hima nai")).

→ 3. T: <u>Hima ja^ arimasen</u>
         you're not free. ((corrects form to "hima ja arimasen"))

  4. K: Oh ja arim[asen
         Oh cop neg

→ 5. C: [°°<u>hima ja^ arimasen</u>°°
                   °°not free°° ((correct form))

In Excerpt 3, the teacher is teaching new vocabulary related to shopping for shoes. Here, the teacher is taking students through a sequence of boxing and wrapping shoes. In Line 3, Andrew has difficulty with the verb *tsutsumu* 'to wrap' and does not complete it. He also chooses the wrong grammatical particle, the dative *ni* instead of the accusative *o*. The teacher recasts in Line 4. Andrew, who is being addressed, does not repeat the recast, but Candace whispers the recast in Line 5. The relevant verbs are underlined for easy identification.

Excerpt 3, Candace, February 28

  1. S: Uh hako ni kutsu o ireru
         Uh you put the shoes in the box

  2. T: Un hako ni kutsu o ireru. Jaa: Andrew-san?
         Yes, I put the shoes in the box. Um: Andrew?

  3. A: Uh <u>tsutsu</u> (..) hako (.) ni <u>tsutsu</u>
         Uh wra (..) in the box (.) wra

4. T: Hako o <u>tsutsumu</u>. [((writing on board)) Ne?
          To wrap the box ((writing on the board)) see?

→   5. C: [°°Hako o <u>tsutsumu</u>°°.
                                  °°to wrap a box°°

6. T: Hai. Hako o <u>tsutsumu</u>. Ne? Hako o <u>tsutsumu</u>.
          Yes. To wrap the box. Right? To wrap a box.

7. C/Ss: Hako o <u>tsutsumu</u>
          To wrap a box.

In all three of these examples, Candace softly whispers her own repetition of the teacher's corrective feedback, showing its salience even though it is addressed to another student, Andrew, who does not respond verbally to the teacher. In Line 6, after writing the expression on the blackboard (Line 4), the teacher repeats the expression for the benefit of the whole class, resulting in a choral repetition by the students in Line 7, with Candace joining in.

Incidental Recasts.   Private speech data also show students to be orally active in formulating their own responses to teacher questions and prompts. As they do this, their own utterances are available to them for comparison with the utterances of the teacher and other classmates, utterances that function as unintentional recasts when the learner's own response is incorrect. Learners form their own responses both in choral contexts, where the teacher's utterance is addressed to the class in general, and also when acting as auditors, in a mode of participation I term *vicarious response* (Ohta, 1998, in press). In the following example, Candace makes her own response to a teacher question directed broadly to the class. It is this vicarious response that then contrasts with that produced by the teacher. In this example, what Candace has difficulty with is forming the past tense of an adjective. Just as adjectives and adjectival nouns inflect differently to show negation, as discussed earlier, they also inflect differently to show past tense, as shown in Table 3.3. Here, in Excerpt 4, Candace used the past form for adjectival nouns for *chiisai*, which is an adjective.

Excerpt 4, Candace, January 24

1. T: Hai soshite (..) suteeki suteeki wa?
        Yes and (..) the steak steak was?

2. Ss: <u>Chiisakatta</u> desu ne
        It was small, wasn't it

TABLE 3.3
Past Tense Marking in Japanese Adjectivals

	Affirmative Form	Informal Past Form	Formal Past Form
Adjectival noun (AN)	hima (having free time)	hima datta AN cop-past	hima deshita AN cop-past (formal)
Adjective (ADJ)	chiisai (small)	chiisa-katta ADJ-past	chiisa-katta desu ADJ-past cop (formal)

    3. T: Oishikatta desu ne. Demo
            It was delicious, right. But

    4. Ss: <u>Chiisakatta</u> [desu
            It was small ((correct form))

→ 5. C: [<u>Chiisai deshita</u>
            It was small ((wrong form))

    6. T: [<u>Chiisakatta desu</u>. Ne? <u>Chiisakatta desu</u>
            It was small. Right? It was small ((right form))

→ 7. C: °ah°

    8. T: Ne. <u>Chiisakatta</u> desu ne? Ookiku arimasen deshita. Ne? Hai ja rokuban.
            Right. It was small wasn't it? It wasn't big. Right? Okay, number six.

In this choral example, Candace has heard several students say the correct answer *chiisakatta desu* 'was small' but formulates her own, incorrect answer, *chiisai deshita*, in Line 5. Her own answer, then, contrasts with that of the teacher in Line 6. Candace notices this discrepancy, as evidenced by her utterance of the change-of-state token (Heritage, 1984) "ah," in Line 7.

Incidental recasts also result from other types of corrective feedback. In the following example, Excerpt 5, Kuo-ming's soft response to the teacher's recast of the Japanese pronunciation of "Capitol Hill" is caught on his individual microphone. The teacher's corrective feedback, however, although functioning for Kuo-ming as a phonological recast, is actually an elicitation designed to get the students to produce a more complete answer, which other students do. In Line 2, Kuo-ming mispronounces the first syllable of the word *kyapitoru*.

Excerpt 5, Kuo-ming, November 18

    1. T: Doko no chizu desu ka?
             Which map?

2. Km: <u>Capitoru</u> [(hill) hmfhmf hehe
   Capitol   (hill) ((laughter))

3. M: [Capito::ru Hiru

   Capito::l Hill

4. T: Un. <u>kyapitoru</u> hiru no:?
   Un. A what of Capitol Hill?

5. Ss: [Chizu/kyapitoru hiru no chizu desu ((various responses))
   A map/a map of capitol hill

→ 6. Km: [°°<u>Kyapitoru</u> h[iru°°
   °°Capitol Hill°°

7. T: [Kyapitoru hiru no chizu desu. Un.
   A map of Capitol Hill. Yes.

Whereas other students respond to the teacher's elicitation, Kuo-ming, instead, responds to a subtle difference between the teacher's pronunciation and his own. His soft response is only available for analysis because he wore an individual microphone.

As shown by the previous examples, private speech provides learners with a forum for trying out their own utterances in a nonthreatening context, where they can then readily compare their production with that of others or of the teacher. In the next example, Excerpt 6, taken from a second-year class, Bryce formulates his own answer, even though the teacher is addressing another student. His wrong answer contrasts with the correct answer given by the student addressed, and provides him with an opportunity to revise his response. The teacher is actually addressing F, who uses an inappropriate verb in Line 2. When the teacher, in Line 3, prompts a reformulation, Bryce whispers *tsukete* 'attach,' which is also wrong—most likely, this is a mispronunciation of the correct verb *tsukutte* 'make.' F then says the correct verb, *tsukutte* 'make' in Line 5, which Bryce correctly follows up with the whispered, *oku* 'to put/place.' The construction verb + *oku* means "to do in advance." *Tsukutte oku* means to make something ahead of time. The teacher then repeats the correct verb phrase in Line 7, which Bryce repeats in a whisper.

Excerpt 6, Bryce, January 27

1. T: Denwa shite okimasu. ((writing)) (.) Denwa shite okimasu (.) Hoka ni wa?
   Call in advance ((writing)). Call in advance (.) And what else?

2. F: Sunakku to sarada o sunakku to sarada o shite oku
        Do snacks and salad, snacks and salads in advance

3. T: Sunakku to sarada o:,
        Do what with snacks and salads?

→ 4. B: °°Tsukete:: °°
          °°attach°°

5. F: Oh tsukutte
        Oh make

→ 6. B: °°°oku°°°
          °°°in advance°°°

7. T: Tskutte okimasu (.)
        Make in advance (.)

→ 8. B: °°°tsukutte oku°°°
          °°°make in advance°°°

Here, the teacher's corrective feedback that is addressed to F in Line 3 is not a recast but a prompt. Bryce's whispered incorrect response in Line 4, however, contrasts with F's response to the teacher's corrective feedback, which she produces in Line 5. F's Line 5 response is incomplete, as she does not add the helping verb *oku*, which Bryce whispers in Line 6. In response to F's incomplete Line 5 response, the teacher, in Line 7, supplies an expansion—a type of recast. Bryce softly whispers this reformulation as well.

When questions are addressed broadly to the class, individual learners have the opportunity to formulate their own responses as loudly or softly as they desire. Choral response activities license participation in private turns. In Excerpt 7, Kuo-ming formulates his own response in a soft voice when the teacher addresses a question about whether or not the test was difficult to the class as a whole. Kuo-ming uses an appropriate word, *yasashii* 'easy,' but does not use the past tense. He catches his own error after the teacher begins saying the correct conjugation in Line 5:

Excerpt 7, Kuo-ming, February 27

1. T: Eto jaa kanji no kuizu arimashita ne::. (.) arimashiTA. (.) ne arimashita ne,
        muzukashikatta desu ka?
        Um there was a kanji quiz wasn't there (.) there was (.) wasn't there,
        was it difficult?

2. Km: °Um°

3. Ss: Iie
        No

→ 4. Km: °Ee:: <u>yasashi</u> desu°
          °Ye::s it is easy°

5. T: Yasa[shikatta desu un
        It was easy

→ 6. Km: [°°Yasashikatta desu°°
          °°it was easy°°

The teacher's Line 5 utterance is an expansion of the students' choral response *iie* 'no' in Line 3. As Kuo-ming reformulates his answer in past tense in Line 6, he has the opportunity to hear the teacher's model response, which contrasts with his misformation and confirms his self-correction.

In Excerpt 8, Sara, another first-year student, answers as part of a chorus to the question of what one does when one has a fever. In Line 2, she says *sundari* "to live" which is incorrect, whereas other students say *yasundari* 'to vacation.' She self-corrects in Line 5, a beat after the teacher.

Excerpt 8, Sara, May 22

1. T: Un. Netsu o hakattari isha ni ittari shimasu netsu o hakatari gakko o? nan desu ka,
        Yes. Take your temperature and go to the doctor. Take your temperature and what about school?

2. Sa: [Sundari
        skip ((missing a syllable))

3. Ss: [Yasundari ((a few students))
        skip ((right pronunciation—a few students))

4. T: Yas[undari shimasu
        Skip school

→ 5. Sa: [Yasundari
          Skip school ((right pronunciation))

6. T: Ne? yasundari, (3) shimasu. ii desu ka? gakko o yasundari shimasu.
        Right? Skip school. Okay? You'd skip school.

Because Sara formulated her own response, the responses of the other students, as well as the teacher's repetition of the correct responses function as recasts, providing Sara with confirmation that her self-correction is, indeed, correct.

CONCLUSION

This study set out to discover what private speech data, voices that have not been attended to in previous research on corrective feedback, might tell us about the salience and efficacy of recasts. Specifically, private speech data were examined for insights into (a) the salience of contrasts presented in recasts, (b) the impact of recasts on members of the class who were not the individual to whom the feedback was addressed, and (c) whether and how learners were able to make use of utterances that contrasted with their own ill-formed utterances. Results show that private speech data make an important contribution to understanding learners' mental activity and give insight into how learners privately make use of contrasting utterances in the classroom setting in these form-focused first- and second-year language classes. More specifically, the data provide evidence of the salience of recasts as seen in the responses of auditors to recasts that were addressed to individuals other than themselves. In addition, the data show that learners were responsive to contrasting utterances that occurred incidentally when learners produced their own responses to utterances addressed by the teacher to the whole-class or to another individual. When learners were addressed in a choral, whole-class context, they produced private speech and other private turns, in response to the contrasting utterances I have termed incidental recasts. Questions and prompts addressed by the teacher to the class provided fertile ground for learners to take private turns, resulting in opportunities for students to experience incidental corrective feedback. Learners' vicarious responses, uttered in private speech when the teacher addressed another individual, also provided this opportunity. These results support the findings of L1 acquisition research, and experimental SLA research that has investigated recasts, by providing additional evidence that recasts are salient and useful to language learners. Child L1 acquisition research, as discussed earlier, has shown a relation between recasts and language acquisition. L1 researchers attribute the effectiveness of recasts in language development to their salience. By extension, the results reported here suggest that the salient contrasts presented by recasts in the L2 classroom impact the language development of the learners who notice and utilize them in their mental activity, even if the learners are not being addressed. Private speech provides powerful evidence of the mental activity triggered by the noticing of contrasts between ill-formed and correct utterances. The efficacy of recasts should not be doubted based on the presence or absence of an overt oral response.

Toward a Learner-Centered View of Corrective Feedback

Previous studies of corrective feedback have made a major assumption: that active involvement can be measured by the oral responses of the addressee to the corrective feedback. However, the data examined here show that traditional teacher-centered data collection methods miss a range of classroom interaction. Results show the utility of examining corrective feedback from the learner's perspective and broaden the notion of corrective feedback beyond utterances that are addressed to the individual who made an error, to all utterances that potentially provide corrective information to a particular learner. Also, the data that are missed when individual learners are not miked has clear potential to reveal classroom SLA processes that have been overlooked in previous studies. The analytic method of prioritizing the oral response of the learner addressed as the sole measure of the effectiveness of corrective feedback not only denies the inner voice of the learner addressed, but also errs in assuming that a particular interaction is for the sole benefit of the student whose ill-formed utterance was corrected. This analytic method ignores two realities—that of each student's ability to covertly and meaningfully participate in classroom interactive events, and the multiple realities of the attentional processes of the individual learners who are legitimate peripheral participants (Lave & Wenger, 1991) in the teacher-fronted interactional event, and who each has his or her own responses to that event. Examination of private speech confirms the autonomy of each learner and the ability of individuals to attend to and make their own productive use of a wide variety of L2 classroom events. Each learner's experience is different, with each individual's unique collection of strengths, weaknesses, and interests shaping what is and is not worthy of attention for that particular student. What is ultimately salient, or what ultimately becomes the focus of attention, is likely to differ significantly from learner to learner. In addition, what is ultimately salient to a particular learner is not determined by the teacher alone, but learners differ in how they capitalize on the affordances of the classroom environment (Ohta, in press; van Lier, 2000). This chapter balances previous teacher-centered work by showing how addressees and auditors alike respond to recasts in settings beyond overt uptake. Results broaden the notion of uptake beyond the addressee response to corrective feedback to consideration of potential covert uptake by both the addressee and by all auditors present in the classroom.

Toward Future Research

How, then, do we determine whether or not a particular corrective feedback technique is effective for SLA? Is there a way to determine, by looking at learner errors, at teacher feedback, and at learner responses to that feedback, and at private speech, that one type of feedback is superior to another in terms of how students utilize the feedback in their developing L2 grammars? I doubt that claims of effectiveness for SLA can be made based only on analysis of corrective feedback in the classroom setting. Inclusion of private speech data is a step forward, but this chapter presents just a beginning in this direction. How learners at different proficiency levels, in classrooms with different structures and goals, use private speech in the classroom has yet to be examined. It must always be kept in mind that private speech occurs when adults are in cognitively demanding situations. Examining private speech in other classroom settings is important to better understand its function in classroom language learning and as a part of corrective feedback sequences. In addition, classroom techniques may not translate immediately into L2 development. Although the effect of particular interactions may be immediately evident (Ohta, 2000), language development continues beyond the interactive events that are its building blocks (Ohta, 1999b). Longitudinal studies of individual learners as well as experimental studies are needed to determine the effect of particular feedback techniques in promoting SLA. Also, claims prioritizing one modality of participation over another, for example, reformulations over repetition or imitation, are likely to lead to oversimplification of SLA processes. Language learning is a complex, multimodal, sociocognitive process. Studies of children acquiring first and second languages have found private speech to be an accurate predictor of the direction of language acquisition—what learners produce in private speech provides a forecast of what the learner will subsequently produce in social speech (Kuczaj, 1983; Saville-Troike, 1988; Weir, 1962). If this is true for L2 learning adults as well, then the presence or absence of private speech indicates not the presence or absence of attention or of salience, or the effectiveness or ineffectiveness of a particular feedback type, but has something important to say about the developmental processes of the particular learner.

REFERENCES

Baker, N., & Nelson, K. (1984). Recasting and related conversational techniques for triggering syntactic advances by young children. *First Language, 5*, 3–22.

Bell, A. (1984). Language style as audience design. *Language in Society, 13*, 135–204.

Camarata, S. M., Nelson, K. E., & Camarata, M. N. (1994). Comparison of conversational recasting and imitative procedures for training grammatical structures in children with specific language impairment. *Journal of Speech and Hearing Research, 37*, 1414–1423.

Chaudron, C. (1977). A descriptive model of discourse in the corrective treatment of learners' errors. *Language Learning, 27*, 29–46.

Chaudron, C. (1986). Teachers' priorities in correcting learners' errors in French immersion classes. In R. Day (Ed.), *Talking to learn* (pp. 64–84). Rowley, MA: Newbury House.

Demetras, M. J., Post, K., & Snow, C. (1987). Feedback to first language learners: The role of repetitions and clarification questions. *Journal of Child Language, 13*, 275–292.

Doughty, C. (1993). Fine-tuning of feedback by competent speakers to language learners. In *Georgetown University roundtable on languages and linguistics 1993* (pp. 96–108). Baltimore: Georgetown University Roundtable.

Doughty, C., & Williams, J. (Eds.). (1998). *Focus on form in classroom second language acquisition*. New York: Cambridge University Press.

Fotos, S. S. (1993). Consciousness raising and noticing through focus on form: Grammar task performance versus formal instruction. *Applied Linguistics, 14*, 385–407.

Heritage, J. (1984). A change-of-state token and aspects of its sequential placement. In J. M. Atkinson & J. Heritage (Eds.), *Structures of social action: Studies in conversation analysis* (pp. 299–345). Cambridge, UK: Cambridge University Press.

John-Steiner, V. (1992). Private speech among adults. In L. E. Berk & R. M. Diaz (Eds.), *Private speech: From social interaction to self-regulation* (pp. 285–296). Hillsdale, NJ: Lawrence Erlbaum Associates.

Kanagy, R. (1994). Developmental sequences in learning Japanese: A look at negation. *Issues in Applied Linguistics, 5*(2), 225–277.

Kanagy, R. (in press). Developmental sequences, second language acquisition and Japanese language pedagogy. In H. Nara (Ed.), *Advances in Japanese pedagogy*. Columbus: Ohio State University, National Foreign Language Center.

Koyanagi, K., Moroishi, M., Muranoi, H., Ota, M., & Shibata, N. (1994, October). *Negative feedback and second language acquisition: An empirical study of the acquisition of Japanese conditional expressions*. Paper presented at the 1994 Second Language Research Forum, Concordia University and McGill University, Montreal, Canada.

Kuczaj, S. A. (1983). *Crib speech and language play*. New York: Springer-Verlag.

Lantolf, J. P. (1997). The function of language play in the acquisition of L2 Spanish. In W. R. Glass & A. T. Perez-Leroux (Eds.), *Contemporary perspectives on the acquisition of Spanish* (pp. 3–24). Somerville, MA: Cascadilla Press.

Lantolf, J. P., & Frawley, W. (1985, December). On communication strategies: A functional perspective. *Rassegna Italiana Di Linguistica Applicata Estratto Dal*, 2–3.

Lave, J., & Wenger, E. (1991). *Situated learning: Legitimate peripheral participation*. New York: Cambridge University Press.

Leontiev, A. A. (1981). *Psychology and the language learning process*. Oxford, UK: Pergamon.

Lightbown, P. M., & Spada, N. (1990). Focus-on-form and corrective feedback in communicative language teaching: Effects on second language learning. *Studies in Second Language Acquisition, 12*, 429–448.

Long, M. (1983). Linguistic and conversational adjustments to non-native speakers. *Studies in Second Language Acquisition, 5*, 177–193.

Lyster, R. (1998). Recasts, repetition, and ambiguity in L2 classroom discourse. *Studies in Second Language Acquisition, 20*, 51–81.

Lyster, R., & Ranta, L. (1997). Corrective feedback and learner uptake: Negotiation of form in communicative classrooms. *Studies in Second Language Acquisition, 19*, 37–66.

Mackey, A., & Philp, J. (1998). Conversational interaction and second language development: Recasts, responses, and red herrings? *Modern Language Journal, 82*, 338–356.

Masur, E. F. (1989). Individual and dyadic patterns of imitation: Cognitive and social aspects. In G. E. Speidel & K. E. Nelson (Eds.), *The many faces of imitation in language learning* (pp. 53–72). New York: Springer-Verlag.

McCafferty, S. G. (1992). The use of private speech by adult second language learners: A cross-cultural study. *Modern Language Journal, 76*, 179–189.

McCafferty, S. G. (1994a). Adult second language learners' use of private speech: A review of studies. *Modern Language Journal, 78*, 421–436.

McCafferty, S. G. (1994b). The use of private speech by adult ESL learners at different levels of proficiency. In J. P. Lantolf & G. Appel (Eds.), *Vygotskian approaches to second language research* (pp. 117–134). Norwood, NJ: Ablex.

Meltzoff, A. N., & Gopnik, A. (1989). On linking nonverbal imitation, representation, and language learning in the first two years of life. In G. E. Speidel & K. E. Nelson (Eds.), *The many faces of imitation in language learning* (pp. 23–52). New York: Springer-Verlag.

Moerk, E. L. (1992). *A first language taught and learned.* Baltimore: Brookes.

Nelson, K. E. (1989). Strategies for first language teaching. In M. Rice & R. Schiefelbusch (Eds.), *The teachability of language* (pp. 263–310). Baltimore: Brookes.

Nelson, K. E., Denninger, M., Bonvillian, J., Kaplan, B., & Baker, N. (1983). Maternal input adjustments and non-adjustments as related to children's linguistic advances and the language acquisition theories. In A. Pelligrini & T. Yawkey (Eds.), *The development of oral and written languages: Readings in developmental and applied linguistics.* Norwood, NJ: Ablex.

Ohta, A. S. (1998, March). *The role of language play in the acquisition of foreign language by adult learners: Evidence from the classroom.* Paper presented at the American Association of Applied Linguistics Annual Conference, Seattle, WA.

Ohta, A. S. (1999a, March). *Broadening the notion of "uptake": What private speech reveals about the role of corrective feedback in L2 development.* Paper presented at the 1999 Annual Conference of the American Association for Applied Linguistics, Stamford, CT.

Ohta, A. S. (1999b). Interactional routines and the socialization of interactional style in adult learners of Japanese. *Journal of Pragmatics, 31*, 1493–1512.

Ohta, A. S. (2000). Re-thinking interaction in SLA: Developmentally appropriate assistance in the zone of proximal development and the acquisition of L2 grammar. In J. P. Lantolf (Ed.), *Sociocultural theory and second language learning* (pp. 52–78). Oxford: Oxford University Press.

Ohta, A. S. (in press). *Second language acquisition in the classroom: Learning Japanese.* Mahwah, NJ: Lawrence Erlbaum Associates.

Oliver, R. (1995). Negative feedback in child NS–NNS conversation. *Studies in Second Language Acquisition, 18*, 459–481.

Philp, J. (1999, March). *Constraints on "noticing the gap": A study of NNS' apperception of recasts in NS-NNS interaction.* Paper presented at the 1999 Annual Conference of the American Association for Applied Linguistics, Stamford, CT.

Pica, T. (1988). Interlanguage adjustments as an outcome of NS–NNS interaction. *Language Learning, 38*, 471–493.

Pica, T., Holliday, L., Lewis, N., & Morgenthaler, L. (1989). Comprehensible output as an outcome of linguistic demands on the learner. *Studies in Second Language Acquisition, 11*, 63–90.

Roberts, M. (1995). Awareness and the efficacy of error correction. In R. Schmidt (Ed.), *Attention and awareness in foreign language learning* (pp. 163–182). Honolulu: University of Hawaii, Second Language Teaching and Curriculum Center.

Saville-Troike, M. (1988). Private speech: Evidence for second language learning strategies during the "silent" period. *Child Language, 15*, 567–590.

Scherer, N., & Olswang, L. (1984). Role of mothers' expansions in children's language production. *Journal of Speech and Hearing Research, 27*, 387–396.

Swain, M. (1985). Communicative competence: Some roles of comprehensible input and comprehensible output in its development. In S. Gass & C. Madden (Eds.), *Input in second language acquisition* (pp. 235–256). Rowley, MA: Newbury House.

Swain, M. (1993). The output hypothesis: Just speaking and writing aren't enough. *The Canadian Modern Language Review, 50*, 158–164.

Uzgiris, I. C., Broome, S., & Kruper, J. C. (1989). Imitations in mother–child conversations: A focus on the mother. In G. E. Speidel & K. E. Nelson (Eds.), *The many faces of imitation in language learning* (pp. 91–120). New York: Springer-Verlag.

van Lier, L. (1988). *The classroom and the language learner: Ethnography and second language classroom research.* London: Longman.

van Lier, L. (in press). From input to affordance: Social-interactive learning from an ecological perspective. In J. P. Lantolf (Ed.), *Sociocultural theory and second language learning* (pp. 247–262). Oxford: Oxford University Press.

VanPatten, B. (1989). Can learners attend to form and content while processing input? *Hispania, 72*, 409–417.

Vygotsky, L. S. (1978). *Mind in society: The development of higher psychological processes.* Cambridge, MA: Harvard University Press.

Vygotsky, L. S. (1987). Thinking and speech. In R. W. Rieber & A. S. Carton (Eds.), *The collected works of L. S. Vygotsky* (Vol. 1; pp. 39–285). New York: Plenum.

Weir, R. H. (1962). *Language in the crib.* The Hague, Netherlands: Mouton.

Spoken Artistry: Performance in a Foreign Language Classroom

Patricia N. Sullivan

In this chapter I examine the discourse of one teacher as he incorporates storytelling and wordplay into his teaching in such a way as to challenge students to broaden their vocabulary and their ways of thinking about the meanings of words. I analyze this teacher's approach to teaching through the lens of performance, and in particular, through storytelling and wordplay as aspects of classroom performance. I first define performance, storytelling, and wordplay, then discuss this type of performance as it relates to second language learning. Finally, I give examples of its use in classroom discourse.

PERFORMANCE

The term *spoken artistry* is borrowed from Bauman (1986), who described performance as "the enactment of the poetic function, the essence of spoken artistry" (p. 3). "Performance," according to Bauman, is

> a mode of communication, a way of speaking, the essence of which resides in the assumption of responsibility to an audience for a display of communicative skill, highlighting the way in which communication is carried out, above and beyond its referential content. (p. 3)

This definition emphasizes three aspects of performance: (a) the importance of audience and setting, (b) the importance of a particular way of speaking, and (c) the importance of seeing referential content as only one aspect of communication. From this perspective, the relationship between a text, a performer, and an audience, as well as an "appreciation of the intrinsic qualities of the act of expression itself" (Bauman, 1986, p. 3) are emphasized.

Performance is one type of communicative event (Hymes, 1972) that can take place in a classroom. Any participant can be involved: teachers, students, native speakers, non-native speakers, adults, or children. In the classroom this communicative event may be either within or outside of the teacher's planned lesson. It is intricately tied to the type of relationship between teacher and students, and the cultures of the classroom, the school, and the community (Holliday, 1994; Kramsch, 1993). Foster (1989), for instance, drew on performance theory when she analyzed the ways that a Black teacher used a discourse style that was familiar to students in her class; that is, expressive talk, a preaching style, and rhythm and intonation that called for active vocal audience response. The teacher was drawing not only on her own expressive mode, but incorporating the cultures of her students. In discussing her analysis of classroom talk, Foster stated that "the more successful performances evoke personal stories and narratives" (p. 18).

My focus is on two types of performance events, storytelling and wordplay, as they are used to focus students' attention on the form and meanings of words. These performance events are defined next.

Storytelling

Storytelling is one type of performance event for which the audience is of primary concern, as is the particular way the story is told. Although there may also be a focus on the content, it is the expression of this content that gives particular meaning to the story. The event of storytelling has related effects on the participants. Storytelling is a primary strategy for creating rapport (Tannen, 1989); it helps bring about a relaxed atmosphere (Norrick, 1993) and it allows a speaker to present a self for ratification by other participants (Goffman, 1959). Humor, which is often intertwined with storytelling, helps to "smooth the work in everyday conversation as well as offering . . . a chance to play: to present a self, test for common ground, and create rapport in an entertaining fashion" (Norrick, 1993, p. 43).

Wordplay

Wordplay can also be a performance. As defined here, it is a supportive, usually pleasurable, activity that often incorporates double meanings. MacHovec (1988) defined wordplay as repartee, that is, "a playful verbal battle of wits between two or more persons enjoying each other or the present situation in an atmosphere of play and mutual stimulation" (p. 20). Norrick (1993) referred to "extended sequences of wordplay" (p. 43) that are produced when conversationalists engage in banter. Both children and adults engage in wordplay, sometimes with a focus on meaning and other times with a focus on sounds.

Wordplay often incorporates repetition; it might include word coinage (i.e., making up a new word for humorous purposes) or playfully using a word in an inappropriate context. Heath (1982/1986) gave examples of wordplay with repetition from children in "Trackton" in terms of a repetition stage and a repetition-with-variation stage: "They [children] incorporate chunks of language from others into their own ongoing dialogue, applying productive rules, inserting new nouns and verbs for those used in adults' chunks. They also play with rhyming patterns and varying intonation contours" (p. 114).

PERFORMANCE AND SECOND LANGUAGE LEARNING

Although the studies just mentioned refer to the ubiquity of storytelling and wordplay as aspects of native language speech, much of the current focus on classroom second language learning disregards this type of speech. Rather, interest in second language acquisition (SLA) has been focused on tasks and task-based learning (Candlin, 1987; Long & Porter, 1985; Nunan, 1989). A task is often advocated so as to bring what is generally considered natural and authentic language into the classroom to focus on meaning. The terms *natural* and *authentic*, however are problematic (cf. Kramsch & Sullivan, 1996; Widdowson, 1994). What, for instance, is natural language in "real life?" What is *authentic*? The production of a task may be one example of real language, but it is not the only one. Cook (1997), for instance, argued that natural or authentic language among native speakers is not always task based, nor is it necessarily focused on meaning rather than form. One example of this is children's enjoyment of repeating rhymes that they do not understand, such as "Diddle Diddle Dumpling, My Son John" or "This Little Piggy Went to Market." Cook also pointed out that many adult conversations between friends

> contain little information, and may be regarded as instances of play and banter. These discourses are not used to solve a practical problem. They are not "task based." They are language for enjoyment, for the self, for its own sake. And they are often fantasies—not about the real world, but about a fictional one in which there are no practical outcomes." (p. 230)

The enjoyment of language, and, in fact, the enjoyment of repetition is apparent not only in conversational exchanges or games among children, but also among adults such as when singing "The Twelve Days of Christmas." Because the real-life language of native speakers includes form-focused and playful language as well as task-based language (cf. Cook, 1998), there should be a place for both in a second language class.

The integration of the social and poetic, as evidenced in performance, is relevant not only to discourse between native speakers in various informal settings, as noted earlier, but also to second language teaching and learning in the classroom. In a second language classroom, storytelling and wordplay can increase intrinsic motivation, serve as mediation in expert–novice interaction, and encourage a focus on form.

Intrinsic Motivation

Intrinsic motivation is the type of motivation for which there is no reward other than the activity itself. Although many researchers as well as language learners say there is a relation between motivation and second language learning, according to researchers that relation is unclear. Ellis (1985), for instance, stated that "there can be little doubt that motivation is a powerful factor in SLA" (p. 119) but he went on to say that the way motivation affects learning is not clear. Crookes and Schmidt (1991) also pointed to the lack of information about motivation, but added, "in the future the field seems likely to accept that the successful SL learner is very involved in learning both at the metacognitive level . . . and the allocation of attention" (p. 479). Brown (1994), in reference to retention, said that he strongly favored intrinsic motivation over and above other types of motivation for long-term retention. In sum, although the relation between intrinsic motivation and second language is not clearly understood, there seems to be agreement as to its importance.

The relation between motivation and performance is also not clear; however, if students are motivated by storytelling and wordplay they may pay more attention to classroom discourse. Longer term benefits may result. The students in the examples given in this chapter were so motivated by the teacher that they formed an English club that met regularly every Friday night for the purpose of talking about their ideas in English.

Expert–Novice Interaction

Social interaction is a key concept of Vygotskyan theory, as is the concept of collaboration with more capable peers (Vygotsky, 1978). The social context plays a dynamic role in the process of internalization because cognitive development originates in the social context as the result of interaction between individuals. According to Vygotskyan theory, this interaction between those who know more, either teacher or other students, and those who know less, leads to learning. As Donato (1994) explained it, "the experienced individual is often observed to guide, support, and shape actions of the novice, who, in turn, internalizes the expert's strategic processes" (p. 37). In terms of classroom performance, the expert might be the teacher, but it might also be any of the students. "The concepts of motive and internalization emphasize the importance of attributing a more dynamic role to the social context than has yet been achieved in the literature on interaction and acquisition" (Donato, 1994, p. 38). In the discourse examples in this chapter, performance in terms of storytelling and wordplay by both teacher and students involves guidance and support among all participants, which leads to a playful attention to words.

Focus on Form

Wong-Fillmore (1985), in her analysis of successful language classrooms, referred to focus on form in terms of repetition: "What we find in these successful lessons . . . is that repetitions are not necessarily identical, but there are small changes in them which may in fact serve to call the learner's attention to places within such expressions where forms can be substituted" (p. 40). Wong-Fillmore went on to say that successful language learning among children includes "richness of language" and "playfulness" that lead to a focus on form:

> The final characteristic of the language used in successful lessons is that of richness and occasional playfulness as well. One might assume that in talking to learners, teachers ought to avoid anything unusual and stick with plain ordinary, unembellished language until the students have gained a degree of mastery over the fundamentals of the new language. In the lessons that we have observed, teachers do try to keep the language simple, but it is in no way stripped-down, unnaturally plain language featured in many ESL courses. The teachers in successful classes tended to use language in ways that called attention to the language itself. (p. 42)

Swain (1995) argued that output leads to "noticing": "Output . . . may be used as a way of trying out new language forms and structures as learners stretch their interlanguage to meet communicative needs" (p. 12). In the performance events described in this chapter, output is encouraged by the teacher and often takes the form of repetition. There is much talk in the classroom as students pick up and repeat both the teachers' and each other's words and phrases.

These aspects of classroom second language learning (i.e., intrinsic motivation, expert–novice interaction, and focus on form) are intricately intertwined with the storytelling and wordplay that are demonstrated in the class sessions described in this chapter.

THE STUDY

Methodology

The data for the classes discussed here are taken from a corpus of transcriptions from recordings of 34 English language classrooms in two universities in Vietnam. The researcher was a participant-observer over a period of 9 months in 1993 and 1994. The data described in this chapter come from two classrooms with the same Vietnamese teacher. The researcher attended every class meeting during a 2-month period in 1994. All classes during that period were observed and audiotaped; some were videotaped. Students and teachers from each class were interviewed. The subsequent notes and transcriptions were shown to the teachers and students for further description, clarification, and analysis. When analyzing the data, attention was paid to the particular way that the participants expressed themselves, as well as their particular audiences and setting.

Classroom Setting

Students were in English classes approximately 4 hours a day, 5 days a week. One of their classes that I participated in was a second-year listening and speaking class consisting of 26 students, which met 4 hours in the morning 2 days a week. The second class was a fourth-year reading class composed of 25 students who were about to graduate. This class also met for 4 hours, but only once a week.

The teacher brought into the class what might be called a customary joking atmosphere (Norrick, 1993). Most people are familiar with this type of person. He or she is usually the joketeller in whatever company he or she is. In this particular class the students were accustomed to hearing the teacher tell jokes, make puns, and relate personal anecdotes. They often responded in kind. The class was teacher centered in that the teacher was usually stationed in front of the class, teaching to the whole class. Classroom exercises were usually based on the textbook.

Findings

The following excerpts taken from two classes (second year and fourth year) during the last 2 months of the spring semester provide evidence of language learning as students and teacher playfully exchange banter that focuses on language form and meaning. The teacher challenges students to stretch their understanding of the meanings of words through a combination of storytelling and wordplay.

Excerpt 1 comes from a class session of the second-year listening and speaking class that was focused on practice using the present perfect tense. The teacher had gone through the exercises in the book, but had just left the book exercises to ask more spontaneous questions of the students.

Excerpt 1: The Duel[1]

1. T: Have you seen the film *Jurassic Park*?
2. S1: Uh no.
3. T: No, you haven't. OK. Now have you watched the film ( )?
4. Ss: Yes.
5. T: OK. When did you first see it? Watch it?
6. Ss: ( )
7. T: Watch it? Four weeks ago? OK. Right. Now have you ever learned French?
8. S1: Uh no.
9. T: Have you ever learned uh linguistics in Vietnamese?
10. S2: I I first learned it last year.
11. T: Last year? Oh right. So
12. S3: Were you ever attacked by a lunatic?
13. Ss: ((laugh))
14. T: Been [attacked by a lunatic?]
15. Ss: [lunatic]
16. Ss: [attacked by a lunatic]
17. T: OK. No, I haven't.
18. Ss: ((laugh))
19. S3: Are you sure?

---

[1]Transcription conventions include the following:

[ ] [ ]	overlapping speech
( )	indecipherable speech
(bed)	guessed word/unclear
(( ))	transcriber's comments
hhh	breathy laugh

20. T: Yes, I'm sure. OK.

21. S4:   So who attacked you actually?

22. T: OK. That's my rival.

23. Ss: ((laugh)) [Rival?]

24. Ss: [ah rival]

25. T: OK. Now ( ) Oh sorry before the duel.

26. Ss: [Duel]

27. S: [(She died in a duel)]

28. T: Yeah. A duel. You shot at me and I shot at you.

29. Ss: Yes. Yes.

30. T: Right. Could we answer the questions in the book. What about you

31.   ((T calls on S5)) How long have you lived at your present address?

32. S5:   I've lived here since ( )

33. T: 18 years. OK. ( ) When did you move there?

34. S5:   Uh I moved

35. T: I moved

36. S5:   Ten years ago.

37. T: Ten years ago. OK. Now how long have you had your present job?

38.   Have you got it?

In Lines 1 through 11, although the teacher is clearly trying to bring in "reality" to the question–answer practice, the questions are not very productive in terms of real conversation. The answers are all fairly short and the questions are not related to each other. It does not approximate a real conversation, but is clearly language practice with a focus on the present perfect tense.

In Line 12, however, one student initiates a question that triggers a more lengthy response as well as the involvement of the whole class and an introduction of new words. This question brings up a topic that had recently been the topic of conversation and joking in this class. She is referring to an incident the teacher had been involved in several weeks earlier in which a rock had been thrown at him by a woman as he was riding his motorcycle home from school. He had been hit in the cheek, and gone to the hospital, and, at this time, still had a bandage over the cut. The teacher had earlier referred to the woman who had thrown the rock as a "crazy" woman.

As shown in Lines 12 through 29, Student 3's question stimulates a playful scenario on the part of the teacher about a duel in which two rivals are shooting at each other. This playful narrative creates rapport in the class; its social function is entertainment. It results in whole-class involvement and at least 16 turns on one topic. Although neither the students nor the teacher have very lengthy turns, the narrative itself has a rhythm and natural flow of speech. Multiple students are actively involved. The narrative also includes a focus on form and meaning, especially in the repetition of new vocabulary. In Lines 12 through 16, for instance, the word *lunatic* is repeated multiple times. Lines 15 and 16, although represented in print by only two lines, indicate that the words and phrases are being bounced from student to student, allowing for pronunciation practice and checking for meaning.[2] Lines 22 through 24 indicate a similar type of exchange with the word *rival*. In Line 25 the teacher throws out the word *duel*, then realizes that he needs to define it further, which he does in Line 28. These instances of repetition demonstrate strategies for actively confronting new vocabulary words and using them in a clear context.

Although the scenario brings in a stimulating playfulness and a focus on new words, Line 30 indicates the teacher's desire to return to the book and to the focus of the lesson; that is, the present perfect tense. Ironically, however, what he is getting back to is less "real" in this setting than his fabricated story. The questions in the text, that is, "How long have you lived at your present address" (Line 31), and "How long have you had your present job" (Line 37) were no doubt brought into the textbook to bring reality to the language lesson. However, in this context, they are "unreal" and forced. Students basically knew where the others lived and no one had a job. The fabricated narrative, on the other hand, is real in that it replicates the kind of narrative humor that one might engage in outside of class. This discourse segment calls into question the meaning and use of the word *reality* in language lessons. It also demonstrates how performance events such as storytelling and wordplay are intricately related to linguistic form and meaning.

The next example comes from the same second-year class as Excerpt 1. The structural focus was on practice with the words *where, how long, how far,* and *how big* along with the superlative, with the teacher asking a series of questions from the course book. Excerpt 2 begins with the teacher asking the third of four questions, which he dismisses as not being relevant (Lines 4–5), after which he asks the fourth question about gardens.

Excerpt 2: The Garden

1. T: OK. That's good. Yeah a long way. Next one ((T reads)) "Who
2.   lives furthest from the shops?"

---

[2]The quality of the recording was not sufficient to transcribe individual responses among the overlapping exchanges.

3. Ss: from the shops

4. T: We have nobody (who lives furthest from) the shops in Vietnam.

5.   In Hanoi. Everywhere you can find the shops. OK. No (   ). OK.

6.   ((T reads)) Who has the biggest garden?

7. S1:   ( )

8. T: (You have a garden?) How large is it?

9. S1:   It's about uh 100 uh square meters.

10. T: (   )OK.

11. S2: ( ) fifteen thousand meters.

12. T: Fifteen thousand?

13. S2: Lenin Park.

14. T: ( )

15. S2: Lenin Park.

16. Ss: ((laugh))

17. T: OK. [T calls S's name] have you got a garden?

18. S3: Yes. [I have]

19. T: [OK]

20. S3: But it's not very big and I build the (   ) for the (bed.)

21. T: The?

22. S3: I build around the the tree trunk.

23. T: (   )?

24. S3: To keep it uh

25. T: Some (low wall?)

26. S3: (Low wall) yeah.

27. T: OK. To protect the root? or to protect the trunk of the trees?

28. S3: Yes.

29. T: Hmmm.

30. S4: My my uncle uncle's garden is the (biggest)

31. Ss: ((laugh))

32. S4: How large is it? How large is it?

33. T: But it's not hers, but her uncle's.

34. S4: (Yeah) ((laugh)) the biggest.

35. S5: But how large is it?

36. Ss: ((Multiple responses, indecipherable, laughter))

37. T: Your uncle's garden is not as big as mine.

38. Ss: Yeah. ((laughter))

39. T: I mean my Uncle Ho.

40. Ss: ((laughter))

41. T: ((to R)) Uh We often call him Uncle Ho.

As in Excerpt 1, the questions posed by the course book are real questions that are aimed at the production of meaningful answers. The teacher and students, however, again play with the reality, turning what might have been a dry practice to a clever exercise in imagination. The first question in the book, "Who lives furthest from the shops," is disregarded by the teacher as being irrelevant and unanswerable because in their neighborhoods many of the homes were combined with stores on the street level. Therefore, as he says, "no one lives furthest from the shops." The shops were all around. By disregarding this question, the teacher also demonstrates that he is concerned not only with reality in terms of how students might answer, but also with questions that, for him, were interesting to talk about.

During the course of answering the question about gardens, the teacher and students play a one-upmanship game that takes the meaning of *garden* from the literal to the figurative. In Lines 7, 8, and 9, S1 was evidently talking about her own family garden. S2 (Lines 11–15) increased the scope of the word by referring to Lenin Park, a large, well-known public park in the city. Student 3's contribution (Lines 18–28) was dealt with by the teacher, but not picked up by the other students. This may have been because the teacher could not make sense of it or that it did not contribute either to the playfulness or the focus on size. S4 (Line 30) again brings in a comment about size, one that is taken up by the teacher (Lines 33–39) to mean the "garden" of Ho Chi Minh, which seems to refer to the whole country. The way the teacher pronounced "your uncle's garden is not as big as mine" in a playful manner focused the students' attention on a new meaning of the word, as evidenced by their laughter. To be sure they got his meaning, he emphasized (Line 39), either to the students or the researcher or both, that he was referring to Uncle Ho. He repeats this again to the researcher in Line 41. The playful broadening of the word *garden* from a part of a home to a public park and then to Ho Chi Minh's domain encouraged students to see one word as having multiple meanings.

In Excerpt 3, the final example from the second-year class, which occurred on the same day as Excerpt 2, the focus was still on question words, but the teacher had left the book exercises and had asked students to ask him questions about his life in Australia. One of the students had asked about university life and whether the students study. This led to a play on words.

Excerpt 3: Stupid

1. T:　　OK. I think the university students there are uh studying quite hard?
2. Ss:　　((laugh))

3. T: All right?

4. S: ( ) the teachers ( )?

5. Ss: ((laughter))

6. T: No, they're very serious. Here.

7. S: They don't (act stupid) ( ).

8. T: ((T looks at R)) OK. Uh there's a a play on words in ( )

9. (Vietnamese way) the word "student"

10. R: Student.

11. T: OK.

12. S: (student that is) stupid.

13. Ss: ((laugh))

14. S: and in Vietnam

15. T: ((T writes the Vietnamese word on the board "stupid = dan"))

16. Stupid and dan. That means students are stupid.

17. Ss: So students are stupid.

18. T: So I put the word "stu"- stupid, OK? and "dan" "dan" the sound. OK?

19. Ss: ((much laughter))

20. R: Student.

21. S: The teacher is a cheater.

22. T: [Cheater]

23. Ss: [((much laughter))]

24. T: A cheater, OK? ((T writes on board "teacher" and "cheater" and "cheetah"))

25. S: Grand cheater.

26. Ss: ((much laughter))

27. T: ((T points to "cheetah" on board)) This one?

28. R: Cheetah? The animal?

29. T: All right. ( )

30. Ss: No. (cheater uh teacher)

31. Ss: ((much laughter))

32. T: (this is called) a cheater. OK? Thank you. So uh what about

33. (yesterday?). Have you been to someplace? Someplace? Yes?

The wordplay in this segment begins when the teacher explains to the researcher the play on words when combining the Vietnamese and the English that results in the "student" being "stupid." This leads a student (Line 21) to recall a previous wordplay with sounds that resulted in the "teacher" being a "cheater." The teacher then carries the play another step by changing "cheater" to "cheetah" (Lines 24–27) and asking students which one they meant. The researcher is a bit lost as to the connection (Line 28), but the students are enjoying it immensely as shown by the class laughter. It was not clear to the researcher whether the students knew the meaning of "cheetah," but as the teacher wrote the word on the board, he was emphasizing both the new word and the similar sounds. He led them to focus on the sound distinction when he asked "this one?" (Line 27). This led to an awareness of words, a noticing of sound differences in the context of repetition and wordplay.

The following three examples were from the fourth-year class. All of them occurred on the same day, the final day of class before the exam. The teacher was reviewing what would be on the exam by going over possible questions on a handout that the students would be asked to respond to in written form. The questions were comprehensive, with examples such as "What do you think are the advantages of imposing stricter laws in Vietnam?" In the following excerpt, teachers and students engage in wordplay that sidesteps the focus on answering questions.

Excerpt 4: Titanic

    1. T: Uh huh? Right. Now 14. "What problems do you think a developing
    2.   country may face in its social and economic development?"
    3. Ss: ((Several repeat the question in Vietnamese)).
    4. R: A major question. h-h-h-h
    5. T: Yes. A very big question uh
    6. S1:   A huge question.
    7. T: Hu:ge question. OK.
    8. Ss: [It's very big]
    9. Ss: [A gigantic question]
    10. T: ((laugh)) A gigantic question. OK.
    11. S: (   )
    12. T: OK.
    13. S2: An enormous question
    14. T: A titanic question. OK. and the last one? "How do we generally
    15.   benefit from modern conveniences?"

In the preceding example, both teacher and students are playing with synonyms. This class, like the second-year class, is engaging in a game of playful, collaborative one-upmanship. The game is unknowingly triggered by the researcher who comments that the question is a "major" one (Line 4). This is picked up by the teacher with the word "very big," and followed by students who expand it to "huge," "gigantic," "enormous," and finally, from the teacher, "titanic." By allowing and encouraging this banter, the teacher contributes to students' breadth of vocabulary, possibly expanding or reinforcing the vocabulary of some students.

The next excerpt is also taken from the focus on exam practice. The teacher had returned to the earlier question about the social problems of a developing country. The students had mentioned economic problems, cultural problems, health problems, and environmental problems. The teacher then asks, "What about politics? It seems to me that almost all the developing countries now in the world are in a system or a policy of military dictatorship. Look at all the countries around Vietnam—Taiwan, South Korea. Even Japan once. " He then mentions the names of Chiang Kai Shek and a few others. Students begin adding names of dictators.

Excerpt 5: Dictator

   1. T: Yes? And Indonesia with Suharto and Sukarno .. Yes? the Philippines with
   2.   uh Ferdinand Marcos. All of the them are dictators. Hmm. And Vietnam too?
   3. Ss: Yes.
   4. T: ((laughs)) Who? Can you can you know who?
   5. S: Yes. YOU.
   6. T: Uh me? ((laughs))
   7. Ss: ((laugh))
   8. T: Yes. I am the dictator. It means I dictate to you. I give you the
   9.   dictation OK?
  10. S: Examination dictation.
  11. T: OK. The examination. Right. OK.
  12. Ss: Dictator.
  13. T: Dictator.
  14. S: ( )
  15. T: OK. (   ). What else? ((T returns to the list of exam questions.))

In this excerpt, the teacher again turns a serious discussion into wordplay by changing the meaning of "dictator" and thereby the tone of the discussion. He sets the stage for a change in tone with his laugh as he asks a question (Line 4). Students respond with "you," which changes the meaning of "dictator" from a national leader to their classroom teacher. In Lines 8 and 9 the teacher carefully glosses the change with two variations of the new meaning of "dictator." One student repeats his meaning, reinforcing the new meaning, after which many students repeat it. After this playful switch in the meaning of "dictator" he returns to the practice questions on the handout.

The final excerpt is evidence of the students' retention of the teacher's play with words. This excerpt comes 187 lines of discourse after the previous excerpt. In the meantime the class had discussed two other exam questions and other aspects of the exam. Just before this excerpt, the teacher had repeated the importance of argumentative writing and backing up a perspective.

Excerpt 6: Dictator Revisited

1. T: So discuss. You can argue or you can counterargue it. Argue for it or
2.   argue against it.
3. S: ( )
4. T: All right? OK? Now. You prove that you are in support of it.
5. S: We have to?
6. T: You have to. You say that it true.
7. S: But I don't think so.
8. T: You don't think so. But you have to.
9. Ss: ((laugh and talk))
10. T: OK. What?
11. Ss: [(   )]
12.   [Either argue for or against]
13.   [dictatorship   ]
14. T: Pardon?
15. Ss: Dictatorship.
16. T: Uh dictatorship dictatorship OK.
17. S: You are a dictator.
18. R: Right. I am. I am. That's why I say you are in the jail yourselves and I am
19.   the jailer. OK? Huh?
20. S: And you send us torting.
21. T: Pardon?
22. S: And you send us torting.
23. T: Tort?
24. S: Torting.
25. T: torment?
26. S: Torting?
27. Ss: Torture. Torture.
28. T: So, torture.
29. S: A torture.
30. T: A torture not torturement. Torture. A torture. OK. Yes. That's all?

In Line 13, a student playfully recalls the teacher's description of himself as a dictator. This dictator, however, is not the dictator of written exercises, as he had referred to himself in Excerpt 5, but a dictator who tells students what they have to do. He agrees, reinforcing the idea that his job is not only to tell them what they have to do, but to give them no choice: They are prisoners. This topic leads to one student to "try out" a new word ("torting," Line 20) that gets bantered around between students (Line 27) who provide the role of more capable others in assisting their classmate. The teacher and students finally accept the word *torture* as the correct form.

Summary

The preceding discourse segments are examples of performance events in the form of storytelling and wordplay. These events contribute to vocabulary expansion through a focus on form and meaning. The switch in the meanings of words as demonstrated by "garden" in Excerpt 2, and "dictator" in Excerpts 5 and 6 challenges students to broaden their understanding and encourages them to move from literal to figurative language. Students are interested and motivated by stories and play, as seen, for instance, when they call out synonyms in Excerpt 4. The playful exchanges add an atmosphere of rapport and group solidarity to the classroom discourse.

This classroom discourse style represents spoken artistry with its fast pace, its overlapping speech, and its playful tone. It includes repetition of words, phrases, and topics that result in attentiveness to others' speech. The storytelling and wordplay serve as building blocks of language learning with their relations to intrinsic motivation, expert–novice interaction, and a focus on form.

IMPLICATIONS

Much classroom research in recent years has been based on an approach to learning that centers on tasks. In this chapter I highlight language learning that instead focuses on playful performance. The discourse excerpts in this chapter also highlight the meaning of reality in terms of classroom discourse. If a teacher is to bring reality into the classroom to prepare students to use the foreign language in a conversational setting, then we should view storytelling and wordplay, even if they seemingly disrupt the lesson, as linguistic preparation for conversation outside the classroom. It is through performance events such as these that people often make their perspectives known, demonstrate their power, show support for others, and increase supportive group feelings. The main purpose of these events is to engage the audience, rather than to practice the language. From this perspective, they are representative of real life. These playful excursions from the planned lesson are an important part of the language learning process, which, in this case, also lead students to an understanding of multiple forms and meanings of words.

REFERENCES

Bauman, R. (1986). *Story, performance, and event.* Cambridge, UK: Cambridge University Press.

Brown, H. D. (1994). *Teaching by principles: An interactive approach to language pedagogy.* Englewood Cliffs, NJ: Prentice Hall.

Candlin, C. (1987). Towards task-based language learning. In C. Candlin & D. Murphy (Eds.), *Language learning tasks.* Englewood Cliffs, NJ: Prentice Hall.

Cook, G. (1997). Language play, language learning. *ELT Journal, 51*(3), 224–231.

Cook, G. (1998, March). *Language play, complex adaptation.* Paper presented at the meeting of the American Association for Applied Linguistics, Seattle, WA.

Crookes, G., & Schmidt, R. (1991). Motivation: Reopening the research agenda. *Language Learning, 41,* 469–512.

Donato, R. (1994). Collective scaffolding in second language learning. In J. P. Lantolf & G. Appel (Eds.), *Vygotskyan approaches to second language research* (pp. 33–56). Norwood, NJ: Ablex.

Ellis, R. (1985). *Understanding second language acquisition.* Oxford, UK: Oxford University Press.

Foster, M. (1989). "It's cookin' now": Performance analysis of the speech events of a Black teacher in an urban community college. *Language in Society, 18,* 1–30.

Goffman, E. (1959). *The presentation of self in everyday life.* Garden City, NY: Anchor Books.

Heath, S. (1986). What no bedtime story means: Narrative skills at home and school. In B. Schieffelin & E. Ochs (Eds.), *Language socialization across cultures* (pp. 97–124). Cambridge, UK: Cambridge University Press. (Original work published 1982)

Holliday, A. (1994). *Appropriate methodology and social context.* Cambridge, UK: Cambridge University Press.

Hymes, D. (1972). On communicative competence. In J. B. Pride & Holmes (Eds.), *Sociolinguistics* (pp. 269–293). Harmondsworth, UK: Penguin.

Kramsch, C. (1993). *Context and culture in language teaching.* Oxford, UK: Oxford University Press.

Kramsch, C., & Sullivan, P. (1996). Appropriate pedagogy. *ELT Journal, 50*(3), 199–212.

Long, M., & Porter, S. (1985). Group work, interlanguage talk, and second language acquisition. *TESOL Quarterly, 19*(2), 207–228.

MacHovec, F. (1988). *Humor.* Springfield, IL: Thomas.

Norrick, N. (1993). *Conversational joking: Humor in everyday talk.* Bloomington: Indiana University Press.

Nunan, D. (1989). *Designing tasks for the communicative classroom.* Cambridge, UK: Cambridge University Press.

Swain, M. (1995, March). *Collaborative dialogue: Its contribution to second language learning.* Paper presented at the meeting of the American Association of Applied Linguistics, Long Beach, CA.

Tannen, D. (1989). *Talking voices*. Cambridge, UK: Cambridge University Press.

Vygotsky, L. (1978). *Mind in society*. Cambridge, MA: Harvard University Press.

Widdowson, H. (1994). The ownership of English. *TESOL Quarterly*, *28*(2), 377–389.

Wong-Fillmore, L. (1985). When does teacher talk work as input? In S. M. Gass & C. G. Madden (Eds.), *Input in second language acquisition* (pp. 17–50). Cambridge, MA: Newbury House.

5

Teachers' Action and Student Oral Participation in Classroom Interaction

Douglas Altamiro Consolo

Classrooms have been studied extensively in the past few years, and a number of their characteristics have been established as both socially determined and largely recurrent. In classroom environments, teachers and students may be seen as members of sociolinguistic contexts in which spoken language has social and pedagogical functions. The functions of classroom language are produced under typical discourse patterns of classroom communication systems (Cazden, 1988), in which the role of language extends beyond the communicating of propositional information, to the establishment and maintenance of relationships in the classroom. Furthermore, the generation of language input by means of classroom interaction is believed to favor language acquisition (Ellis, 1984, 1990; Krashen, 1982). Thus the language spoken in classrooms is not only linked to social and pedagogical aims; it is also "a medium through which much language is learnt, and which for many is conducive for learning" (Bygate, 1987, p. vii).

It has been reported in the literature on discourse analysis and classroom studies (e.g., Burton, 1981; Cazden, 1988; Johnson, 1995; Sinclair & Coulthard, 1975, 1992) that the social and the linguistic aspects of classrooms exhibit patterns that allow a certain amount of prediction and control in managing classroom interaction. Such predictable patterns, revealed by the way students and teachers usually interact in the course of lessons, can contribute to the definition of a system of categories in classroom discourse (CD). Additionally, patterns of CD are believed to correlate with teaching effectiveness and learning (Sinclair & Coulthard, 1975; Wong-Fillmore, 1985).

As teacher–student interaction is a sociolinguistic process that is believed to contribute to learners' language development, my aim here is to report on and discuss some results of a research study I carried out in English as a foreign language (EFL) classrooms (Consolo, 1996a) investigating foreign language classroom interaction and the discourse patterns under which teacher talk (TT) and student speech are developed. One of the major assumptions in my original study is that the quality of teachers' classroom language can contribute to language development, inasmuch as it fosters regular patterns of CD that favor learners' verbal contributions and active participation in discourse (Allwright, 1984; Allwright & Bailey, 1991; Ellis, 1984, 1990). Another assumption in this discussion is that teachers' competence in the target language is a requirement for the "quality" of teachers' management of CD. Hence the comparison, in this chapter, of verbal interaction in lessons taught by native speaker (NS) and nonnative speaker (NNS) teachers as to verify whether there are differences in student participation in their lessons. EFL classroom language is thus analyzed and discussed in relation to teachers' verbal action and learners' contributions to CD, and their implications for foreign language development (FLD).

TEACHER TALK AND PEDAGOGIC DISCOURSE

The characteristics of classroom communication have been extensively reported in the literature (e.g., Johnson, 1995; Lemke, 1989; Stubbs, 1983; Wong-Fillmore, 1985). The main purposes of classroom communication are to instruct and to inform (Coulthard, 1977). The linguistic structural choices and patterns of interaction in CD thus differ from those choices evident in other types of talk, such as everyday conversation, which usually aims at informing and interacting for social purposes (Cheepen & Monaghan, 1990; Stubbs, 1983).

The functions of classroom language have been investigated from a number of sociolinguistic and pedagogical aspects (Cazden, 1988; Cicurel, 1990; Johnson, 1995; Lemke, 1989; Sinclair & Coulthard, 1975, 1992). In a study of classroom discourse in science lessons, Lemke (1989) identified two types of tension in language use. The first is the tension between the use of language to teach content and that to manage social interaction. According to Lemke, once teachers maintain control of discourse and patterns of interaction to follow their teaching agenda, the responses of students can be seen as pro forma, often nothing more than mere repetitions of what has already been said. The other type of tension is that observed between "'scientific' ways of saying things" (p. 15) and the use of more colloquial, everyday language in the classroom. This second type of tension is exemplified by a teacher's deviation from typical classroom language use, which resulted in a "more playful or more personal" (p. 15) atmosphere, and caused the students to be more attentive to what the teacher says. This suggests that the use of language by teachers and students in the classroom does not have to be restricted to the formal register nor to the maintenance of asymmetrical verbal exchanges. Rather, the desired atmosphere (cf. Allwright & Bailey, 1991) for a class may be attained by means of teacher and student management of CD, and the switching of conversational roles in pursuit of interactional goals. From the perspective of student contributions to CD, my position here is that interaction is better accomplished when negotiation takes place; that is, when the verbal roles taken up by classroom interactants (a teacher and his or her students) are nearly symmetrical, in "attempts to reach decisions by consensus rather than by unilateral decision-making" (Allwright, 1984, p. 160).

In typical classroom communication, however, unilateral decisions occur because the teacher usually follows a plan of action in agreement with his or her views of teaching and learning and aims and course objectives. Not only does the teacher manipulate classroom interaction through his or her agenda as he or she uses language for classroom management. He or she also plays a significant role in topic management (Burton, 1981) and controls the social system of interpersonal relations in the classroom through the speaking rights (Cazden, 1988) entrusted to him or her by the schooling context (Cicurel, 1990; Lemke, 1989).

Whereas in other types of everyday speech encounters interlocutors usually share the control and management of topic, turn-taking, and the orientation of talk, the pedagogical agenda may prevent verbal exchanges from even resembling natural conversation. In some cases, teachers and their students may simply follow ritualistic classroom action and, in a way, fail to exploit the capacity of the mind to make sense of the environment and the real context of language lessons, therefore failing to meet the interactants' needs (Breen, 1985).

In pursuit of verifying how the management of CD engenders verbal interaction, and if the characteristics of such interaction can foster student participation, the study reported here attempts to answer the following questions:

1. In whole-class instruction, are there observable features of TT that foster EFL students' contributions to CD?

2. If so, how do NS and NNS EFL teachers compare concerning these features?

INVESTIGATING STUDENT SPEECH IN EFL LESSONS WITH NS AND NNS TEACHERS

The discourse features of classroom language and teacher–student interaction in monolingual EFL classes are analyzed here with the focus on student oral production as dependent on and affected by the teacher's language. Lessons taught by NS and NNS teachers in Brazilian school contexts are compared in an attempt to identify possible significant differences between patterns of student speech in connection with the classroom talk of these two groups of teachers.

Before proceeding toward a description of the study reported here, I present a brief account of NS and NNS teachers' linguistic profiles, based on Consolo's (1996a, 1996b) discussion on EFL teachers in Brazil. Consolo showed that, in the area of English language teaching, teachers are generally assigned into two categories: NS (Category 1) and NNS teachers (Category 2). The NS teachers either speak English as their first language (and that usually means they were born and educated in English-speaking countries), or were born in Brazil, from English-speaking ancestors and brought up as bilinguals in English and Portuguese. The NNS teachers are mostly nationals who have once been EFL learners. Among these teachers, some have a high level of proficiency in English, developed not only in teacher education courses (e.g., undergraduate studies on English language and literature), but also (and mainly) because of experiences in learning and using the language (first as students, then as teachers) in private language courses (as reported, e.g., in Gimenez, 1994) and as a result of visits to English-speaking countries. The linguistic profile of those teachers is generally of a fluent language user.

The contrast between NSs and NNSs of a given language is, however, a controversial matter (Kramsch, 1995; Lee, 1995) and cannot be viewed in a simplistic way. Although it seems valid to label a person born and educated in an English-speaking country (henceforth Country A) as an NS of English, once this speaker has moved to a non-English-speaking country (henceforth Country B) where he or she has been living for a considerably long time, his or her command of English is bound to be different. It may differ, for example, at discourse and phonological levels, from the English proficiency of speakers who have always lived in Country A. Therefore, if these differences are considered, the speakers formerly assigned into one category, that of NSs of English, can in fact be classified into two subcategories. Moreover, the NSs of English living in Country B may have developed such a level of competence in the language(s) spoken in that country (e.g., Portuguese in Brazil) to characterize them as a very good users of that language as well, perhaps with bilingual competence in both languages. By the same token, Brazilians who speak EFL may have reached a near-native level of competence in English due to years of language study and experience of living abroad, like most of the individuals in this study, and be sometimes considered bilingual speakers of English and Portuguese.

Finally, even though NS teachers "are potentially more accomplished users of English than non-native speakers" (Medgyes, 1994, p. 12), because of the nature and the demands of pedagogic discourse, specific aims of classroom language imply modifications in teachers' speech. Therefore, and in particular at the level of discourse, features of NS and NNS teachers' TT may be more similar to one another than everyday speech produced by native and non-native speakers of English (Consolo, 1996a).

Because a thorough discussion on English speakers would fall beyond the scope of this chapter, and to narrow down the theoretical background to fulfill the aims of this discussion, two levels of analysis are delimited: discourse and sociocultural issues. Lexis and pronunciation per se are not analyzed here. Consequently, lessons taught by NS and NNS teachers are compared in terms of discourse and sociocultural issues concerning classroom language and teacher–student interaction.

Research Design and Methodology

The data were collected in two private language schools (LS1 and LS2) and at a university (UNIV1) in two large cities in Brazil. The participants were nine EFL teachers (NS1, NS2, NS3, NS4, NNS1, NNS2, NNS3, NNS4, and NNS5) and their students, in classes ranging from intermediate to advanced levels of English instruction. Participants at the three institutions were selected according to the following criteria: (a) at least one NS teacher and one NNS teacher were engaged in teaching the same course (each teacher in a different class), (b) both teachers followed roughly the same syllabus and teaching methodology, and (c) the courses were not taught simultaneously, so that a single observer could attend both to collect data. For the purpose of comparison, lessons taught by NS2 were investigated at two different levels: at ADV1 (to be compared to

TABLE 5.1
EFL Courses and Levels Investigated

Class	Institution	Level of Students	Teacher Assignments
INT1	UNIV1	Intermediate	NS1, NNS1
ADV1	LS1	Upper intermediate	NS2, NNS2
ADV2	LS2	Advanced (post-Cambridge FCE examination)	NS3, NNS3 NS4, NNS4
ADV3	LS1	Advanced[a]	NS2, NNS5

[a]ADV3 is the last term of the general English course at LS1. Students can then choose to proceed to a preparatory course for the University of Michigan Certificate of Proficiency in English examination. Although students at ADV3 have had fewer classroom contact hours than students at ADV2, their level of oral proficiency is generally higher. This explains why the courses have been labeled here as ADV2 and ADV3, respectively.

NNS2) and at ADV3 (to be compared to NNS5). The four levels of classes, student levels, and teacher assignments are presented in Table 5.1.

The data corpus discussed here comprises two or three EFL lessons with each teacher,[1] observed by a nonparticipant observer and recorded on audio. Field notes were recorded during the observations to complement tape transcripts and clarify the different phases of the lessons and the classroom activities. Once classroom observation had finished, the teachers and their students answered questionnaires to provide complementary data concerning previous EFL experience and their awareness of their own needs in the use of language for communication in the classroom.

From the total of approximately 42 hours of recorded lessons, a whole lesson and an extract from another lesson taught by each teacher were selected for transcription and analysis. Lessons of the same level and on approximately the same content were selected for comparison. In nearly all cases, NS and NNS teachers dealt with the same activities and tasks, generally in compliance with suggestions of the course books. These portions of the lessons were labeled *lesson segments*.

The EFL Students

The 87 students (49 female and 38 male) in the classes investigated were EFL learners trying to develop a command of English for educational or professional purposes, either for traveling abroad or for using the lan-

[1]Three lessons taught by NS1, NS2 at ADV1, NS3, NS4, NNS1, NNS2, NNS3, and NNS4; two lessons taught by NS2 at ADV3, and two lessons taught by NNS4 at ADV2.

guage locally. Their ages varied between 13 and 44, and their previous experiences in learning English varied between 1 and 13 years. Most learners were full-time secondary and university students (33.3% and 48.8%, respectively), and the other 17.9% were employed in one of the following professions: architecture (2 students), banking (3), computing (2), engineering (1), language teaching (2), sales (1), and secretarial work (2). Due to their individual needs and expectations (Cardinalli & Fraga, 1990; Fraga, 1993) the students—mainly the adult ones—had probably chosen to take EFL lessons, as opposed to students who have compulsory English lessons as part of their school curriculum. Therefore, their willingness to develop language skills in English, especially for oral communication (Cardinalli & Fraga, 1990), is assumed. Classes in which English is a compulsory school subject, such as in secondary schools and in some undergraduate courses, were not considered in this investigation.

Classes were quite small (*Mdn* = 7 students), which may favor whole-class instruction and teacher–student verbal interaction. Moreover, previous experience as EFL learners (*Mdn* = 6 years), level of maturity (mostly young adults and adults, *Mdn* age = 20), and level of language proficiency (intermediate and upper intermediate) are believed to have influenced the quality of their participation in classroom oral interaction, as further discussed in the next section.

Categories for Analyzing Classroom Interaction

A typology of discourse categories from earlier studies on CD and classroom interaction, especially that of Sinclair and Coulthard (1975, 1992), was adapted for the comparison of the discourse patterns in lessons taught by NS and NNS teachers. Language is broken down into *acts*, the units of analysis at the lowest rank of discourse, which label the functional properties of utterances. Acts structure the next higher ranks of discourse categories, defined as *moves* and *exchanges*. Moves frequently involve the interactional initiation–response–follow-up (IRF) structure of the typical lesson, in which teacher initiations (I) predict student responses (R) and the teacher's follow-up (F) evaluation. In such analysis, the discourse value of an item depends not only on what acts and moves have preceded it, but also what is expected to follow and the way acts and moves relate to each other.

In this study, a differentiation is made between TT and student speech by using the labels I, Rt, and F for moves produced by teachers, and Is, R, and Fs for moves produced by students. The labels for acts, as in Consolo

(1996a), are based on categories presented in Burton (1981), Francis and Hunston (1992) and Sinclair and Coulthard (1975, 1992). Thirty-five act types were used, as listed in Table 5.2.

The moves and acts in the coded lesson transcripts were counted with the aid of the Longman Mini-Concordancer (Chandler, 1989), a software package for analyzing large quantities of computer-readable texts. The data were analyzed statistically using a one-way analysis of variance

TABLE 5.2
Acts in Teacher and Student Talk: Average for Whole Lessons

	NS Teachers		NNS Teachers	
Category: ACTS	Teacher Talk	Student Talk	Teacher Talk	Student Talk
Markers	42	3	52.4	5.8
Starters	35.2	1	49.2	2.4
Elicitations	115.4	15.8	181.8	26.4
Rhetorical questions	2.4	—	1.6	—
Comprehension checks	31.2	—	60.8	0.6
Confirmation checks	18	5	35.2	4.6
Clarifications	10.8	4.4	19.8	2.6
Directives	29.8	—	50	—
Informatives	159.6	26.2	151.2	46.8
Comments	24	1.4	39.6	6.4
Clues	21.4	0.6	27.2	—
Models	15.4	0.4	27.4	0.4
Bids	—	2.4	—	1.2
Nominations	6.2	1	21.4	3
Acknowledgments	45.2	32.8	106.8	29.2
Affirmative replies	3.8	19	7.2	20
Negative replies	1.8	5.4	3.2	7
Choice replies	—	13.2	—	0.6
Repetition replies	—	4.6	—	8.6
Informative replies	45.8	107	48.8	173.2
Offer replies	—	1	—	1
Reactions	0.6	19.2	11.6	12.6
Protests	—	2.8	5.8	8.8
Corrections	4.6	—	11.2	—
Evaluates	21.4	0.4	30	0.8
Metastatements	13.2	—	15.6	—
Apologies	0.8	—	1.2	0.6
Thanks	0.2	—	0.4	—
Encouragements	0.2	—	2.4	—
Conclusions	9	0.4	4.8	0.4

(Continued)

TABLE 5.2 *(Continued)*

| | NS Teachers | | NNS Teachers | |
Category: ACTS	Teacher Talk	Student Talk	Teacher Talk	Student Talk
Terminates	6	—	14.4	—
Greetings	0.2	0.4	1.8	—
Partings	1	—	1	—
Asides	1	—	2.33	—
Translations	0.6	0.2	0.2	0.8
Total of Means	666.8	267.6	986.33	363.8

(ANOVA) and a chi-square test. Because the interest here is student participation in classroom interaction, the frequencies of moves categorized as typical of TT and student speech were compared to see whether significant differences existed between lessons taught by NS and NNS teachers.

Findings

Teachers' and Students' Management of Whole-Class Interaction. In the data analyzed in this study, TT and student speech followed typical IRF patterns, and all types of moves were found in the lessons analyzed. In related NS- and NNS-taught classes, the percentages of TT and student speech were distributed similarly between interactants within each group (with the exception of the lesson taught by NNS1), as shown in Table 5.3. Similarities also applied to the percentages of TT and student speech when compared in the corpus as a whole.

Statistical Treatment of Data at the Rank of Moves and Acts. At the rank of moves, the results of the ANOVA showed that lessons taught by NS and NNS teachers were significantly different only in relation to F and Fs moves, indicating a higher frequency of Fs moves in lessons taught by NS teachers. A subsequent analysis of the types of acts constituting followups in student speech (Fs) indicated that no strong claims could be made about the types of acts occurring in Fs moves at different levels, or between lessons taught by NS and NNS teachers, except for a slightly greater variety of acts produced by students taught by NS1 in INT1 and by NS2 in ADV1. These encompass comments, informatives, and evaluates, which tend to be less typical of student speech. On the whole, Fs moves most frequently consist of acknowledges, reacts (laugh), and repetitive replies; other con-

TABLE 5.3
Percentages of TT and Student Speech

	TT	Student Speech
NS1	57%	43%
1NS2	51%	49%
NS3	65%	35%
NS4	55%	45%
3NS2	53%	47%
M	56.2%	43.8%
NNS1	74%	26%
NNS2	62%	38%
NNS3	52%	48%
NNS4	53%	47%
NNS5	51%	49%
M	58.4%	41.6%

stituents found in the data are comments, confirmation checks, conclusions, evaluates, informatives, informative replies, models, protests, and thanks.

At the rank of acts, the average frequency of the 35 types of acts represented in the lessons and lesson extracts are presented in Table 5.2.

A chi-square test was carried out for the frequencies of acts occurring in student speech for all pairs of classes, to verify the likelihood of their occurrence as a significant contrast between NS- and NNS-taught lessons. The acts analyzed were elicitations, informatives, acknowledgments, affirmative and negative replies, repetition replies, informative replies, and reactions. The value of χ^2_{obs} for the acts analyzed by means of chi-square (10.799) is nonsignificant for the frequency of acts compared (χ^2_{crit} = 12.592), suggesting that, for most of the language in student contributions to CD, communicative functions used do not correspond to the linguistic background of the teachers.

A categorization of utterances in student speech at the rank of acts reveals that classroom communication consists mainly of the exchange of information between interactants (Coulthard, 1985), as shown by the high frequency of informatives and informative replies (Table 5.2); moreover, the high frequency of elicitations in TT support the view that teachers manage classroom interaction mostly by eliciting through questioning (Banbrook & Skehan, 1990; Long & Crookes, 1987; Long & Sato, 1983).

Having examined the patterns of classroom interaction at the levels of both moves and communicative acts, in lessons taught by NS and NNS teachers, it can be concluded that there are no significant differences in discourse features in TT or in student speech when NS and NNS EFL teachers are compared under the conditions established in this investigation. This provides an answer to the second question posed earlier in this chapter: How do NS and NNS EFL teachers compare concerning features of classroom discourse? The results of such quantitative analysis may be explained by the following reasons.

Although recent methodologies emphasize communication in foreign language teaching, it seems that this tendency has not significantly modified the roles of teachers and students when they interact in the classroom. Conversely, despite the willingness to increase the amount of student participation in classroom discourse and promote less asymmetrical verbal interactional, students and teachers often fall short of this goal because the interaction "remains at the instructional end" (Kramsch, 1987, p. 28), as reiterated by the results obtained here. Besides, EFL teachers seem to be highly influenced by the guidelines of the chosen English Language Teaching (ELT) methodology and the language imported into their lessons by the materials adopted, especially course books, which is reflected in the way they conduct their lessons. This may also have been a reason for the type of classroom language and interaction observed in the classes investigated. Moreover, teachers' individual differences in the management of classroom interaction may be blurred by these influences, which tend to standardize patterns of teacher–student communication.

In response to the first research question that oriented this investigation, the statistical results have not identified any specific combination of discourse categories in TT that foster the oral production of students, other than the typical IR pattern, even though students occasionally initiate exchanges and provide follow-up moves. Although not statistically significant, there seems to be a trend to more teacher–student interaction and student contribution to CD in the lessons taught by two of the NNS teachers. A qualitative analysis of lesson segments reveals that the characteristics of classroom interaction found in lessons taught by NNS3 and NNS4 represent, to a certain extent, teaching as interaction (Allwright, 1984), and can be seen as beneficial in terms of both language comprehension and production to aid FLD (Long & Crookes, 1987; Malamah-Thomas, 1987).

NNS3 gives significant importance to students' verbal contributions, which she elicits intensely. Not only does she follow her agenda for the lesson, but she also develops the topic being discussed, according to the students' opinions. NNS4 teaches along similar lines, and her lessons reveal a good amount of student participation, as indicated by a fairly balanced distribution of teacher moves and student moves in her lessons (see Segment 2 later).

It may be suggested here that contributing factors for the quantity and quality of student contributions to CD may include (a) the amount of student involvement with the subject matter (i.e., the topic of interaction), and (b) the teacher's ability in both topic management and rhetorical strategies to acknowledge students' contributions to motivate further participation. As indicated by the qualitative analysis, such behavior was more evident in the lessons taught by NNS3 and NNS4, in which a greater frequency of various types of acts in student speech was also observed, as illustrated in Segments 1 and 2.

Segment 1 (from the lesson taught by NNS3)[2]

570.	St3:	(ah,) I think for women, thirty, thirty-two
571.	T:	THIRTY-TWO YOU'RE A SPINSTER? ah, {chuckle}
572.	St3:	(unintelligible)
573.	T:	I don't know. I'll kill myself
	Ss:	{laugh}
574.	T:	(I'd like to know what's) the word that comes after spinster {chuckle}ok, what is the how old is a spinster in Brazil? thirty-two you said?
575.	St1:	forty
576.	St2:	(no)
		. . . . .
590.	T:	Frank, how old is a spinster in your opinion?
591.	St4:	(for women) For womens or for men?
592.	Ss:	{laughter}
593.	St1:	(it's a social)
594.	St3:	(unintelligible)

---

[2]The following transcription symbols are used for this and subsequent segments.

+	Pauses of less than 1.0 second
[1]	Pauses between 1.0 and 2.0 seconds
=	In final position (babies=): A speaker's utterance that is categorized as one act but separated graphically to accommodate intervening interruption or overlapped speech. In initial position (=think): The continuation of an utterance, started in an earlier turn.
{FS}	False start
SPINSTER	Stressed word
[RISE]	Rising intonation
[ ]	Overlapped speech
( )	What was possibly said
(UNINT)	Unintelligible speech

595. T: it's a social. I don't think it's a social (unintelligible)
             I think it's a CULTURAL [characteristic]
596. St1:   [I (yeah)   ] it's (unintelligible)
597. St2:   (forty-five)

In Segment 1, the teacher (T) and her students are discussing a word list (new vocabulary) in preparation for a unit in their course book that dealt with issues related to young and old age. Prior to Segment 1, in Turn 564, T had asked the question "How old is a bachelor in Brazil?" aiming at defining the meaning of *bachelor* and *spinster*, two items in their word list. The first point to be made is that, rather than teaching words straightforwardly, for example, by asking questions such as "What's the meaning of . . . ?" as observed in the lesson taught by her NS counterpart, NNS3 attempts to motivate a discussion (i.e., verbal interaction) around meanings implied by what students say (Turn 595). She personalizes classroom language and creates a humorous atmosphere in the classroom, as in Turns 571, 573, and 574.

Because the atmosphere favors student participation, they probably feel at ease to negotiate meanings (Turn 591), and even to disagree with what is said by the teacher or by other students (Turn 576). Likewise, in the lesson taught by NNS4, students seem to be at ease to express themselves, disagree with what the teacher says, and, to a certain extent, attempt a less asymmetrical role in CD.

Segment 2 (from the lesson taught by NNS4)[3]

383. T: why do you think they, they like that? [1] I'm not sure but I think that's because they LEARN, they are beginning to realize that they are different from their mother they are another person because when they are babies they think that [1] they are the same as their mothers.
384. St1:   I disagree
385. T: yeah? I don't know. I just read it {chuckle}
386. St1:   I think that babies=
387. T: uhm [RISE]
388. St1:   =think that er the word THEIR word are really what they see
389. T: their what?
390. St1:   their word is [(unintelligible)]
391. T: [world?] world or word?
392. St1:   world

---

[3]Up to this point the discussion was about young age and the teacher had asked the class why babies liked to play a kind of hide and seek with their caretakers.

393. T: world?
394. St1:   yes [1] is only what they, they see at that moment
395. T: yes

One of the students (St1) disagrees with the teacher (Turn 384) and carries on expressing his point of view through two exchanges (Turns 386–395). When St1 mispronounces *world* (Turn 390), however, the discourse structure changes to the typical IRF sequence, in which the teacher takes up her role of correcting students' mistakes. Once the problem is solved, St1 manages to go back to the topic being discussed (Turn 394). Segments 1 and 2 also contain a variety of student acts typically found in TT: markers, informatives, elicitations, acknowledges, and protests. Such acts differ from replies and clarifications, the acts mostly found in student speech.

This interactive style indicated by NNS3 and NNS4 cannot be attributed to the teachers' native language. Rather, for these two teachers, the management of classroom interaction is in line with the construction of interpersonal meaning. In this sense, Kramsch (1987) suggested that "only by broadening their discourse options in the classroom can learners stop being foreign-language consumers and become the active architects of interpersonal and cultural understanding" (p. 28).

Similar claims are made by Almeida Filho (1993) on the use of the target language for communication in the foreign language classroom. Gradually, he stated, the artificial atmosphere and foreign characteristics of interaction initially brought in by the foreign language, should give way to meaningful interaction, lowering the learners' affective filter (as in Krashen, 1982), and, by means of using target language authentically, fulfill communicative goals pursued by teachers and students.

One factor for student contribution to CD is the configuration of social and affective factors in classroom, which affect each speaker's psychological profile and his or her performance in classroom interaction (Garau, 1995; Krashen, 1982; Scarcella, 1990). In the case of Brazil and other countries where interactants are immersed in a culture that emphasizes informality, in both verbal and nonverbal behavior, EFL students may respond better to teachers whose speech style matches the cultural characteristics of oral interaction in their first language, for example, Brazilian Portuguese. Such characteristics find their way into the classroom language of NNS teachers as they externalize their Brazilian cultural background while speaking English to conduct EFL lessons. This informality was characteristic of NNS2, NNS3, NNS4, and NNS5, in contrast to the style of their NS counterparts. On the other hand, the more formal style of NNS1 may have been the cause of less student participation in her lessons than in those of NS1, who adopted a more relaxed and rather humorous posture when conducting his lessons.

CONCLUSION

This chapter focused on student contributions to CD in EFL lessons taught by NS and NNS teachers. The data analysis showed little significant difference between the language as produced in lessons taught by teachers who speak English as their mother tongue and the language used by NNS teachers who have mastered English as a foreign language, as very similar patterns of CD discourse structures were encountered in lessons taught by both groups of teachers.

Despite the statistical results, however, the study has contributed to a better understanding of classroom communication and the status of student speech in foreign language lessons. There was a trend for greater teacher–student interaction and more student contributions to CD in the lessons taught by one NS teacher (NS1) and two NNS teachers (NNS3 and NNS4). This was confirmed by means of a qualitative analysis of the lessons taught by those teachers. It may be suggested that individual teaching style makes a difference, rather than the teacher's mother tongue.

Classroom oral language use may fall short of teachers' and students' expectations for oral interaction due to constraints imposed on the verbal behavior of the students by the features of CD. Most of the time, teachers and students rigidly observe their part in the socially defined classroom roles. Although they may engage in a spoken discourse that resembles conversational English, they do so to achieve their teaching and learning goals. Moreover, it is still the teacher's agenda that determines the characteristics of CD. With minimum variation, the classroom communication in the EFL lessons investigated shows that teachers dominate both the content and the patterns of interaction in lessons, even though there is usually room for students to contribute to, and less frequently to intervene in, the interactional structure.

The belief that speaking a language implies the construction of interpersonal meaning seems to be relevant for language lessons that will motivate more engagement in CD on the part of students. Such engagement presupposes the taking up of active roles in verbal interaction by the students, as for example, the initiation and finishing of exchanges, as well as having some sort of control over topics dealt with. It seems that some improvement in teacher–student interaction in language lessons may be achieved if the interactants can be made aware of the characteristics of the sociolinguistic process in which they are engaged in the management of relationships in the classroom.

REFERENCES

Allwright, R. (1984). The importance of interaction in classroom language learning. *Applied Linguistics, 5*(2), 156–171.

Allwright, D., & Bailey, K. M. (1991). *Focus on the language classroom: An introduction to classroom research for language teachers.* Cambridge, UK: Cambridge University Press.

Almeida Filho, J. C. (1993). *Dimensões comunicativas no ensino de línguas* [Communicative dimensions in language teaching]. Campinas, Brazil: Pontes.

Banbrook, L., & Skehan, P. (1990). Classrooms and display questions. In C. Brumfit & R. Mitchell (Eds.), *Research in the language classroom* (ELT Documents No. 133, pp. 141–151). London, UK: MET in association with The British Council.

Breen, M. (1985). Authenticity in the language classroom. *Applied Linguistics, 6*(1), 60–70.

Burton, D. (1981). Analysing spoken discourse. In M. Coulthard & M. Montgomery (Eds.), *Studies in discourse analysis* (pp. 61–81). London: Routledge.

Bygate, M. (1987). *Speaking.* Oxford, UK: Oxford University Press.

Cardinalli, M. I. and Fraga, M. C. S. (1990). O curso de inglês geral do Centro de Ensino de Línguas da Unicamp: implicações e problemas [The general English course at Centro de Ensino de Línguas—UNICAMP: implications and problems]. Campinas, Brazil: UNICAMP (mimeo.).

Cazden, C. B. (1988). *Classroom discourse.* Portsmouth, NH: Heinemann.

Chandler, B. (1989). *Longman mini-concordancer.* Harlow, UK: Longman.

Cheepen, C., & Monaghan, J. (1990). *Spoken English: A practical guide.* London: Pinter.

Cicurel, F. (1990). Elements d'un rituel communicatif dans les situations d'enseignement [Elements of a communicative ritual in teaching situations]. In L. Dabène, F. Cicurel, M. -C. Lauga-Hamid, & C. Foerster (Eds.), *Variations et Rituels en Classes de Langue* [Variations and Rituals in Language Classes] (pp. 23–57). Paris: Hatier-Crédif.

Consolo, D. A. (1996a). *Classroom discourse in language teaching: A study of oral interaction in EFL lessons in Brazil.* Unpublished doctoral thesis, CALS, University of Reading, UK.

Consolo, D. A. (1996b). A panorama of tendencies and evidence about NS/NNS teachers in ELT. In *Annals of the IV Congresso Brasileiro de Lingüística Aplicada* (pp. 465–473). Campinas, Brazil: UNICAMP.

Coulthard, M. (1977). *An introduction to discourse analysis.* Harlow, UK: Longman.

Coulthard, M. (1985). *An introduction to discourse analysis* (2nd ed.). Harlow, UK: Longman.

Ellis, R. (1984). *Classroom second language development.* Oxford, UK: Pergamon.

Ellis, R. (1990). *Instructed second language acquisition.* Oxford, UK: Basil Blackwell.

Fraga, M. C. S. (1993). Abordagens de ensino de segunda língua e o ensino de língua estrangeira [Approaches in second and foreign language teaching]. *Letras, 12*(1 & 2), 139–161.

Francis, G., & Hunston, S. (1992). Analysing everyday conversation. In M. Coulthard (Ed.), *Advances in spoken discourse analysis* (pp. 123–161). London: Routledge.

Garau, P. (1995, November). *The emotional switchboard*. Talk presented at the TESOL-Italy Annual Convention, Rome, Italy.

Gimenez, T. (1994). *Learners becoming teachers: An exploratory study of beliefs held by prospective and practising EFL teachers in Brazil*. Unpublished doctoral dissertation, Lancaster University, Lancaster, UK.

Johnson, K. E. (1995). *Understanding communication in second language classrooms*. Cambridge, UK: Cambridge University Press.

Kramsch, C. J. (1987). Interactive discourse in small and large groups. In W. M. Rivers (Ed.), *Interactive language teaching* (pp. 17–30). Cambridge, UK: Cambridge University Press.

Kramsch, C. J. (1995, April). *The privilege of the nonnative speaker*. Talk presented at the TESOL Conference, Long Beach, CA.

Krashen, S. D. (1982). *Principles and practice in second language acquisition*. New York: Pergamon.

Lee, W. R. (1995). Natives and non-natives: Much ado about something? *IATEFL Newsletter, 126*, 8–9.

Lemke, J. L. (1989). *Using language in the classroom* (2nd ed.). Oxford, UK: Oxford University Press.

Long, M. H., & Crookes, G. (1987). Intervention points in second language classroom processes. In B. K. Das (Ed.), *Classroom-oriented research in second language acquisition* (pp. 177–203). Singapore: Regional English Teaching Conference.

Long, M. H., & Sato, C. J. (1983). Classroom foreigner talk discourse: Forms and functions of teachers questions. In H. W. Seliger & M. H. Long (Eds.), *Classroom-oriented research in second language acquisition* (pp. 268–285). Rowley, MA:Newbury House.

Malamah-Thomas, A. (1987). *Classroom interaction*. Oxford, UK: Oxford Univerisity Press.

Medgyes, P. (1994). *The non-native teacher*. London: Macmillan.

Scarcella, R. C. (1990). Communication difficulties in second language production, development and instruction. In R. C. Scarcella, E. S. Andersen, & S. D. Krashen (Eds.), *Developing communicative competence in a second language* (pp. 337–352). New York: Newbury House.

Sinclair, J., & Coulthard, M. (1975). *Towards an analysis of discourse: The English used by teachers and pupils*. London: Oxford University Press.

Sinclair, J., & Coulthard, M. (1992). Towards an analysis of discourse. In M. Coulthard (Ed.), *Advances in spoken discourse analysis* (pp. 1–34). London: Routledge.

Stubbs, M. (1983). *Discourse analysis: The sociolinguistic analysis of natural language*. Oxford, UK: Basil Blackwell.

Wong-Fillmore, L. (1985). When does teacher talk work as input? In S. Gass & C. G. Madden (Eds.), *Input in second language acquisition* (pp. 17–50). Rowley, MA: Newbury House.

6

Repetition in Foreign Language Classroom Interaction

Patricia A. Duff

One of the mainstays of second language teaching in the days of audio-lingualism was drills with frequent repetition of target structures. Considered a means of helping learners develop good language learning "habits," these drills were led by teachers or an audiotaped stimulus to which students would respond on cue (Brown, 1994; DeKeyser, 1998; Hadley, 1993). In more recent theory (e.g., McLaughlin, 1987; Skehan, 1998) and teaching methods informed by cognitive psychology (Hadley, 1993; Skehan, 1998), the benefits of repetition are not viewed in terms of behaviorist habit formation. Rather, repetition is viewed as a way of providing learners greater access to language forms—for example, by repeating forms for learners (Chaudron, 1977)—and as a means of enabling learners to develop automaticity in the target language as they proceed from highly controlled language use to more automatic or spontaneous production of internalized forms. Indeed, the importance of having learners reproduce forms they have heard to help them notice gaps between their own and others' production is underscored in several current accounts of language acquisition (see, e.g., Schmidt & Frota, 1986; Skehan, 1998, following Swain, 1985).

Similarly, in Slobin's cognitive-interactionist approach to language development (cf. Andersen, 1990; Slobin, 1985), in subsequent connectionist accounts of language acquisition (e.g., Gasser, 1990), and in research on language learning strategies (e.g., Chamot, 1987), the importance of repetition in language learning—either of formulaic or nonformulaic speech and as spontaneous or planned production—is clear: Frequency of exposure to input is a fundamental factor in determining its saliency and the likelihood that it will be noticed and acquired or that significant connections between forms and meanings will be made. In language assessment, as well, dictation and elicited repetition have been used as means of determining first and second language learners' grammatical proficiency because, it is argued, the ability to reproduce sentences that exceed a particular number of syllables or phrases requires not just an echoing of the original stimulus, but a decoding and reprocessing of the sentence for production purposes, based on long-term, stored knowledge of grammar (Bley-Vroman & Chaudron, 1994).

Summarizing some of the second language (L2) cognitivist literature, Skehan (1998) wrote:

> Repetition in what we hear means that the discourse we have to process is less dense; repetition in the language we produce provides more time to engage in micro and macro conversational planning. In acquisitional terms, repetition in conversation can serve to consolidate what is being learned, since the conversation may act as an unobtrusive but effective scaffold for what is causing learning difficulty. (p. 33)

Unlike earlier accounts of the role of repetition in foreign language (FL) learning, however, most current accounts acknowledge that it should be meaningful and relevant to the learners—a form of negotiation of messages and texts—and not merely (or entirely) a mechanical or rote parroting of structures that does not ultimately enhance students' proficiency in the target language.

In this chapter, I outline some of the ways repetition has been analyzed in previous acquisition and interaction research and then consider a broader, more socially contextualized research perspective. This perspective is based on language socialization principles (e.g., Duff, 1995; Schieffelin & Ochs, 1986) and constructivist approaches to educational discourse (e.g., McGroarty, 1998), and supported by discourse analysis. I first present examples analyzing repetition in young children's language learning, then present examples of linguistic interactions involving repetition in FL classrooms with adolescent and young adult learners. The analysis focuses not only on the types of constructions that are repeated, by whom, and in what contexts, but also the implications of the repeated language forms for learning, for effecting solidarity among the members of the class, and for helping them to construct knowledge together through their use of an

FL. The chapter shows the range of uses of repetition in classrooms for a combination of disciplinarian, social, cognitive, linguistic, and affective purposes. Beyond psycholinguistic and other curricular reasons for the use of repetition, I also illustrate how repetition can either further students' social and affective interests or, when used excessively, frustrate students, resulting in their diverting classroom discussion in other directions to avoid further repetition.

PSYCHOLINGUISTIC (COGNITIVE-INTERACTIONIST) VERSUS SOCIOCULTURAL AND AFFECTIVE PERSPECTIVES ON REPETITION

Despite the arguments and evidence that exist in support of the psycholinguistic value of certain kinds of repetition in interaction within classrooms and other social contexts, little research has examined its sociocultural, discursive, and affective roles in education, and the ways in which certain kinds of repetition can enhance or impact language, content, and communal learning. Cognitive accounts pertain primarily to individual language learners and their acquisition and production of language. That is, they highlight learners' interactions with language, rather than their interactions with other learners, although there is naturally an implicit understanding that interlocutors exist, especially when repetition is being examined. Following Tannen (1989), however, Skehan (1998) also noted the collective, cohesive, even deictic origins and functions of repetition, pointing out, in particular, its role in signaling cognitive and affective participation or involvement in contextualized discourse (oral conversations as well as other, e.g., literary, genres) and its rhetorical effectiveness from "the resonances which it strikes with previous conversations" (p. 34).[1] Repetition signals not only that one is engaged in discussion with others, but it also indexes a history of interactions with one's interlocutors:

> Repeating the words, phrases, or sentences of other speakers (a) accomplishes a conversation, (b) shows one's response to another's utterance, (c) shows acceptance of others' utterances, their participation, and them, and (d) gives evidence of one's own participation. (Tannen, 1989, p. 34, cited in Skehan, 1998, p. 34).

---

[1]One has only to watch episodes of television programs such as *Seinfeld* to observe the extent to which repetition is used in (scripted) discourse for dramatic and comedic effect and as a means of providing textual and interpersonal cohesion.

Like Tannen (1989), Johnstone (1994) examined repetition in language use from a variety of perspectives, including clinical therapeutic contexts where echoing and mirroring are pervasive. What is apparent is that repetition plays many different discursive roles in everyday language interactions among peers, in first language (L1) development, in therapeutic and professional discourse (e.g., among pilots), among the elderly with language disabilities, and in classrooms with FL learners and teachers. Although some of the discursive functions of repetition have been examined elsewhere, its role in fostering social cohesiveness and communities of learning has received less attention.

In connection with L1 acquisition, Greenfield and Savage-Rumbaugh (1993) discussed children's use of "repetition to stimulate more talk in their conversational partner" (p. 1). Their use of repetition plays both pragmatic and discursive roles by providing cohesion, signaling discourse topics, and providing counterclaims, denials, agreements, and verbal play. In addition, it is argued that repetition helps young children acquire grammar (see also Bennett-Kastor, 1994). It is also a pervasive and multifunctional discourse phenomenon in monolingual content-based classrooms. In an example from an L1 classroom in Britain (Excerpt 1), Edwards and Westgate (1994) showed that the purpose of repetition may simply be to check whether a student (P in Excerpt 1) is paying attention. However, given the delays and difficulties the teacher (T) encounters in obtaining the definition of *community*, the excerpt becomes an extended attempt to have P, and perhaps her classmates as well, internalize the definition that the teacher has provided. That is, although the use of repetition may have started out being managerial, it ended up being didactic.

Excerpt 1: L1 Content Class

1. T: Right, I'll read there and then you read that. 'Tristan da Cuhna is an island where about 300 people live. Why are we learning about Tristan da Cuhna? A group of people who live together are called a **community**.' . . . What's a **community**?

2. P: (Mumbles)

3. T: What's a **community**?

4. P: Er . . . (Silence)

5. T: Were you listening? (Pause) You weren't? (Laughs; he reads the passage again) So what's a **community**?

6. P: A group of people.

7. T: Who . . .

8. P: That live on the island there, er, about three years ago.

9. T: Well, it's a group of people that live together. So a **community** is a group of people who live together. Right? What's a **community**?

10. P: When people live together.

11. T: A group. (emphasized)

12. P: A group of people who live together.

13. T: That's right. It could be any group of people, not just Tristan but any group of people who live together—and we call that a **community**. (Edwards & Westgate, 1994, p. 107; emphasis and line numbers added)

The use of repetition in this excerpt clearly extends beyond its management function. It is used to ensure students' cognitive involvement in the instructional discourse on communities, in this case, that they understand that community involves the three fundamental concepts of people, group, and living together.

In a recent analysis and conceptualization of repetition in L1 classrooms, drawing particularly on sociocultural theory, O'Connor and Michaels (1996) examined teachers' "revoicings" of students' contributions, specifically those connected with theorizing about scientific phenomena (e.g., how scales balance depending on where weights are placed). Revoicing in their analysis involves the teacher's reformulation of part or all of a student's utterance to clarify content, to reinforce new terminology, and to amplify students' contributions by "rebroadcasting the students' utterance to reach a wider audience" (p. 74). Revoicing may or may not involve verbatim repetition, although it recasts what has been said in a new way, giving the student who made the original contribution credit, to some degree, for the reformulation. Revoicing may be used to create alignments and oppositions in arguments within particular participant frameworks. It is also an important means of incorporating reported speech and critical thinking into classroom discourse, as students' contributions are reported back to the class and students are asked to agree or disagree with the teacher's or each other's reformulation. Repetition and revoicing, they noted, are part of academic and linguistic socialization in the act of inferencing and the "explication of reasoning" (p. 75).

Most previous L2 and FL classroom research has examined repetition in codeable, structural discursive terms—as a recognizable feature of teacher talk, corrective feedback, confirmation moves, and so on (see Chaudron, 1988) and includes analyses of students' immediate uptake of teacher talk through repetition of correct forms supplied by the teacher. Alternatively, repetition has been analyzed in teachers' repetition of student forms, as part of the typical three-part initiation–response–evaluation (IRE) sequence, where evaluation (or feedback, as it is sometimes labeled) might simply be the teacher's repetition of a student's correct reply. More recent discourse analysis has tended to examine repetition of lexical or syntactic forms in task-based L2 exchanges as interactional or modification features between interlocutors who are either native speakers (NSs) or non-native speakers (NNSs) of the target language. Many examples of controlled experiments involving dyads of learners (and sometimes NSs) interacting on tasks have also examined types, roles, and results of repetition in the discourse surrounding the tasks. These often require participants to describe objects in a particular spatial configuration to others but tend to be rather limited in terms of the content, cognition, affect, affiliation, extended discourse, linguistic structures, and so on that they engender (e.g., Tomlin, 1994; see also Gass & Mackey, 1998).

Disclaimers are also made about the value of repetition in L2 discourse and instructional interaction. For example, Gass and Selinker (1994) provided examples of NNSs repeating lexical items produced by their NS partners in ways that would seem to be appropriate, but without having comprehended them. The researchers obtained retrospective comments from the participants about their state of knowledge of the terms and their comprehension at the time that confirmed this observation. Lyster (1998) cautioned that students' repetition of teachers' utterances (e.g., provided in response to incorrect utterances produced by students) in no way ensures that students will learn the forms they have repeated. Rather, as Allwright and Bailey (1991) observed, "simple repetition or modelling of the correct form may be useless if the learners cannot perceive the difference between the model and the erroneous forms they produce" (cited in Lyster, 1998, p. 54). Instead, they recommended self-correction by students. Similarly, a teacher's repetition of a student's correct utterance may be ambiguous and thus ineffectual. It may indicate the teacher's confirmation of the student's contribution or signal agreement or appreciation, without providing differentiated feedback between ill-formed versus well-formed utterances (i.e., corrective vs. noncorrective). However, in Lyster's study a teacher's corrective repetition (with questioning intonation) of an incorrect utterance tended to result in self-correction by the student more than half the time. Chaudron's (1977) account is consistent with this view, noting that teachers' repetitions with emphasis or reduction drawing attention to problems in students' ill-formed utterances provided potentially more effective intake for students than teachers' more implicit recasts or expanded, correct versions of student speech.

Valuable though these psycholinguistic analyses may be, there has been a lack of research on the role of repetition (or other aspects of linguistic interaction) in the construction of discourse (or Discourse, in Gee's [1996] use of the term) by communities of classroom FL learners. Also, there has been limited analysis of the role of repetition in the construction and negotiation of knowledge of the world (beyond syntactic forms), particularly when students are discussing substantive topics over a prolonged period of time.[2] As Tomlin (1994) asserted, repetition is a "social act with cognitive consequences" (p. 174; see also DiCamilla & Anton, 1997); yet the social aspect is frequently minimized in Tomlin's and other interactionists' research, both in analyses of acts and their consequences.

Among the few to examine the sociocultural properties of repetition in FL pedagogy (albeit in a lab-based study), DiCamilla and Anton (1997) claimed that "repetition is an important means by which students construct and hold in place scaffolded help while achieving and maintaining intersubjectivity, which are two critical elements of successful collaboration within the [Vygotskyan Zone of Proximal Development]" (p. 614). Their study involved the discourse of 10 adults studying Spanish as an FL in an intensive program for which they were asked to do collaborative writing assignments. The authors reported that approximately one third of all utterances produced in relation to the assignments involved repetition (in English or Spanish, where repetition was defined as a restatement of the content or form of a previous utterance) and that these repeated target forms helped scaffold the ultimately correct production of erstwhile problematic Spanish constructions (e.g., *almorzamos*, for 'we have lunch'). They also highlighted the graduated nature of the help or scaffolding among peers with unequal levels of L2 proficiency and discussed the joint authorship, voice, and hence ownership of texts produced for the task as a result of intersubjective repetition:

> Viewing verbal interaction within the zone of proximal development as scaffolding, we observe that the role of repetition is to distribute the scaffolded help throughout the activity, and thereby hold the scaffold in place, as it were, creating a cognitive space in which to work (e.g., think, hypothesize, evaluate), and from which to build (i.e., generate more language). (p. 628)

---

[2]To his credit, Lyster's ongoing research is longitudinal and situated in content-based French immersion classrooms, which is a departure from typical form-focused, classroom-oriented research.

In a similar vein, Knox (1994) and Bean and Patthey-Chavez (1994) highlighted the affective, poetic, affiliative, and constructivist roles of repetition in discourse involving NNSs. Knox (1994) illustrated how repetition signals shifts in topics and participant roles, explaining that "the formal redundancy of repetition does not imply a poverty of meaning, but instead exposes the rich pragmatic potential of the linguistic form . . . [which shifts] the work of constructing coherent and meaningful text from a codification process to an interpretive process" (p. 205). Repetitions and related moves such as redrafts and shared utterances are, in Bean and Patthey-Chavez's (1994) analysis, reflective of "the texture of joint cognition" (p. 211). Like Knox, they identified the cooperative potential or orientation of repetition, especially in repetitions of others (allo-repetition) by novices. In a bilingual reading lesson excerpt, they noted that the teacher used repetition to "elicit an array of responses, to acknowledge possible responses, and to reinforce timely information in both her own questions and the students' responses" (p. 218). The teacher's use of repetition-expansion, they pointed out, also modeled "a more thorough and complex way of displaying information" (p. 218). They also observed ways in which affective goals, in addition to cognitive ones, are served through repetition.

In FL content-based classrooms, as in L1 classrooms, the purposes of repetition may be multiple but also limited by the extent to which truly contingent discourse can take place. Repetition may be used to direct students' attention (and involvement), discipline students, help students practice difficult terminology, reinforce meanings, and so on. Repetition also has rhetorical uses and provides discursive cohesion and topical coherence (Halliday & Hasan, 1976; Levinson, 1983; Tannen, 1989), through the repetition of lexical items, phrases, or linked concepts. Beyond the textual functions, Day (1998) examined the "affiliative" function of repetition in her study of a kindergarten English as a second language (ESL) student's use of others' words during interactions with peers to "gain entry and establish affiliation with the girls and boys in his class, counter subordination, reposition himself, and gain power."

Not all repetitions are equal, however. Sometimes repetition is sanctioned, required, and successful; and other times, it is not. Therefore, part of learning to be part of a discourse community involves understanding how to (re)produce and interpret utterances appropriately. In a study of first-grade children in an ESL language arts class, for example, Toohey (1998) pointed out that in the discussion period following students' sharing-time contributions, "both the teacher (gently) and the children (often forcefully) made it known that repetitions were illegitimate contributions" (p. 76). One excerpt she provided shows how students were asked to guess numbers, but after "one million" had been uttered by one student, and "one thousand" by another, a third student who volunteered "one million" was told that that number had already been guessed and was therefore illegitimate. Toohey observed:

> At the beginning of the year, there were many instances when the bilingual students orally repeated like this, but there are no such instances in my field notes or in the videotaped data from after Christmas. It appeared that the children had learned effectively not to repeat in this way. (p. 76)

Copying or repeating was "an affiliative practice of flattery . . . as evidence of friendship" (p. 76) but one that was discouraged within the classroom.

In addition to the cognitive and social benefits of memorizing and reciting chunks of language and then learning to analyze the component parts and integrate them within one's own linguistic repertoire, there may be concomitant affective consequences, both negative, as in Toohey's (1998) study, and positive, as Cook (1994) claimed:

> Repetition and learning by heart, though condemned by pedagogic and acquisition theorists, are two of the most pleasurable, valuable, and efficient of language learning activities, and they can bring with them the sensations of those indefinable, overused yet still valuable goals for the language learner: being involved in the authentic and communicative use of language. (p. 133)

The data I present in this chapter are meant to add to what we know about the role of repetition in FL learning. In what follows, I present data from FL classroom research to answer the following question: What are the discursive, sociocultural, and affective roles, characteristics, and consequences of repetition in FL classroom interaction? The data were collected as part of larger studies in Europe and America. They are not meant to be representative of the entire corpus of data from which they were taken. Rather, they have been selected to illustrate principles regarding the theoretical and analytical treatment of repetition in FL classroom research.

SOCIOCULTURAL AND AFFECTIVE DIMENSIONS
OF FOREIGN LANGUAGE INTERACTION

High School Language Immersion Classes

In my research on English as a foreign language (EFL) content-based high school classes in Hungary (e.g., Duff, 1995, 1996), I found repetition used extensively for affiliative social purposes even in discussions about history, the subject matter of EFL immersion courses I observed and video-taped for several months in the early 1990s. The classes in question were not language classes and there was relatively little explicit focus of a met-alinguistic nature.[3] Yet, the cohesive, paradoxical, and even comedic uses of particular EFL forms seemed to have a reinforcing effect both psy-cholinguistically and socioculturally, indexing their multiple prior occur-rences in the same discourse context. Several excerpts from one class fol-low, where the topic was making generalizations about Russian autocracy versus Western absolutism. In the entire text from which these examples are taken, the word *general* was produced 10 times, *generalization* four times, and *exception* nine times. However, other terms that provided cohe-sive links across speakers and turns were also evident. In Excerpt 2, for example, with the use of *terror* (Turns 1 and 2), *mental(ly)* (Turns 8 and 11) and the comment *that happens* (Turns 10 and 11). The repetition of these terms provided connectivity or contingency throughout the text and across speakers, and also served to validate the concepts by showing that the teacher ratified earlier comments (to a certain extent).

Excerpt 2: EFL History Class (Kati = Teacher)[4]

1. Jan: The Russian autocracy provided **terror in general** while in Western abso-
          lutism (it has/there's) no **terror. Terror.**

---

[3]The classes were taught by Hungarian L1 teachers and taken by Hungarian L1 stu-dents, but the language of instruction was English, their FL. The students had studied EFL intensively for a year prior to resuming the standard Hungarian high school curriculum in English and the examples here are taken from the equivalent of Grade 10 and 11 classes. They continued to study EFL as a course for a few hours each week.

[4]The following are the transcription conventions used in this and all subsequent excerpts.

Participants	T = teacher; S = student; SS = two students; SSS or Ss = many students. Initial(s) or unique identifiers used for students identifiable by name (e.g., M, SZ, J; or S1, S2, S3) rather than S.

 2. Kati: No(t) [**terror**
 3. S: [Was it **general**? <u>Was it</u> **general**?
 4. Kati: [Aha.
 5. SS: No=
 6. Ss: =Yes=
 7. Kati: =J?
 8. Judy: I don't think it was. It was just the **mental** disease of the ruler.
 9. Kati: Aha. (.6) Of <u>one</u> ruler.
10. Jan: Yeah. But I was - **that happens**=
11. Kati: =But - yeah. I mean. **That happens**. But an absolutist ruler can be
            - **mentally** disor-
12.   ((. . . some turns later . . .))
13. Jan: No but that's so- nothing can be (x) by **general rule**

Left bracket ([)	The beginning of overlapping speech, shown for both speakers; second speaker's bracket occurs at the beginning of the line of the next turn, rather than in spatial alignment with previous speaker's bracket
Equal sign (=)	Latched utterance; speech that comes immediately after another person's with no intervening pause; shown at end of one speaker's utterance and beginning of another's.
(#)	Marks the length of a pause; (.2) is 2/10 of a second, (2.0) is 2 seconds
(Words)	The words in parentheses ( ) were not clearly heard; (x) = unclear word; (xx) = two unclear words; (xxx) = three or more unclear words.
Underlined words	Spoken with emphasis
CAPITAL LETTERS	Loud speech
Double parentheses	Comments, like ((laughs)); details pertaining to interaction
Colon (:)	Sound or syllable is unusually lengthened
Period (.)	Terminal falling intonation
Comma (,)	Rising, continuing intonation
Question mark (?)	High rising intonation, not necessarily at the end of a sentence
Unattached dash (-)	A short, untimed pause (e.g., less than half a second)
One-sided attached dash (word-)	A cutoff often accompanied by a glottal stop (e.g., a self-correction); a dash attached on both sides reflects spelling conventions
Boldface	Focal utterance or point of discussion for analytical purposes
Italics	English translation

14. Kati: You are right. You discovered a very great=

15. Val: =No **there was absolutism that's what general means**

16. Kati: But because- it is meant to=

17. Zoli: =Certain points but [we've discovered it

18. Kati: [to ease understanding

19. SSS: What? What?

20. Kati: **Generalization**

Thus, by repeating a sequence of terms, the students and teacher indicate not only that they are processing the utterances lexically or syntactically, but that they are also building on the content of the utterances to formulate principles regarding the nature of absolute government in general terms as opposed to specific instances of it.[5]

In Excerpt 3, the same teacher, Kati, gives an explanation that appears to be somewhat paradoxical, juxtaposing general and exceptional aspects of political movements, which elicits laughter. Concluding the same passage, Kati rebukes the students for not taking the point seriously enough, for making fun of the contradiction. Another student picks up on the word *fun* and remarks that "history is fun," which as a matter of fact was a fairly widespread view of that subject, and which also suggests a certain rapport between the students and teacher, perhaps even a hint of flattery of the teacher regarding the course. Here, then, students' use of repetition is seen to be a way of potentially undermining the seriousness with which Kati expects them to approach the concepts and the discussion of the points in class. However, it is their play with the language by means of repetition and their enjoyment of the perceived contradictions that helps affiliate them more with the subject and with others in their community of learning.

Excerpt 3: EFL History Class

1. Kati: So first you have to- have to **generalize** to understand the **exceptions**

2.   ((laughter))

3. S: **Exceptions**

4. Zoli: **Generalize**

5. SS: **Generalize**

---

[5]Lapkin and Swain (1996) similarly highlighted one exemplary Grade 8 French-immersion science teacher's practices of "repetition, the use of multiple synonyms in their characteristic syntactic frames, revisiting words in a variety of contexts and in different parts of the lesson" (p. 248).

6. SSS: ((laughing and discussing the problem))
7. Kati: Well, you are making **fun** of (x)
8. S: History is **fun**

Group membership and affiliation were thus inculcated and indexed by means of active participation in this FL discourse through the use of repetition of others' utterances, and through humor and repartee. Continuing with this theme, in Excerpt 4, Val recounts her understandings about general principles of absolutism. Approvingly, in Line 8 Kati acknowledges that Val has produced a very general statement. Kati's use of this expression then prompts what appears to be a common refrain: "X (Spain, England) is an exception . . . *to the general rule*" (Turns 12, 19–20, 26), which induces laughter. Yet this repetition does not succeed in subverting the discussion underway—if indeed that was intended (i.e., in addition to playing with the language and revealing the teacher's penchant for emphasizing the point about generalizations)—and the talk resumes quite seriously afterward.

Excerpt 4: EFL History Class

  1. Val: So ah in Western absolutism So France and England ah they had a very well developed economy it was needed for absolutism
  2. Kati: Yeah
  3. Val: While in Russia hm it was underdeveloped
  4. Kati: Aha
  5. Val: And it didn't really x so it didn't make any progress.
  6. Kati: Is it clear?
  7. S: ((whispering)) Yes.
  8. Kati: Yes? **This- this this I mean this was very general statement.**
  9. Val: Yes.
  10. Zoli: Should we discuss it?
  11. Kati: **Very general**. No. As soon as
  12. Val: Spain is- [Spain is **an exception**
  13. Kati: [We understand what Val meant by well-developed and underdeveloped then it's okay.
  14.   ((many turns later . . .))
  15. Kati: Yeah. Around the turn of the 16th 17th century. When - did the first absolutist ruler appeared in England?
  16. Val: The same
  17. Kati: Earlier. [Okay so
  18. S: [((laughing, surprised)) So=
  19. Val: =**England is the exception**

20. Judy: **To the general rule**
21. SSS: ((laughter))
22. So: Ah what about Spain
23. Val: Spain=
24. Kati: =And what about France
25. SSS: ((laughter))
26. Zoli: **It's an exception**

In one last excerpt concerning this theme of links between discoveries, absolutism, precapitalism, and reformation, Excerpt 5, the notion of general rules and exceptions again surfaces. Questioning students about the general effects of war initially (e.g., eliciting "dissatisfaction" from one student in Turn 4), Kati then makes use of a student's contribution about weaknesses (Turn 7). In the manner described by O'Connor and Michaels (1996), Kati revoices and expands on the notion of weakness, making a coherent academic generalization about one aspect of war. This follow-up by Kati indirectly gives some credit to Al for having volunteered the lexical item, and also models for the students a legitimate, general assertion.

Excerpt 5: EFL History Class

1. Kati: What was the **general effect** of the wars?
           (1.8)
2. Al: The (2.5) country (was) economically - exhausted.=
3. Kati: =Aha. Yeah. That's a very good effect of the war but - if we want to be <u>very</u>
           generally we <u>might</u> say that the <u>wars</u> (1.4) wha- how can we put it? To be <u>very</u>
           <u>very</u> **general**.
           (3.0)
4. K: **Wars meant dissatisfaction**
5. SSS: ((laugh))
6. Kati: Aha=
7. Al: =Showed the **weakness** of the (country)=
8. Kati: =Aha. So war:rs brought to the <u>surface</u> a:ll the **weaknesses** - of the system -
           economic, social, political.

Discourse has its own sociohistorical context, one that is perhaps even more complex and textured when the discussion itself is about historical and geographical contexts and is being discussed in an FL. I illustrate the historical aspect of discourse and repetition in Excerpts 6 and 7 by showing how chunks of discourse are repeated across excerpts for largely symbolic, affective reasons. In Excerpt 6, the teacher answers a student's question, "What is in Siberia?" with the literal but ironic utterance "Cold and - and prisoners," a response that, although perhaps true, is unrelated to the topic of natural and other material resources in Russia under discussion. Another student adds *snow* to the list. The group is, therefore, engaging in playful banter about less desirable associations with Siberia.

Excerpt 6: EFL History Class

1. S5:   What was in Siberia?
2. Kati: **Cold**=
3. S8:   =**Cold** ((laughs))
4. Kati: **Cold and - and prisoners** ((laughing)) **Cold** and [uh **prisoners**
5. S5:   [**Snow**

When the class discussion following Excerpt 6 moves away from a teacher-led format to student group-based discussion and reporting later that lesson, the phrases *cold, prisoners, snow,* and other associations with Siberia mentioned previously are reinvoked and accompanied by laughter, as we see Excerpt 7.

Excerpt 7: EFL History Class

1. S2:   [The secret police in Russia] censored all the book and newspapers and uh - arrested political groups and people who criticized the government, and this people, were usually **sent to Siberia ha ha**
2. S1:   Where it was **cold**.
3. S2:   Yeah and there was [**snow**
4. S3:   [There was **no government**=
5. S2:   =**And prisoners** ((laughing))

This repetition and laughter are emblems of students' collective memory or "common lore" (Freeman, 1992, p. 76) linked to their previous jointly produced oral texts that had also elicited laughter from Kati and her students in the first instance. And, despite the seriousness of the topic under discussion—natural resources, political persecution, and industrialization, topics that Central Eastern Europeans knew about very well—the hardships of Siberia trigger humor, not horror. However, the humor is derived not so much from the content as from the act of repeating something associated with an unexpected element in the previous discourse context, thus indexing that occurrence once again.

Sometimes a student's phrasing of an utterance is repeated or marked in some way by the rest of the class, either because it is too general (e.g., "wars indicate dissatisfaction," in Excerpt 5) or because it is perceived to be somewhat flippant or humorous. Thus the repetition of such a phrase signals a number of things: that others have taken note of it (for whatever reason) and that it is subject to further comment. In Excerpt 8, during group work involving about six students, one student (S9) lightheartedly repeats his classmate's expression "everything like," which he has used to terminate a list of the consequences of hardships on peasants in prerevolutionary Russian. An expression such as "everything like" is a set-marking tag, which "[tells] an interlocutor to interpret the tag's antecedent as an example of some other more general set/class of items" (Ediger, 1996). Perhaps the repetition here is meant to draw attention to the set-marking tag itself—a banal but colloquial expression for a class of nominals representing severe deprivation—and it also calls into question the more general set or class of items to which *famine* and *starvation* might belong.

Excerpt 8: EFL History Class

> S1: this had to be concluded in 49 years. So you had 49 years to pay t- that 100 forints. Uh but uh these given lands were usually not big enough, and (4.8) therefore the- the peasants were - in a quite bad situation. So uh famine and starving and **everything like that**.
>
> S9: ((laughing)) **Everything like**

Excerpt 9, from a different lesson, shows how the repetition of a student's phrase, "cos they were enlightened," in reference to people who were politically active prior to the French Revolution, elicits a number of subsequent exchanges by the teacher and by other students. Some of these turns signal that *enlightenment* is neither a sufficiently serious nor analytical reason or explanation for the phenomenon in question. Then, when the teacher does pursue a more in-depth explanation regarding people's enlightenment, students begin to play with the term and its lexical associations with light, fire, burning, matches, electricity, and so on. Hence, the repetition of the utterance in the teacher's question prompts a series of playful moves by these students in English, their FL, about the lexical semantics of the construction that has been volunteered. This excerpt illustrates how language play in this context is valued and appreciated by students (and also by the teacher as in Excerpt 6) because it demonstrates the students' metalinguistic facility with and enjoyment of using their L2.

Excerpt 9: EFL History Class

1. Kati: That's a good - question. What were these meetings for - and why did peo-ple bother - going to clubs or meetings of the sections. Why didn't they stay at home - [and why didn't they lead a happy family life and so on

2. S: [Cos they were interested in politics

3. Pete: **Cos they were enlightened?**

4. Kati: **Because they were enlightened?**

5. SSS: ((**laughter**))

6. Uh they were interested in politics

7. Zoli: (xx) <u>had been</u> **enlightened.**

8. (1.7)

9. Val: (x) all **burning**

11. SSS: ((**laughter**))

12. Kati: That's an interesting idea and **what made them so enlightened**

15. Val: Well maybe a **match**

16. Z: **Inven[tion of electricity**

17. Kati: [Yes - I mean do you think they - I mean the (x) shopkeepers were - sitting behind the counter reading Rous- Rousseau and Voltaire

18. SSS: ((**laughter**))

To summarize, the preceding excerpts highlight several types and roles of repetition in "collectively scaffolded" FL discourse (Donato, 1994) at an advanced proficiency level, in this case in the negotiation of historical understandings. The observed uses of repetition involved language play (and perhaps rehearsal to a lesser extent), references to previous occur-rences of phrases or concepts for socioaffective reasons, and selective attention to part of a previous speaker's utterance for both instructional and affiliative purposes. Thus, knowledge of the social and discourse con-texts in which the repetition occurred, and analysis of it within and across excerpts as opposed to within adjacent pairs of utterances alone, provides a means of understanding potentially cohesive, communal, and construc-tive functions of repetition in FL use within content classrooms.

Repetition in University FL Classrooms

In this section, I present a different analysis of repetition, this time using data from classroom research in FL classrooms at a U.S. university. The excerpts come from second-term courses in first-year university courses in German and Hebrew, respectively, that were audiotaped as part of a larger study of FL use across a range of language courses (see Duff & Polio, 1990; Polio & Duff, 1994). Unlike the FL immersion activities and discourse in the previous section, interaction in the university FL classes is necessarily more basic and also more form-focused because the courses are language courses with no overriding thematic content other than mastery of grammar and language skills. Repetition is pervasive but, unlike the preceding examples, is not used as much for play and joint affiliation. Rather, some language play and other discussion occur as a consequence of extended repetition; that is, to offset the tedium and difficulty of concentrating on repeated syntactic or lexical forms for a prolonged period of time. Whereas the previous examples highlighted the community-building aspects of repetition, the following examples illustrate some contingency and affect accompanying repetition; however, the class's seemingly ambivalent or negative response to repetition in form-focused interactions is perhaps even more remarkable.

In the first example (Excerpt 10) in a German FL class, after the teacher asks Janet about what she does in the morning and she describes some activities in sequence, the teacher checks to see if Janet's classmate Gord has been listening or paying attention (much like the example of community seen in Excerpt 1). Apparently, he has not (Turns 5–6). It seems unlikely that Gord does not comprehend the verb (*ziehe mich an* '[I] get dressed'), because no translation or other means of explaining the activity is indicated. This lack of attention to Janet's narrative on Gord's part then gives rise to an extended sequence in which the teacher gets Janet to repeat what she has said and in which the teacher confirms that the form is correct (*ich ziehe mich an*; Turns 8–10).

Excerpt 10: German FL Class

1. T: Was macht ihr alles am Morgen? Janet, was machst du Morgens?
   What all do you do in the mornings? Janet, what do you do in the morning?

2. J: ((describes when she gets up and showers, over several turns))

3. T: Was machst du dann, Janet?
   What do you do next, Janet?

4. J: Um, ich ich **ziehe - mich an.**
   I get dressed.

5. T: Mhm. Gord. Was machst sie dann?
   Mhm. Gord. What does she do then?

6. G: Um, ich weiss nicht.
   Um I don't know.

7. T: Was- was machst du dann, Janet?
What do you do then, Janet?

8. J: Ich **ziehe- ich ziehe mich an.**
I get dressed.

9. T: Mhm. **Ziehe mich an.**
Get dressed.

10. J: Ich **ziehe mich an.**
I get dressed

In Excerpt 11, the teacher then asks another student (S1) about the activity Janet referred to (i.e., getting dressed). However, S1 does not get the third-person conjugation correct, substituting *zeht* for *zieht* in Turn 2 in the following, then omits the correct reflexive pronoun for third-person singular (*sich*) and the second part of the two-part verb, *an* (Turns 4, 10–14).

Excerpt 11: German FL Class

1. T: Mhm. Was machst sie?
What does she do?

2. S1:   Uh, sie **zeht**?
She dresses ((mispronounces third-person form))

3. T: **Zieht.**
Dresses.

4. S1:   **Zieht dich an.**
Dresses yourself.

5. T: Mhm. **Zieht.**
Dresses.

6. S1:   **Zieht.**
Dresses.

7. T: **Zieht sich an.**
Dresses herself

8. S1:   **Zieht sich an.**
Dresses herself.

9. T: Sie **zieht sich an.** Wann **ziehst du dich an**, morgens? Wann **ziehst du dich an**?
She gets dressed. When do you get dressed in the morning? When do you get dressed?

10. S1:   Um, ich **ziehe**, ich **ziehe**?
          I dress, I dress

11. T: Mhm.

12. S1:   mich uh um sieben Uhr.
          Myself at seven o'clock.

13. T: An
          On ((second part of verb))

14. S1:   *An*

15. T: Wann **ziehst du dir** die Schuhe **an**? Wann **ziehst du dir** die Schuhe **an**?
          When do you put your shoes on? When do you put your shoes on?

16. S1:   Uhm, ich **ziehe mir die Schuhe** um sechs Uhr **an**.
          I put my shoes on at six o'clock.

17. T: Uhhuh. Um sechs Uhr.
          Uhhum. At six o'clock.

The effect of this extended sequence of repetition is apparent in Excerpt 12. Following the series of repeated utterances in Excerpt 11, designed to elicit grammatically correct forms (even to the point of sounding a bit silly, e.g., "What time do you put your shoes on?"), students seek a meaningful outlet in which to contextualize the discourse not only for the sake of clarity but also in recognition of the social context in which they are speaking. In this case, S1, who has focused on why he must get up and get dressed (put on his clothes, shoes) so early, adds in English that he actually has to get up at five o'clock. Another student, S2, then asks why he must get up so early (Turn 5) and S1 replies in English and then German that it is because he commutes and otherwise cannot get parking (Turns 6–11). That is, despite the numerous repetitions surrounding the production of the correct form for getting dressed, that act itself is not currently central to S1's intended message or S2's question, which is that S1 must get up and leave for school very early in the morning because of limited access to parking.

Excerpt 12: German FL Class

1. S1:   I get up at five, it's true.

2. T: es ist sehr fruh. Warum **ziehst du dir die Schuhe** um um sieben um sechs Uhr
          an?
          It's very early. Why do you put your shoes on at seven- at six o'clock?

3. S1:   Um.. ich - stehe - um - funf Uhr auf.
          I get up at five o'clock.

4. T: Mhm.

5. S2:   Warum? Warum stehst du - um funf Uhr auf?
         Why? Why do you get up at five o'clock?

6. S1:   Cause I commute.

7. T: In Deutsch?
         In German?

8. S1:   Um, ich muss zur Schule fahren.
         I have to drive to school.

9. T: Mhm.

10. S2:   Um sechs?
          At six?

11. S1:   If you didn't have parking, you'd know.

Without detracting from the potential value of form-focused intervention by the teacher, extended repetition sequences also appear to have their limits, at least in this interaction. S1 switches to English to emphasize that the meaning he is trying to convey is true and then, when prompted, attempts to give an explanation for that fact (in both English and German). In other words, it may be because of the repetition of forms and the students' attendant concentration on the forms that additional social and linguistic interaction takes place between students to provide both justification and a deeper level of communication than the repeated FL forms alone allow.

Next I present an unrelated series of interactions and excerpts that nonetheless shares the potential for having students use repetition as a launch for socioaffective communication and cohesion. It comes from a Hebrew FL class, where laughter and group cohesiveness coincide with students' attempts to derail a classmate's protracted explanation about hospitalization, constituting a kind of counterdiscourse to the instructional discourse underway. Two students (M and K) are presenting a role-play dialogue in Hebrew about forest fires in a nearby valley. K has been asked to tell M about a fire that started burning earlier that week; M responds to the dialogue that K initiates. It is unclear to what degree this has been preplanned, although from the number of questions involved throughout, it appears to be relatively spontaneous. To contextualize Excerpt 13, considerable negotiation has already taken place during the lesson regarding the Hebrew word for *hospital*, which proved very problematic. For example, K asked M something like: "I you lives hom- the hou- the hospital?" [*b'beit uh: xolim*]. M replied that she "Never hou- in a houspitol [sic] [*b'bayit xolim*]"; the teacher intervened and after five turns M repaired her utterance saying she "was never in a houspital" [sic] [*b'bayt xolim*]. K asked M if she lived near the mountains, but when the teacher asked the class what *harim* 'mountains' means, a student replied in English, "hospital." The teacher then provided the Hebrew word for mountains. Having established that M lives near the mountains, K tells her that there are many fires in the mountains. Several dozen turns later, K asks M whether she has seen the fire(s). She replies that although she has not seen the fires, she has friends who live close to the mountains who saw them. K then asks whether their houses were affected. M replies that several of their houses had actually caught fire.

Excerpt 13 begins at this point, from what would have been Turn 139 in the original sequence of this speech event, as M tries to explain that one of her friends who tried to put out a house fire was burned and needed to be hospitalized as a result. K later asks if the other friends are now living at M's house or whether they are still in the hospital. As in Excerpt 10, taken from the German class, there is an extended series of interactions involving the elicitation and repetition of a correct form, here for the word *hospital* (*beit xolim*) or phrase "in the hospital" (*b'veit xolim*) in Turns 3 through 12, 14 through 16, 20 through 25, and 33 and 34.[6]

Excerpt 13: Hebrew FL Class

  1. M: Um V' – v' um, v'ha Xaver exad um ho- halax halax lo=
             And and and the and the One friend who- went went tu=

  2. T: =[xx] Mhm!

  3. M: Xa- **batei batim xole**
             Frie- houses of houses sick

  4. T: ((snaps fingers)) Eix omrim?
             How do we say it?

---

[6]Considerable negotiation takes place prior to this excerpt, dealing primarily with Hebrew vocabulary items, equivalent to *burn, fire, the fire burned, live/d, hospital, far (away), mountains, isn't that right?, fire in the mountains, friends, their houses, caught on fire, extinguish, put out,* and other related terms. It would be fairly easy to conclude that the task greatly exceeds students' linguistic competence and it is therefore questionable how much intake and integration of these new forms will occur, regardless of the amount of repetition. In fact, the short dialogue involves a total of more than 220 turns, 138 of which occur prior to Excerpt 13, and then nearly 100 additional turns, as indicated in the excerpt (with some turns intentionally deleted). Those turns are distributed among M, K, the teacher (T), and an assortment of other students.

5. M: Aval **beit xole.**
       But house of a sick person

6. T: **Be:::it?**
       House of?

7. M: **Haxole**
       The sick person

8. T: **Be::it?** Eix omrim. **Beit xole?**
       House of? How do we say it? House of a sick person?

9. SSS: **Xolim.**
       Sick people

10. T: **Beit xolim**
       Hospital; lit: 'house of the sick'

11. M: Oh. **Beit xolim.**
       Hospital

12. T: **Beit xolim.** ((pause)) Okay? Finish
       Hospital

13.   ((7 turns later))

14. K: Aval heim tamid **b'- b'beit xole.**
       But are they always in- in the sick house?

15. T: **Beit xolim.**
       Hospital

16. K: **B' - beit xolim.**
       Hospital

17.   ((pause))

18. T: Od pa'am
       Once again

19.   ((10 turns later))

20. K: O heim:: - tamid **b':: b'veit?**
       Or are they always in- in the hosp-

21. T: **B'veit=** ((repeating correct phonology 'v' after preposition affix 'b'))
       In the hosp-

22. K: **=B'veit xolim?**
       In the hospital?

23. T: Ma ze 'o'? O:::?
       what does 'or' mean? Or:::?

24. SSS: Or.

25. T: Or! Kein, Heim babayit shelax o **b'veit xolim**, haxaverim.
           Yes (go on), are they at your house or in the hospital, your friends?

26. M: Uh:m ((short laugh))

27. T: At m'vina::? Ah- Ma hash?eyla? Ma hash?eyla?
           Do you understand? Uh- what's the question? What's the question?

28.   ((15 turns later, after some work on the plural form of "friends"))

29. T: Babayit shelax? B'beiteix?
           In your house?

30. S: Uh:: - in your house,

31. T: O::
           Or::

32. S: Or

33. T: **B'beit xolim.**
           In the hospital

34. S: Or **in the hospital**.

Exasperated, in Turn 37, a student (S1) recommends that M simply say the "people died" (i.e., are no longer in hospital). This draws laughter from the class, unifying them in their desire not to have to repeat the target item for *hospital* anymore. Another student (S2), drawing on relevant cultural scripts and schemata, jokes in Turn 40 that they should call the rabbi (because the victims are dying or have died), which again elicits laughter.

35. M: Oh::: ((laughs)). U::m.

36.   ((3 turns later))

37. S1:   **Say they died.**

38. SSS: ((big laugh))

39. T: Kein,
           Yes

40. S2:   **Just call for the rabbi.**

41. SSS: ((laugh))

42. T: Get to the point.

43. M: U:m.

44. T: Kein?
         Yes?

45. M: Kol haxaverim u:m - **meitu**.
         All the friends uh died.

46. T: **Meitu::::**
         Died::::

47. SSS: ((laugh))=

48. M: =((laughs))

The teacher herself goes along with this conclusion and in Turn 46 corrects the student's use of the term for died (*meitu*); she then notes that this conclusion will provide closure to the dialogue (in Turn 49). Another student jokes that this then solves the housing problem for K as well, and the English word *problem* is repeated several times (Turns 50, 54, 57). The excerpt ends with the teacher providing the Hebrew word for *problem* and then, in English, asking whether there are any problems with grammar. She thus reverts to a discussion of grammar. The deliberate repetition of problem as a linguistic pivot back into a focus on form has apparent discursive relevance to the students, at least one of whom laughs in Turn 59.

49. T: **Okay, Ze natan lanu 'closure'**=
         Okay that gave us closure

50. S: =That way there's no **housing problem**.

51. T: Ma ma?
         What What?

52. M: ((laughs))

53. T: What?

54. K: I don't know how to say it in Hebrew, but Kax [*that way*] there's no **housing problem**.

55. T: There's no house what?

56. S2:   Sh! ((to other students))

57. S: **Housing problem**.

58. T: Oh::: Ein ba'aya- Oh **Ba'aya** [*problem*] we don't know. Shel batim.
         Okay. Okay! Uh:: Any **problem** with the grammar?

59. S: **((laughs))**

To summarize, the German and Hebrew examples illustrate not only how pervasive repetition is in fairly low-level FL classrooms, but also its effect on classroom interaction, particularly as the groups grow increasingly weary with the focus on forms. To compensate, students engage in side sequences that allow them to find a meaningful way out of the series of repetitions. In the German example, a student asked the speaker why he got up so early, to which he replied it was necessary for the sake of parking. In the Hebrew example, after having excessive difficulty with the production of phrases related to hospitals, two students offer an alternative: Simply say the people have died and call the rabbi instead. It is by means of this act of assistance and comic relief that students and even the teacher seize the opportunity to terminate the extended dialogue and return to the grammatical points that must be covered in the lesson. Thus the repetition unites the students in their experience of difficulty and apparent frustration with the terms that have been introduced (both planned and unplanned by the teacher). They also seem united in their desire to finally abandon the topic and move onto something perhaps less taxing. Whereas a psycholinguistic assessment of the interaction might suggest that there had been a considerable amount of negotiation of input and interaction together with the repetition, the analysis presented here also shows how the class rallied together to overcome the burdens posed by that level of interaction.

DISCUSSION

In this chapter, I have provided examples of some of the ways in which repetition in FL classes goes beyond the psycholinguistic needs of language learners, signaling some of the following features: students' shared lack of competence in an FL and their unwillingness to proceed with further repetitions of forms for their own sake (e.g., in the German and Hebrew examples), or conversely, their competence in it (e.g., EFL in Hungary); and their desire to circumvent a lesson's extended focus-on-form activities by providing a meaningful context for the utterances (again, in the German and Hebrew examples) and communicative closure. Repetition is also used by teachers to provide cohesion and uptake of student utterances (e.g., EFL and Hebrew lessons), and by students to index prior interactions that were somehow significant (e.g., ironic, humorous), again to provide social, intellectual, and discursive cohesion in FL classroom interaction. Repetition can be sanctioned or required (as in the university FL classes), prohibited (as in content-based primary school interactions when only novel contributions are sought), or tolerated (to varying degrees) because the students enjoy the superficial language play and are strong students who also appreciate deeper academic concepts.

The observed academic uses of repetition were to draw students' attention to key concepts or linguistic forms (as in the L1 and EFL examples), especially if they have not been listening; to "revoice" a student's contribution, to correct it, or to affirm its validity (as in the German, Hebrew, and EFL classes); and to provide a cohesive thread that runs through a lesson (as in the EFL discussion of generalizations and the dangers of Siberia). For learners, the academic and cognitive benefits of repetition are to hear multiple occurrences of a potentially problematic term, to practice articulating the term, and to join together with other classmates in the common pursuit of new knowledge, even to the point of diverting attention from the intended formal focus of the lesson.

CONCLUSION

This analysis has shown that studies of repetition in FL classroom contexts have up until now tended to focus on their role in the three-part IRE sequences, where R may constitute a form that the teacher repeats in E, verbatim, with emphasis, correction, or expansion. I have attempted to show in a preliminary way some of the sociocultural and other functions of repetition in the construction of discourse communities; in the management of students by focusing their sometimes wandering attention; and in the service of humorous side sequences that humanize and energize the discussions, providing a much-needed affective dimension to classroom learning. However, for students who spend many hours a day in classrooms and whose attention span is heavily taxed, hairsplitting attention to detail (either linguistic or conceptual) and excessive repetition may have other interactional and sociocognitive consequences, at odds with the instructional goals of the teacher. As several scholars have noted, it is time to reexamine repetition in classrooms, not as a feature of behaviorist pedagogical methods, and not only as a means of providing sufficient psycholinguistic opportunities to individual students to acquire competence in the target language, which in itself is a worthy enough goal. Rather, future analyses should pay greater attention to repetition as an element of discourse that potentially unifies students (and teachers) in their common pursuit of learning within particular communities of language users and learners, that scaffolds their learning by means of their interactions with other learners and with the teacher, and that socializes them into other academic and nonacademic uses of language, such as for humorous, affiliative, or rhetorical purposes.

REFERENCES

Allwright, R., & Bailey, K. (1991). *Focus on the language classroom.* New York: Cambridge University Press.

Andersen, R. (1990). Models, processes, principles and strategies: Second language acquisition inside and outside of the classroom. In B. VanPatten & J. Lee (Eds.), *Second language learning—Foreign language learning* (pp. 45–68). Clevedon, UK: Multilingual Matters.

Bean, M., & Patthey-Chavez, G. (1994). Repetition in instructional discourse: A means for joint cognition. In B. Johnstone (Ed.), *Repetition in discourse: Interdisciplinary perspectives* (Vol. 1, pp. 207–220). Norwood, NJ: Ablex.

Bennett-Kastor, T. (1994). Repetition in language development: From interaction to cohesion. In B. Johnstone (Ed.), *Repetition in discourse: Interdisciplinary perspectives* (Vol. 1, pp. 155–171). Norwood, NJ: Ablex.

Bley-Vroman, R., & Chaudron, C. (1994). Elicited imitation as a measure of second-language competence. In E. Tarone, S. Gass, & A. Cohen (Eds.), *Research methodology in second-language acquisition* (pp. 245–261). Hillsdale, NJ: Lawrence Erlbaum Associates.

Brown, H. D. (1994). *Teaching by principles.* Englewood, Cliffs, NJ: Prentice-Hall.

Chamot, A. (1987). The learning strategies of ESL students. In A. Wenden & J. Rubin (Eds.), *Learner strategies in language learning* (pp. 71–83). Englewood Cliffs, NJ: Prentice-Hall.

Chaudron, C. (1977). A descriptive model of discourse in the corrective treatment of learners' errors. *Language Learning, 27,* 29–46.

Chaudron, C. (1988). *Second language classrooms: Research on teaching and learning.* Cambridge, UK: Cambridge University Press.

Cook, G. (1994). Repetition and learning by heart: An aspect of intimate discourse, and its implications. *ELT Journal, 48,* 133–141.

Day, E. M. (1998, March). *Ethnographic study of kindergarten ESL learners: The roles of repetition and language play.* Paper presented at the meeting of the American Association for Applied Linguistics, Seattle, WA.

DeKeyser, R. (1998). Beyond focus on form: Cognitive perspectives on learning and practicing second language grammar. In C. Doughty & J. Williams (Eds.), *Focus on form in classroom second language acquisition* (pp. 42–63). New York: Cambridge University Press.

DiCamilla, F., & Anton, M. (1997). Repetition in the collaborative discourse of L2 learners: A Vygotskian perspective. *Canadian Modern Language Review, 53,* 609–633.

Donato, R. (1994). Collective scaffolding in second language learning. In J. Lantolf & G. Appel (Eds.), *Vygotskian approaches to second language research* (pp. 33–56). Norwood, NJ: Ablex.

Duff, P. (1995). An ethnography of communication in immersion classrooms in Hungary. *TESOL Quarterly, 29,* 505–537.

Duff, P. (1996). Different languages, different practices: Socialization of discourse competence in duallanguage school classrooms in Hungary. In K. Bailey & D. Nunan

(Eds.), *Voices from the language classroom: Qualitative research in second language education* (pp. 407–433). New York: Cambridge University Press.

Duff, P., & Polio, C. (1990). How much foreign language is there in the foreign language classroom? *The Modern Language Journal, 74*(2), 154–166.

Ediger, A. (1996, March). *Set-marking tags in English: A discourse marker.* Paper presented at the annual meeting of the American Association for Applied Linguistics, Seattle, WA.

Edwards, A. D., & Westgate, D. P. G. (1994). *Investigating classroom talk* (2nd ed.). London: Falmer.

Freeman, D. (1992). Collaboration: Constructing shared understandings in a second language classroom. In D. Nunan (Ed.), *Collaborative language learning and teaching* (pp. 56–80). New York: Cambridge University Press.

Gass, S. M., & Mackey, A. (Eds.). (1998). The role of input and interaction in second language acquisition [Special issue]. *Modern Language Journal, 82*, 3.

Gass, S., & Selinker, L. (1994). *Second language acquisition.* Hillsdale, NJ: Lawrence Erlbaum Associates.

Gasser, M. (1990). Connectionism and universals of second language acquisition. *Studies in Second Language Acquisition, 12*, 179–199.

Gee, J. (1996). *Social linguistics and literacies: Ideology in discourses* (2nd ed.). Bristol, PA: Falmer.

Greenfield, P., & Savage-Rumbaugh, E. S. (1993). Comparing communicative competence in child and chimp: The pragmatics of repetition. *Journal of Child Language, 20*, 1–26.

Hadley, A. O. (1993). *Teaching language in context* (2nd ed.). Boston: Heinle & Heinle.

Halliday, M., & Hasan, R. (1976). *Cohesion in English.* New York: Longman.

Johnstone, B. (Ed.). (1994). *Repetition in discourse* (Vols. 1 & 2). Norwood, NJ: Ablex.

Knox, L. (1994). Repetition and relevance: Self-repetition as a strategy for initiating cooperation in nonnative/native speaker conversations. In B. Johnstone (Ed.), *Repetition in discourse: Interdisciplinary perspectives* (Vol. 1, pp. 195–206). Norwood, NJ: Ablex.

Lapkin, S., & Swain, M. (1996). Vocabulary teaching in a grade 8 French immersion classroom: A descriptive case study. *Canadian Modern Language Review, 53*, 242–256.

Levinson, S. (1983). *Pragmatics.* New York: Cambridge University Press.

Lyster, R. (1998). Recasts, repetition, and ambiguity in L2 classroom discourse. *Studies in Second Language Acquisition, 20*, 51–81.

McGroarty, M. (1998). Constructive and constructivist challenges for applied linguistics. *Language Learning, 48*, 591–622.

McLaughlin, B. (1987). *Theories of second language acquisition.* London: Arnold.

O'Connor, M. C., & Michaels, S. (1996). Shifting participant frameworks: Orchestrating thinking practices in group discussion. In D. Hicks (Ed.), *Discourse, learning, and schooling* (pp. 63–103). New York: Cambridge University Press.

Polio, C., & Duff, P. (1994). Teachers' language use in university foreign language classrooms: A qualitative analysis of English and target language alternation. *Modern Language Journal, 78*(3), 313–326.

Schieffelin, B., & Ochs, E. (1986). Language socialization. *Annual Review of Anthropology, 15*, 163–191.

Schmidt, R., & Frota, S. (1986). Developing basic conversational ability in a second language: A case-study of an adult learner. In R. Day (Ed.), *Talking to learn* (pp. 237–326). Rowley, MA: Newbury House.

Skehan, P. (1998). *A cognitive approach to language learning*. Oxford, UK: Oxford University Press.

Slobin, D. (Ed.). (1985). *The crosslinguistic study of language acquisition*. Hillsdale, NJ: Lawrence Erlbaum Associates.

Swain, M. (1985). Communicative competence: Some roles of comprehensible input and comprehensible output in its development. In S. Gass & C. Madden (Eds.), *Input in second language acquisition* (pp. 235–253). Rowley, MA: Newbury House.

Tannen, D. (1989). *Talking voices: Repetition, dialogue and imagery in conversational discourse*. Cambridge, UK: Cambridge University Press.

Tomlin, R. (1994). Repetition in second language acquisition. In B. Johnstone (Ed.), *Repetition in discourse: Interdisciplinary perspectives* (Vol. 1, pp. 172–194). Norwood, NJ: Ablex.

Toohey, K. (1998). "Breaking them up, taking them away": ESL students in grade 1. *TESOL Quarterly, 32*, 61–84.

7

Social Interaction and Language Development in a FLES Classroom

Etsuko Takahashi
Theresa Austin
Yoko Morimoto

Recently, in addition to the programs in middle schools and high schools, there is an increasing interest in starting the study of foreign languages in the early grades. Consequently, there are more Foreign language in elementary schools (FLES) programs throughout the United States.[1] The interest in implementing early foreign language education programs reflects the general tendency in the United States to recognize the importance and necessity of studying foreign languages. Indeed, more states in the nation are setting up new foreign language requirements. According to Rosenbusch (1995), this trend is influenced in part by research indicating the benefits of early study of a second language in terms of cognitive development, academic achievement, and positive attitudes toward diversity. Yet one cannot overlook the political context of educational reform in the United States and the impetus for educational practices to equip us for the approaching challenges of a new century. Education 2000, a U.S. policy initiative, incorporated foreign languages along with traditional subjects such as math, science, and social studies into the core

---

[1]According to demographic information provided by the Center for Applied Linguistics (Branaman & Rhodes, 1998, cited by Schulz, 1998), the number of FLES programs increased nearly 10% in the last decade, and the number of students in FLES programs has risen to as many as 4 million out of a total of 27.1 million students.

curriculum. In addition, national standards for foreign languages have been established.[2] Currently performance standards—how well students should demonstrate their proficiency—are being developed in several states. As the interest in foreign language learning in the early grades continues to rise, so does the need to develop practitioners' understanding of effective pedagogical approaches for promoting foreign language learning among children.

In the past two decades, the teaching focus has shifted away from a traditional approach emphasizing particular language skills such as grammatical structures, vocabulary, and pronunciation (Schulz, 1998). Instead, the current trend has become more holistic, aiming at an overall communicative proficiency and learning content through language, defined as the ability to communicate in the target language about the real-world topics (Rennie, 1998; Schulz, 1998). To enhance communicative proficiency, the practice of classroom interaction itself has to be communicative. As Clipperton (1994) noted, teaching has to be purposeful, interactive, and creative. Indeed for foreign language learning, or any learning to be successful, the teacher has to be able to tailor instruction and guide complex interactions for a variety of learners.

In recent years there has been a growing understanding and acknowledgment of the contributions made by research on second language learning, in particular those studies that examine student–teacher and student–student interactional patterns and their impact on language development. Yet Swain (1995) was critical of the limited focus of past psycholinguistic research that examined input given to the learners (i.e., input hypothesis by Krashen, 1985) and the output produced by the learners (i.e., output hypothesis by Swain, 1993). Swain argued that this focus does not necessarily capture the most important aspects of the processes involved in language learning. As an alternative, Swain pointed to sociocultural research, which acknowledges and deals with the complexities of the classroom learning and provides insight into the moment-by-moment processes used by teachers and learners in achieving goals. Swain stated that mere observation of the input and the output does not clearly explicate the actual nature of interaction. Chaudron (1988) and Johnson (1991) supported the

---

[2]The American Council on Teaching of Foreign Languages (ACTFL) announced the completion of "Standards for Foreign Language Learning: Preparing for the 21st Century" in November 1995. Whereas the ACTFL Proficiency Guidelines reflect performance standards, Standards for Foreign Language Learning are content standards consisting of five Cs, communication, communities, comparisons, connections, and cultures.

notion that foreign language learning and sociocultural contexts are inseparable. Thus, to understand the development of learners' competence the intricate interconnections between the social contexts for additional language learning and the learners' strategies, processes, and attitudes toward learning must be taken into consideration. The notion of learning language as a constructive process situated in particular social and cultural contexts opposes the concept of the individual learners acquiring "knowledge & cognitive skills as transferable commodities" (Salomon & Perkins, 1998, p. 2). Highlighted is the notion that each particular classroom offers specific opportunities for learning that defy prior prescription of sequences of skills or language outcomes.

In foreign language classroom research, few studies have focused on the sociocultural learning processes that affect what and how learners achieve. Focusing on the contexts of learning would provide examples of how conditions jointly created by teachers and learners promote certain types of language learning. Our study investigates the sociocultural nature of classroom interaction and its impact on language development over time in a Japanese FLES program. It sheds light on the role that all participants' interaction plays in constructing "the lesson" and demonstrates how understanding about language, its use, and how to learn it are integral to the outcomes of the lesson. Specifically this study describes the following processes: (a) how students learn about the Japanese language (forms and use) over time, and (b) how they learn and become competent in the interactional patterns of the classroom. In the illustrations we provide, we demonstrate how members of this classroom group jointly construct knowledge, understandings, and actions. In the next section we explain the tenets of sociocultural theory, the theoretical framework of this study, and how instructional conversations (ICs) function.

SOCIOCULTURAL THEORY

Vygotsky, a Russian psycholinguist, established the foundational concepts of sociocultural theory. Underlying his theory is the belief that human beings are social by nature, and thus, human cognition develops first through social interaction. That is, a child is born into a certain society and learns about his or her world, including social conventions and cultural knowledge, through participation in experiences constituted within that world. This belief led Vygotsky to formulate the general law of cultural development, which is explained as follows:

Any function in the child's cultural development appears twice, or in two planes, first it appears on the social plane, and then on the psychological plane, first it appears between people as an *interpsychological* category, and then within the child as an *intrapsychological* category. This is equally true with regard to voluntary attention, logical memory, and the formation of concepts, and the development of volition. (Vygotsky, 1981, p. 163, italics added)

The interpsychological dimension or the social plane indicates that learning first takes place between a child or a novice and a more capable peer (or peers). This dependent nature of learning transforms to something more independent (i.e., intrapsychological) at a later phase. For instance, young children might be largely dependent on other individuals, most probably parents, in the early stages of development. As they grow, however, they gradually become less dependent on others, because they become more capable of achieving things by themselves (Lantolf & Appel, 1994). Furthermore, when a child or novice is able to accomplish a certain task independently (i.e., the child's or the novice's actual level), he or she can achieve something even more difficult and complex, if given appropriate assistance by a more capable peer (or peers). This area of growth was defined as the *zone of proximal development* (ZPD) by Vygotsky (1978): "It is the distance between the actual developmental level as determined by independent problem solving and the level of potential guidance or in collaboration with more capable peers" (p. 86).

Development occurs as a novice or a child and an adult or a more capable peer engage in dialogic interactions in which the more capable participants guide the learners in accomplishing specific tasks. Through their regular interactions over time, learners internalize the skills and abilities needed to be able to function independently. This shift from interpsychological to intrapsychological planes is referred to as "regulation" (Wertch & Hickmann, 1987).[3] The use of language in this process is key to learning and development.

In examining foreign language from a sociocultural perspective, we are looking at language as both a product and process of social interaction

---

[3]A child, in the early stage of cognitive development, relies on the environment to accomplish certain tasks. This stage is called *object regulation*. The next stage is *other regulation*, in which a child depends on his or her parent or a more capable peer for assistance. A child will then grow into the *self-regulation* stage. A child is finally independent and capable of exerting control over his or her environment. This is not to say, however, he or she has total control over all the tasks for all time (Lantolf & Appel, 1994).

(Gee, 1992; Moll, 1992). In this perspective language is dynamic and multiple-functional. It requires active human agents making use of available resources for purposeful interaction and cannot be understood decontextualized from this interaction. In other words, what we communicate and can understand happens because we mutually accomplish and act through language. From this viewpoint, language functions as a system that people use to construct meaning. This position is in direct contrast with the view of language as an idealized system independent from its actual use. Agar (1994) referred to this latter view as the definition of "linguistic that narrows its view to grammar and dictionary" (p. 47). He further asserted that this view draws a "circle around language" that excludes culture. This distinction is important because, from a sociocultural perspective, language cannot be viewed as having any fixed meaning independent of its context of interaction. This means people are socially constructing the nature of reality through language at any particular moment of history.

INSTRUCTIONAL CONVERSATIONS

The concept of ICs is based on a sociocultural perspective of development. They provide clear evidence of how language mediates learning through social interactions (Tharp & Gallimore, 1991). Through ICs, teachers and students construct practices that form a part of the daily rituals of learning at school. The teacher's role is to facilitate learning by drawing on prior or background knowledge of the students and encouraging a variety of responses. That is, it is not to transmit correct answers, but to guide students to higher levels of understanding through their joint participation in the interaction. Through their extended participation, teachers and students together establish a common foundation of understanding.

ICs are important to language teaching in more ways than solely being the conveyer of language content. Rather it is through the process of interacting that learners come to understand how to use language to build knowledge and achieve shared notions of interpretation. Patthey-Chavez and Clare (1996) stated that "learning to use language means coming to understand when particular choices are appropriate and implicitly learning and accepting rules and values about language choices that originate in the larger community of speakers" (p. 517). Through their participation over time, learners not only develop expectations of the content focus of the lesson; just as important, they learn about the process of communication itself. Thus by examining the ICs of a classroom we can identify the understandings the participants are developing in relation to what they are doing. Analyses of

ICs also allow us to know what language resources are considered appropriate, what activities are valued, and what beliefs are voiced.

There are also quality issues to be addressed in carrying out ICs because these conversations are the principal means for structuring learning opportunities (Goldenberg, 1991; Rueda, Goldenberg, & Gallimore, 1992). The conversations that take place in classrooms are different from ordinary exchanges between passersby or exchanges typical of chit-chatting with friends. Conversations that teachers have with students have a learning goal that must be met. They are similar, however, in the sense that they seem natural and spontaneous. Unlike recitation script-type instruction, IC has been proposed "as a generic term encompassing central features of a more recent, and still evolving, conception of teaching methods that attempts to go beyond recitation to challenge students and to propel them toward higher planes of knowing" (Tharp & Yamauchi, 1994, p. 7). Goldenberg (1991) advocated that ideal ICs scaffold learning for students by engaging students and integrating their comments in the discussion. The instructional talk should augment, challenge, or draw out complex language and expression, and thereby help to promote learning.

Through the analysis of ICs we can see how teachers and students construct knowledge about ongoing events, how they bring past knowledge into learning, and how they create a communal sense of what counts. Certainly in analyzing these conversations, it is important to recognize the many types of constraints, as these indicate the conditions that influence the learning potential. For example, teachers generally steer, if not command, the exchange to flow along certain lines to get the students to practice using, gaining, and creating knowledge within a limited amount of time. In addition, spatial constraints can restrict the movement of the students and teacher within a certain room. Also, there are behavioral and linguistic constraints in terms of procedures that are permitted and those that are not. Analysis of these characteristics of ICs is important because it reveals to us the values, knowledge, and skills important to learning and created in the conversations between students and teachers. Thus by scrutinizing the nature of ICs, we can identify particular contexts and the variety and complexity of the participants' developing understandings and ways of making sense.

The focus of the study we present here is on how ICs unfold in one Japanese as a foreign language (JFL) elementary classroom and the developmental consequences that result from student participation in them. In the following section we describe the setting, the participants, and the methods for collecting and analyzing the data.

THE STUDY

Setting

Our study takes place in the Japanese FLES Program at Falk School in Pittsburgh, Pennsylvania. With a current population of approximately 300 students, Falk School has been the University of Pittsburgh's laboratory school since 1931. At the time of this study, the population of the school consisted of approximately 77% European American, 9% African American, and 14% Asian American or other minorities (Antonek, Donato, & Tucker, 1994). Falk School features a unique system of mixing students of neighboring ages so that each class consists of children of two different grades. Thus, one class might consist of kindergartners and first graders, and another class might consist of first graders and second graders. Approximately half of the students are children of university employees.

The students are taught in a multiage classroom setting by modified team teaching with nongraded instruction (Antonek et al., 1994). The Japanese FLES program began in the summer of 1992. Yoko Morimoto, one of the authors of this chapter, has been teaching in this program since August 1994. The program consists of a 15-minute lesson a day, 5 days a week. Morimoto originally developed the curriculum and materials based on proficiency-oriented instruction (Omaggio, 1986; Shrum & Glisan, 1994),[4] and more recently on the National Standards for Foreign Language Learning (National Standards in Foreign Language Education Project, 1996).

Participants

To examine how foreign language acquisition develops from the introductory level, we observed the youngest cohort of JFL students for this study. The first two sets of data come from the class consisting of kindergartners and first graders, and the third set of data from the class of first and second graders. The class of kindergartners and first graders, observed at Times 1 and 2, consisted of 2 African American, 4 Asian American, and 18 European American students. The class of first and second graders, observed at Time 3, had 1 African American, 3 Asian Amer-

---

[4]Proficiency-oriented instruction is based on three interrelated criteria underlying the proficiency descriptions: context, function, and accuracy. ("Functional Trisection of Oral Proficiency Levels" put forth by the American Council on Teaching Foreign Languages; Buck, Byrnes, & Thompson, 1989).

ican, and 19 European American students. These children had started studying Japanese on a daily basis (a 15-minute lesson a day, 5 days a week) in August 1994, approximately 1 month prior to the first observation (Time 1). There were no children who had had any exposure to Japanese prior to starting this program.

Data Collection and Analysis Procedures

The data for this study are longitudinal. The first period of observation took place in September 1994 (Time 1), at the beginning of the school year. The second took place at the end of the school year in May 1995 (Time 2), approximately 9 months after Time 1. The third period of data collection was held in March 1996 (Time 3), 9.5 months after Time 2. Although the same students were observed at Time 1 and Time 2 in the same school year, it was unfortunately impossible to follow exactly the same individuals at Time 3, the following school year. This was due to the fact that the mixture of the students was rearranged at the beginning of the new school year. Thus, the results reported here are for the class consisting of a combination of kindergartners and first graders (total of 24 students) at Time 1 and Time 2 (in the same school year, 1994 to 1995), as well as a combination of first and second graders (total of 23 students) at Time 3 (the following school year, 1996). Of this group of students, 12 were part of the group observed at Times 1 and 2.

The class was conducted in a naturalistic way without any interference by the researchers. Each class was videotaped and transcribed for analysis. Additional information was obtained from interviews of the teacher of the class and also from field notes recording the details of the classroom events. Three protocols were selected for analysis from the data sets: Protocol A was taken from the data obtained at Time 1, Protocol B from Time 2, and Protocol C from Time 3. These excerpts were chosen because they are representative of the types of conversations observed at each point in time.

In our analysis of the transcripts of the class lessons we were interested in how both teacher and students used language during their lessons. This entailed identifying how the teacher guided the students and how the students interacted during classroom activities. In these activities we were specifically interested in identifying both vocabulary and syntax development across time and the patterns of interaction used by the teacher and students in the joint construction of knowledge.

Findings

Linguistic Development and Its Context.   In the transcript labeled Protocol A, we present an example of a typical vocabulary lesson observed during Time 1. In this instructional conversation the teacher often brought in pictures to serve as stimuli for the naming practice, one in which the students identified objects or actions depicted in graphics. This characteristic was more prominent during the class at Time 1.

Protocol A: Class of Kindergarten and Grade 1 (Time 1, September 1994)[5]

A1.	T:	Hai, ii desu ka. (Showing a picture of a father.)
		OK, are you ready?
A2.	SS:	Okaasan!
		Mother!
A3.	T:	Okaasan? (Raising her eyebrows)
		Mother?
A4.	SS:	Otoosan! (laugh)
		Father!
A5.	T:	Hai, ii desu ne. Otoosan. Hai.
		Right, good. Father. OK.
A6.	SS:	Otoosan.
		Father.
A7.	T:	Otoosan.
		Father.
A8.	SS:	Otoosan.
		Father.
A9.	S1:	Otoosan!
		Father.
A10.	S2:	Otoosan!
		Father.
A11.	T:	Hai!
		All right!

---

[5]The following abbreviations are used in this and subsequent protocols: T = teachers; SS = students; S1, S2, and so on = individual students.

Because students were practicing the vocabulary for family members, the teacher showed a picture of a man, expecting the students to answer *otoosan* 'father.' The students made a mistake in referring to father and instead produced the word *okaasan* 'mother.' The incorrect response by the students elicited the teacher's feedback—raised eyebrows and an echo of what the students had just said, "Okaasan?" with rising intonation (Line A3). Understanding this cue, students quickly realized that their response was not correct. They were able to self-correct producing the appropriate answer, *otoosan* 'father' (Turn A4). The utterances at Turns A2 and A4 were responses to the teacher's question. Yet the segment did not end here because the students' level of participation was extremely animated. They continued to respond to the teacher's evaluation and confirmation, as we see in Turn A5, and exerted their control by maintaining the floor through repetition of the correct answer. Due to both their limited linguistic knowledge and the inherent restrictions of the interactional game for naming, the students' utterances were either echoes of the teacher's utterances or elicited responses that were kept at the one-word level.

By Time 2, it was evident that the students were quite familiar with this particular IC, and they became even more active in responding to the teacher. With respect to sentence structure, the students started to create many more utterances consisting of two or more words with particles, rather than just producing a single word at a time. In Protocol B, we see that the game required different morphological inflections of verbs, such as "he or she eats something," "he or she ate something," or "he or she wants to eat something," not explicit in the picture stimuli.

Protocol B: Class of Kindergarten and Grade 1 (Time 2, May 1995)

B1. T: Hai. (shows a picture of a man eating an apple.)
         Here you go.

B2. S1: Denisu wa ringo o tabemasu. Masu!
         Dennis eats an apple. Eats!

B3. T: Denisu wa ringo o tabemasu, ii desu ne. Mary (=S2). (Showing a picture of a boy who is thinking about an apple.)
         Dennis eats an apple. Good. Mary (=S2).

B4. S2: Denisu wa ringo o tabe
         Dennis an apple ea

B5. T: Tabe?
         Ea?

B6. S2:   Tabemasu.
          He eats.

B7. S3:   Tabetai. Tabemasu Tabemasen!
          He wants to eat. He eats. He doesn't eat!

B8. S2:   . . .

B9. T: Remember this song? Tai, tai, tai . . . (Starts singing a song of "Tai (want)")
          Remember this song? I want, I want, I want . . .

B10. SS: Ta, tai tai, nomitai, tabetai, hon yomitai. netai, kaitai, terebi mitai!
          (The students join the teacher and start singing the song.)
          Ah, I want, I want, I want to drink, want to eat, want to read, want to buy,
          want to watch TV!)

B11. T: Haaaai, tabetai! Ii desu ka? Tabetai.
          Goooood. He wants to eat! All right? He wants to eat.

B12. SS: Tabetai.
          He wants to eat.

B13. T: Tabetai, hai, Mary.
          He wants to eat. Here you go, Mary.

B13. S2: Denisu wa ringo o tabetai.
          Dennis wants to eat an apple.

B14. T: Hai, ii desu ne!
          Yes, that's great!

Prior to this segment, all the students had created sentences in chorus. The protocol begins with the teacher calling on individual students. Student 1 answered the teacher's question right away (Turn B2), but when Mary, Student 2, was called on (Turn B3), she could not produce the correct sentence, *Denisu wa ringo ga tabetai* 'Denise wants to eat an apple' (Turn B4). She was confused as to the form needed to end the sentence. The teacher then tried to elicit more from her by repeating what she had just said (Turn B5) but Mary ended up producing the most basic structure *tabemasu* 'he or she eats' (Turn B6), which was consistent with the action represented in the picture cue. Then Student 3 chanted several verb conjugations that they had learned before (Turn B7), although the teacher did not give any cues to do so. The teacher looked at Mary at this point, giving Mary the opportunity to extract a more appropriate sentence from the cues given by Student 3's utterance. However, Mary kept silent (Turn B8). Then the teacher started singing a song that contained the pattern Mary was to use, a song of "tai (want to)," which had been created by the teacher and sung often to practice the *tai* 'want to' form (Turn B9). Consequently we see in Turn B13 that Mary was now able to independently produce the targeted response, "He wants to eat an apple."

It should be noted that Mary reached this successful formation of the linguistic structure as a result of all the scaffolding that took place in this IC. First, Mary was helped by Student 3's chanting of the verb endings, "Tabetai. Tabemasu . . . Tabemasen" (Turn B7). Although this was unsolicited, Student 3's chanting helped Mary remember the pattern she needed to produce. Second, the teacher helped refresh Mary's memory of the target form by singing a mnemonic song "tai (want to)." Thus, although Mary's actual level did not allow her to accomplish this particular task independently, spontaneous guidance from her peers and teacher enabled her to perform at the higher level, her potential level. The exchange exhibited in Protocol B is a clear case of the teaching and learning that take place in the ZPD. The observed segment of the IC not only demonstrates the teacher–student interaction that promotes the student's performance level, but it also shows that peer collaboration, if permitted to happen, plays a considerable role in scaffolding learners' language use. This is consistent with the research findings of Adair-Hauck and Donato (1994) and Donato (1994).

In Protocol C the students were learning the existence construction, such as "There is XXX on the desk." This construction is often pointed out as a stumbling block for learners of Japanese in general (Traphagan, 1997). In this protocol we see a clear example of the intrinsic link between social interaction and language learning.

Protocol C: Class of Grades 1 and 2 (Time 3, March 1996)

C1. T: Soshitara nee. Eeto. Akachan wa doko ni imasu ka? Akachan wa?
        (Showing a picture of a baby in a house.)
        Well then. Let's see. Where is the baby? The baby?

C2. SS: Akachan wa (They start creating a sentence to answer the teacher's question.)
        The baby is

C3. T: Akachan wa? Tom (=S1).
        The baby is? Tom.

C4. S1: Tsukue!
        The desk!

C5. T: Tsukue? Hai, tsukue
        The desk? Yes, the desk

C6. S2: Ue!
        Top!

C7. T: Ue
Top

C8. S3: Ue ni!
On top!

C9. S1: Akachan imasu![6]
There is the/a baby!

C10. S4: Akachan wa tsukue no ue ni
The baby is located on top of the

C11. S1: Arimasu. (Trying to finish up S4's sentence.)[7]
Exists.

C12. T: Arimasu ka?[8]
The baby is there?

C13. SS: Iie! Imasu![9]
No! The baby is there!

C14. S2: Akachan, i, ma, su (Starts singing the song of "The baby is there.")
The baby is th-e-re

C15. All: Akachan ga i, ma, su. Akachan ga i, ma, su. Akachan ga teeburu no ue ni i, ma, su! (The teacher and the students sing the song together.)
The baby is th-e-re. The baby is th-e-re. The baby is on the table!

C16. T: Hai, ii desu ne. Hai, akachan wa Tom?
All right, great. OK, the baby is Tom?

C17. S1: Akachan wa tsukue no ue ni i, ma, su! (Singing the ending part just like the song.)
The baby is on top of the desk!

In Turns C2 to C8, the students' utterances were made at the one-word level. When Student 2 came up with the location word *ue* 'top' (Turn C7), it became the trigger for Student 3 to respond with the proper particle that marks the location, *ni* 'on' (Turn C8). Then Student 1 took a turn again to say *Akachan imasu* 'There is a baby' or 'The baby exists,' which was a two-word utterance (Turn C9). However, this sentence lacked the particle, *wa*, which should mark the subject *akachan* 'baby' as in "Akachan wa tsukue no ue ni imasu." Student 4 then attempted to produce a full sentence to describe

---

[6]The particle *wa/ga*, which should mark *akachan* 'baby' is missing.

[7]"Arimasu" is used for inanimate objects and so is not suitable here.

[8]The teacher repeats the wrong verb produced by the student with a rising intonation.

[9]Here, the students use the correct form of the verb.

where the baby was, "Akachan wa tsukue no ue ni . . ." (Turn C10). His three-word utterance with two particles was flawless; that is, he successfully used the locative particle *ni* 'on' and the subject marker *wa*. However, he stumbled at the end of the sentence and failed to finish it. Student 4's incomplete sentence was finished by Student 1, who applied the verb to indicate the existence of inanimate objects, *arimasu* (Turn C11).

After the teacher questioned Student 1's answer by repeating it (Turn C12), other students detected the error in verb selection and corrected Student 1's mistake by saying "imasu" to express the existence for animate subjects (Turn C13). Whether or not Student 1 could have produced the complete sentence to describe the given picture at this point was unclear because he was not really given an opportunity to speak out then. Immediately following Turn C13, Student 2 started singing the song of "Akachan ga imasu (The baby is there)" (Turn C14). Following the song, Student 1 was called on by the teacher, and he then could successfully describe that the baby was on top of the desk. The way he finished the sentence, singing the ending "i-ma-su," showed that he was applying what he had just relearned in the song with the help offered by Student 2.

Throughout, the teacher was observed taking the lead in guiding the students to reach a higher level of linguistic achievement. With the teacher's guidance, the students responded with vigor and experimented with the language. Indeed, although individual students each contributed a little bit, it was as a whole class that they coconstructed this difficult structure. At first pass, this was something they could not have done individually. Thus, the assistance given in the ZPD was provided not only by the teacher but again by the peers, as in the case of Protocol B. As in Protocol B, the teacher played a crucial role in providing the guidance that resulted ultimately in timely help for the called-on student, assistance that the student uses to accomplish the task. This dynamic participation by students symbolizes the students' approach to self-regulation—the students are proceeding from dependence to independence, becoming more autonomous learners in the process.

To summarize, we found three important points. First, the linguistic development achieved in the observed period of time is notable—from a simple word-level utterance at Time 1 to a complex sentence structure at Time 3. Second, such linguistic development was made possible by the guidance given by the teacher and the peers in the ZPD. The students successfully solved the problems they could not individually complete when given appropriate assistance. Finally, underlying this development is the pervasive use of ICs, which allowed such mutual assistance to take place. In the next section we examine how the students' learning was shaped and enhanced by learning how to learn in this particular social and cultural context.

Interaction and Construction of Meaning. In addition to learning language forms, students were developing pragmatic competence specific to classroom learning to become effective learners. Johnson (1995) stated that "full participation in classroom activities requires competence in both the social and interactional aspects of classroom language" (p. 6). This is defined as "classroom communicative competence" by Wilkinson (1982, p. 6). Students need to be aware of the social and interactional norms of particular classes to fully participate and benefit from the ICs in the classroom.

Returning to Protocol A, although the teacher did not explicitly say "wrong," students were tuned into the teacher's gestures (raising her eyebrows) and replied with another answer (Turn A3). Clearly, the students picked up the teacher's signal that something was amiss and rectified their responses accordingly. They were learning to monitor their responses by reading the teacher's responses. In other words, they were developing a sense of what their roles were in the lesson and how to perform in the valued or correct way. For successful ICs, such learning in an academic community is requisite for building shared experiences and higher understandings.

The teacher's affirmation of the right answer with a "Hai" (Turn A5) and her repetition of the correct answer to ensure everyone's understanding, opened up opportunities for other students to also repeat the correct answer and be affirmed as knowers. In response to the children's correct answer, the teacher repeated it once again and thereby fueled another cycle of student repetition. Clearly this was not the direction the teacher wanted to take. Yet two individual students continued the repetition until, in responding to these last children's correct answers, the teacher asserted her authority to end the student's calling out with a "Hai" (Turn A11). Because of the time constraints, the teacher needed to control the pace of the introduction of items in the lesson. Clearly they each had particular roles to enact; when the students sustained their own repetition of the correct answer beyond the teacher's desired length of time, their communication conflicted. Consequently, the teacher reestablished her authority.

Closely examining this episode shows a level of student comprehension not initially viewed. The simple utterance, "Hai," can be interpreted in many possible ways. In this classroom it was used by the teacher for getting the children's attention, eliciting their participation, recognizing answers, and ending the interaction. Moreover, it was also used when the children responded appropriately. However, no one had explicitly translated the implicit meanings for them. Rather, the students were acquiring these meanings through the interactions with their teacher. By paying attention to cuing systems, such as differences in intonation and syntactic markers, the children were learning how to do things with the language in addition to learning particular language forms.

This short excerpt in Protocol A demonstrates how one student's correct answer gets picked up or echoed by various students so that all students interacted to complete the lesson. It also shows that the students were learning implicit rules such as how to deal with the teacher's indirect style of correcting their errors, when to respond, and when to stop repeating their utterances. By identifying the teacher's and the students' moves in this IC, we can identify the students' reading-between-the-lines knowledge: knowledge of how to play the IC games, recognition of the various cues that alert them to strangeness, their ability to self-correct, and to respond to the same word "Hai" in its multiple meanings in context. The students were learning much more than the correct vocabulary items, and yet, rarely are these kinds of knowledge and skills explicitly recognized in the foreign language class.

We can also see in Protocol B some of the pragmatic knowledge and skills important to the learning environment into which the children were being socialized. As we see in Turn B2, Student 1 produces an utterance, "Denisu wa ringo o tabemasu. Masu!" ('Denis eats an apple. Eats!'). In Japanese, the beginning part of a verb is the root and the ending is the inflection that determines the mood and aspect. Student 1 smoothly produced the sentence "He or she eats an apple" in Japanese and he confirms his use of a particular form by repeating the ending part of the verb, "masu." It seems reasonable to suggest that the student's repetition of "masu" indicates that he was actively monitoring and confirming his choice of linguistic form. Thus, in addition to learning the teacher's cues for signaling the right answer, the students are learning to monitor the grammatical forms of their responses. In this way, they are learning how to be bona fide members of their academic community, and in doing so, how to advance their own learning of the subject matter.

Another important aspect of learning into which the students were being socialized was learning to use the tools made available by the teacher. Protocol B is a good example of how students learned to make use of the teacher's tool for remembering—the mnemonic song, "Tai (I want)." Breaking into a loud song during a normal conversation would be unthinkable. Yet that the teacher broke into song in the observed classroom did not confuse or surprise the students (Turn B9). Instead, they joined in (Turn B10). The singing helped to foreground the needed information for the student whose turn it was and permitted her to make use of it (Turn B13). The existence of scaffolding in the singing and the help it provided to the students' development are plain to see. The scaffolding worked primarily because it belonged to a set of practices that the children had already engaged in and could do rather independently (i.e., sing the song). Thus, we see that students had learned another resource to use to complete their roles as active learners in their ICs.

We can see the active use of this tool by the students; that is, using a song to remember and thus participate in an IC, in Protocol C. Here, the teacher's verbal and perhaps nonverbal (i.e., rising intonation) signals (Turn C5), and other students' bit-by-bit contributions (Turns C6, C8, C9, and C10) together helped to build the IC. At Turn C14, to provide assistance for the other students in selecting the appropriate form, Student 2 began to sing a song that contained the needed information. The use of a song to remember certain syntactic features is evidence of the linguistic forms the students were learning. It also illustrates the skilled manipulation of a particular learning strategy by a learner, and thus provides evidence that the students had internalized a means used by the teacher to offer assistance. This type of learning indicates that the student was gaining what some cognitive researchers have called executive control strategies over learning (Bereiter & Scardamalia, 1989; Perkins, 1993).

Students learn and adopt the teacher's ways of interacting and guidance provides evidence of an important outcome of socialization in classrooms. As pointed out by Cook-Gumperz and Gumperz (1982), Tharp and Gallimore (1988), and Wilkinson (1982), the students do not simply learn the subject of a class, they learn much more. They learn, to a large degree, how to learn in a given environment. The classroom environment is in fact, as Brooks (1993) discussed, a particular culture that becomes co-constructed and constantly defined and modified in the course of activities that take place as part of daily life. It is through their interactions in the classroom that the students can gain mastery in how to mediate their own and each other's learning.

CONCLUSION

In this study we used a framework informed by Vygotskyan theory on learning to illustrate the developmental process of young learners of Japanese and to examine the nature of social interaction and language development. In particular, two areas were focused on.

First, we examined what the students were indeed learning in the cultural environment of the foreign language classroom. We found that the teaching and learning that took place in these classrooms was not restricted to the linguistic content of the subject matter. Instead, what the students learned was as much due to how they experienced learning as it was with the content of the lessons. Although not prescribed, their lessons included metalearning, learning about learning, and learning about social content; that is, how to interact with each other through language. As seen here, then, underlying language use in all settings is a social and cultural network that links language, cultural practices, and knowledge building. The language class needs to examine these connections in a much closer way than it has in the past if we wish to create classroom practices in which students become autonomous learners and users of a target language. Students need to be aware of the social and interactional norms of particular classes to fully participate and benefit from the ICs in the classroom.

Second, we found that students who struggled to produce the target structures of the lesson on an individual basis could in the end be successful when given appropriate assistance in the ZPD. In other words, the collaboration in the ZPD allowed these young learners of Japanese to outperform their current linguistic level, or their actual level, and to reach their potential level. Assistance was not only provided by the teacher, but also by the way the teacher sanctioned having other students provide one another with assistance during classroom activities. As we noted, over the time from Time 1 to Time 2, and then to Time 3, students' participation grew much more active and dynamic. Whereas the students' utterances were mere echoes of the teacher's utterances at Time 1, the students started to produce freer responses and to take turns more vigorously at Times 2 and 3. Moreover, the students demonstrated that they could indeed extend their communicative dynamics by responding to the teacher's question through coconstructed elaboration with peers, without the teacher's control.

Further research on learner development of target language sociocultural knowledge and skills through their collaboration in language learning needs to be conducted in foreign language classroom settings. Findings from this research can help us determine how to improve the teaching and learning of socioculturally appropriate communicative behaviors that extend far beyond the classroom.

ACKNOWLEDGMENTS

This research was partly supported by a grant from the Falk Humanities Award, Carnegie Mellon University, given to Etsuko Takahashi. We would like to express our gratitude to Dr. Rick Donato at the University of Pittsburgh for encouraging us to develop this study, and Dr. G. Richard Tucker at Carnegie Mellon University and Dr. Janis Antonek at the University of North Carolina who, along with Dr. Donato, implemented the Japanese FLES program in Falk School, and thus made this research possible.

REFERENCES

Adair-Hauck, B., & Donato, R. (1994). Foreign language explanations within the zone of proximal development. *Canadian Modern Language Review, 50,* 532–557.

Agar, M. (1994). *Language shock: Understanding the culture of conversation.* New York: Morrow.

Antonek, J., Donato, R., & Tucker, G. R. (1994). Japanese in the elementary school: Description of an innovative Pittsburgh program. *Mosaic, 2,* 5–9.

Bereiter, C., & Scardamalia, M. (1989). Intentional learning as a goal of instruction. In L. B. Resnick (Ed.), *Knowing, learning & instruction: Essays in honor of Robert Glaser* (pp. 361–392). Hillsdale, NJ: Lawrence Erlbaum Associates.

Branaman, L. E., & Rhodes, N. C. (1998). *A national survey of foreign language instruction in elementary and secondary schools* (Final report submitted to U.S. Department of Education, Office of Postsecondary Education). Washington, DC.

Brooks, F. B. (1993). Some problems and caveats in communicative discourse: Toward a conceptualization of the foreign language classroom. *Foreign Language Annals, 26,* 233–242.

Buck, K., Byrnes, H., & Thompson, I. (1989). *The ACTFL oral proficiency interview tester training manual.* New York: American Council on the Teaching of Foreign Languages.

Chaudron, C. (1988). *Second language classrooms: Research on teaching and learning.* New York: Cambridge University Press.

Clipperton, R. (1994). Explicit vocabulary instruction in French immersion. *Canadian Modern Language Review, 50,* 736–749.

Cook-Gumperz, J., & Gumperz, J. J. (1982). Communicative competence in educational perspective. In L. C. Wilkinson (Ed.), *Communicating in the classroom* (pp. 13–24). New York: Academic Press.

Donato, R. (1994). Collective scaffolding. In J. Lantolf & G. Appel (Eds.), *Vygotskian approaches to second language research* (pp. 33–56). Norwood, NJ: Ablex.

Gee, J. (1992). Sociocultural approaches to literacy (literacies). *Annual Review of Applied Linguistics, 12,* 31–48.

Goldenberg, C. (1991). *Instructional conversations and their classroom application* (OERI Grant No. R117G10022). Santa Cruz: University of California, Santa Cruz, National Center for Research on Cultural Diversity and Second Language Learning.

Johnson, D. M. (1991). *Approaches to research in second language learning.* White Plains, NY: Longman.

Johnson, K. E. (1995). *Understanding communication in second language classrooms.* New York: Cambridge University Press.

Krashen, S. (1985). *The input hypothesis: Issues and implications.* Torrance, CA: Laredo.

Lantolf, J., & Appel, G. (1994). Theoretical framework: An introduction to Vygotskian approaches to second language research. In J. Lantolf & G. Appel (Eds.), *Vygotskian approaches to second language research* (pp. 1–32). Norwood, NJ: Ablex.

Moll, L. (1992). Literacy research in community and classrooms: A sociocultural approach. In R. Beach, J. L. Green, M. L. Kamil, & T. Shanahan (Eds.), *Multidisciplinary perspectives on literacy research* (pp. 211–244). Urbana, IL: National Council on Teachers of English.

National Standards in Foreign Language Education Project (1996). *Standards for foreign language learning: Preparing for the 21st century.* Yonkers, NY: National Standards in Foreign Language Education Project.

Omaggio, A. C. (1986). *Teaching language in context.* Boston: Heinle & Heinle.

Patthey-Chavez, G. G., & Clare, L. (1996). Talk, talk, and text: The influence of instructional conversation on transitional bilingual writers. *Written Communication, 13*(4), 515–563.

Perkins, D. N. (1993). Person plus: A distributed view of thinking and learning. In G. Solomon (Ed.), *Distributed cognitions: Psychological and educational considerations* (pp. 88–110). New York: Cambridge University Press.

Rennie, J. M. (1998). Current trends in foreign language assessment. *Eric Review, 6,* 27–31.

Rosenbusch, J. M. (1995). Language learners in the elementary school: Investing in the future. In R. Donato & R. Terry (Eds.), *Foreign language learning, the journey of a lifetime* (pp. 22–57). Lincolnwood, IL: National Textbook.

Rueda, R., Goldenberg, C., & Gallimore, R. (1992). *Educational practice reports, No. 4, Rating instructional conversations: A guide.* Washington, DC: National Center for Research on Cultural Diversity and Second Language Learning Center for Applied Linguistics.

Salomon, G., & Perkins, D. (1998). Individual and social aspects of learning. In P. D. Pearson & A. Iran-Nejad (Eds.), *Review of research in education* (pp. 1–24). Washington, DC: American Educational Research Association.

Schulz, R. A. (1998). Foreign language education in the United States: Trends and challenges. *ERIC Review, 6,* 6–13.

Shrum, J., & Glisan, E. (1994). *Teachers handbook: Contextualized language instruction.* Boston: Heinle & Heinle.

Swain, M. (1993). The output hypothesis: Just speaking and writing aren't enough. *Canadian Modern Language Review, 50,* 158–164.

Swain, M. (1995, March). *Collaborative dialogue: Its contribution to second language learning.* Plenary paper presented at the Annual AAAL Conference, Long Beach, CA.

Tharp, R. G., & Gallimore, R. (1991). *Rousing minds to life: Teaching, learning, and schooling in social context.* New York: Cambridge University Press.

Tharp, R. G., & Yamauchi, L. A. (1994). *Effective instructional conversation in Native American classrooms* (Educational Practice Rep. No. 10). Washington, DC: The National Center for Research on Cultural Diversity and Second Language Learning.

Traphagan, T. (1997). Interviews with Japanese FLES students: Descriptive analysis. *Foreign Language Annals, 30*, 98–110.

Vygotsky, L. S. (1978). *Mind in society: The development of higher psychological processes*. Cambridge, MA: Harvard University Press.

Vygotsky, L. S. (1981). The development of higher forms of attention in childhood. In J. V. Wertsch (Ed.), *The concept of activity in Soviet psychology* (pp. 189–239). Armonk, NY: M. E. Sharp.

Wilkinson, L. C. (1982). Introduction: A sociolinguistic approach to communicating in the classroom. In L. C. Wilkinson (Ed.), *Communicating in the classroom* (pp. 2–12). New York: Academic Press.

II

*Classroom Interaction
and Second Language
Learning*

8

How Teachers Can Build on Student-Proposed Intertextual Links to Facilitate Student Talk in the ESL Classroom

Maureen Boyd
Valerie Miller Maloof

Students learn through talking (Britton, 1990; Gambrell & Almassi, 1996; Goldenberg, 1992–1993; Palinscar, 1986; Rubin, 1990; Swain, 1994; Vygotsky, 1986; Wells, 1990) and there is a documented need for more student talk in the classroom (Ernst, 1994; Johnson, 1995; Nystrand & Gamoran, 1991; Smagorinsky & Fly, 1993). Furthermore, the importance of student talk in the target language has been increasingly recognized in second language learning (Lantolf, 1994; Pica, 1987, 1991, 1994; Platt & Brooks, 1994; Swain, 1994). Through talk we learn not only the structural components of a language but also the communicative application of them. Swain (1994) proposed three functions of talk that promote second language learning: noticing of structural characteristics, practice in using them, and opportunities to reflect on them. However, not all talk exploits these potential functions.

In this chapter we focus on ways the classroom teacher can orchestrate and support a kind of classroom discourse that engenders active student talk that leads to second language learning. We examine the classroom discourse patterns of one sheltered English university language and culture class and show ways the default discourse pattern of U.S. classrooms (the teacher initiation, student response, and teacher evaluation [IRE] sequence) is disrupted to promote exploratory epistemic student talk. Exploratory epistemic talk is student-directed talk that explores connections between what students know and what is being taught. We highlight teacher instructional practices that promote and sustain epistemic student talk by building on student-proposed connections with what is being studied or discussed (student intertextual links) and incorporating them into the classroom discourse and making them socially significant. We uncover the kinds of intertextual links the students propose and some ways the teacher explicitly builds on and extends what the students have introduced.

RESEARCH ON CLASSROOM TALK
AND LANGUAGE LEARNING

The dominant pattern of classroom talk is the IRE sequence (Cazden, 1988; Ernst, 1994; Mehan, 1979; Wells, 1993). This discourse pattern can provide scaffolds to encourage structured one-word or limited participation in the target language in the classroom, particularly with beginning speakers of English. Furthermore, the teacher evaluation utterance may function as follow-up to, as opposed to evaluation of, the student utterance in teacher initiation, student response, teacher follow-up (IRF) sequence (Wells, 1993). However, most IRE or IRF sequences direct students into reproducing information in the response participation slots assigned. Such teacher-driven discourse socializes students into short, paradigmatic utterances that recite known information (Mosenthal, 1984) or choppy, tentative utterances (Gutierrez, 1994; Nystrand, 1997). As shown by some research (Gutierrez, 1994; Ernst, 1994; Johnson, 1995), a teacher-centered, sentence-level meaning, recitation, or IRE or IRF sequence of structures, which focuses on grammatical or content accuracy as students respond in the allocated participation slots, pervades most English as a second language (ESL) classrooms. This can be problematic for ESL students as such presentational talk provides few opportunities for developing communicative competence (Canale & Swain, 1980; Celce-Murcia, Dornyei, & Thurell, 1995; Hymes, 1972) through exploratory, reflective or responsive-collaborative talk (Barnes, 1969/1990; Gutierrez, 1994; Palinscar, 1986; Rubin, 1990; Wells, 1990).

It is now generally accepted that proficiency in another language requires more than knowledge of a linguistic code (grammatical competence). It includes the ability to say the appropriate thing in a certain social situation (sociolinguistic competence); the ability to start, enter, contribute to, and end a conversation, and the ability to do this in a consistent and coherent manner (discourse competence); the ability to communicate effectively and repair problems caused by communication breakdowns (strategic competence); and the ability to convey and understand communicative intent (actional competence). Such a notion of communicative competence entails the ability to interpret and enact appropriate social behaviors and requires the active involvement of the learner in the production of the target language (Canale & Swain, 1980; Celce-Murcia et al., 1995; Hymes, 1972). However, for talk to build communicative competence the learner needs to do more than supply one-word answers in the target language or recite isolated sentences. The learner needs to be actively engaged in constructing and clarifying meaning. Students can learn through talk and students can learn about the target language and through the target language by producing it.

Extended discourse can provide opportunities for students to develop and practice elements of communicative competence. Students can practice what, when, and how to communicate. If the discourse focus is on negotiating meaning, the target language becomes the vehicle for communicating ideas rather than the content focus for instruction. Furthermore, if the talk builds on what is previously uttered, a discourse coherence is established (Carrell, 1982). The teacher can play a significant role in promoting discourse coherence.

Teachers can foster classroom conditions that encourage or restrict successful student participation (Bruner, 1986; Ernst, 1994; Gee & Green, 1998; Gutierrez, 1994; Johnson, 1995; Mehan, 1979; Mosenthal, 1984; Nystrand, 1997; Smagorinsky & Fly, 1993). Teacher instructional practices shape the extent of student engagement, and teacher ideology shapes what counts as knowledge or experience as manifest through selective privileging of particular student utterances (Bloome & Egan-Robertson, 1993). When teachers take students seriously and validate their ideas by incorporating their responses into subsequent discourse, they allow students to direct and elaborate on the topic and scope of discussion (Nystrand & Gamoran, 1991). In such classrooms the students are actively involved in classroom talk. Research demonstrates how student talk in classrooms can be increased by teachers acknowledging and building on what students know and providing opportunities for students to contribute to what is being discussed (Bloome & Egan-Robertson, 1993; Goldenberg, 1992–1993). On the other hand, teachers can cut short student comments with a flat declarative (Bruner, 1986). The teacher can create explicit opportunities for students to actively participate in the classroom discourse by focusing on a topic that is of interest or relevance to students, and can provide opportunities for extended student-directed discourse by encouraging students to make connections with what they know or what is of interest to them (Moll, 1992).

The importance of making connections with what is known is underscored by schema theorists. They stress the importance of the reader and the reader's prior knowledge in reading a text (Carrell, 1984, 1987). This is of particular relevance when dealing with ESL students. Comprehension and retention are enhanced when new information is related to personal experience, especially when students do this in their own words (Nystrand & Gamoran, 1991). As students articulate their own thinking, they are motivated to use their resources to communicate. Coherent meaningful interaction—when students are relating new information to what is known and applying it and transforming it by applying it from one schema domain to another—promotes communicative competency in its fullest sense. This epistemic mode of engagement "in which meaning is treated as tentative, provisional and open to alternative interpretations and to revision—fully exploits the potential of literacy to empower the thinking of those who use it" (Wells, 1990, p. 369). We make sense by relating things to what we know—by making intertextual links—and when teachers recognize student intertextual links and make them socially significant by acknowledging and building on them, we create an environment where students are encouraged to articulate their own thinking, often in extended utterances.

Potential of Literature to Engender Student Talk

Our experience suggests, narrative and reading response theorists claim (Britton, 1969/1990; Bruner, 1986; Rosenblatt, 1938/1995, 1978/1994; Scholes, 1989), and research confirms (Gambrell & Almasi, 1996; Langer, 1995; McGinley et al., 1997; Short, 1992; Wells, 1990) that literature has the potential to engender a kind of quality talk that is characterized by reflection and exploring intertextual connections. By introducing substantive issues through literature, and encouraging students to relate them to their experiences and perspectives, teachers can facilitate opportunities for students to compare and contrast, to make connections with other literary texts and other experiences of their lives. These potential epistemic connections can then become texts to which other class members respond.

Literature has the potential to engage students and provide creative interfaces for exchange. However, local classroom conditions can encourage or restrict this potential because they regulate opportunities for and accept types of student talk. Much first language research on literature-based instruction has focused on the role of small group discussion in promoting student talk (Eeds & Wells, 1989; Gambrell, 1996; McMahon & Raphael, 1997; Smagorinsky & Fly, 1993). Discussion is defined as "cognitive engagement to the extent that the participants are *actively* involved in a conversation with one another rather than passively reciting answers to questions that may not be personally meaningful" (Almasi, 1996, p. 2, italics added). However, the act of establishing small groups does not by itself engender student discussion (Nystrand, Gamoran, & Heck, 1993; Smagorinsky & Fly, 1993). By the same token, the presence of the IRE sequence does not preclude the presence of meaningful exchange. It is the function of the student utterance, not the structure in which it is embedded, that provides evidence of thinking and engagement (Wells, 1993). Likewise, language learning is not so much tied to the structure of an activity (e.g., pattern of discourse sequence or size of student groups), although particular structures predispose us to particular types of talk, but tied to the participant role enacted by the learner. Students need many and varied participant role experiences. They need to act as, for example, questioners, reflectors, and responders as opposed to the static role of mainly responding to teacher recall and display questions and offering what they perceive as acceptable to the teacher (Almasi, 1996; Britton, 1969/1990; Ernst, 1994; Gutierrez, 1994; Johnson, 1995; Rubin, 1990).

This study recognizes the documented need for "more extended discourse, more meaning focused interactions and self-initiated participation in the ESL classroom" (Johnson, 1995, p. 17) and "a broad range of interactional and conversational roles and relationships that helped them [students] construct extended oral and written texts" (Gutierrez, 1994, p. 362) in the ESL classroom. Mindful of this, this study examines the classroom discourse in an ESL classroom and focuses on the role of the teacher in facilitating extended discourse. It uncovers what the students are talking about (the types of intertextual links the students are proposing) and the ways the teacher builds on and incorporates the proposed student intertextual links into the classroom discourse (the interactional roles and strategies the teacher adopts).

THE STUDY

The students in this study are international graduates and undergraduates studying at a large university in the southern United States. This 10-week course on American language and culture is an elective offered once a year. Students are required to have met an English language proficiency (TOEFL) requirement to enter the university. The purpose of the course is to foster academic competence in English through a variety of listening, speaking, reading, and writing activities. This particular teacher's class was chosen because the teacher's focus and main objective was classroom participation. The session under examination occurred at the beginning of the course and was the group's first class discussion on literature. Prior to this, the teacher had focused on academic competency skills such as note taking and had used articles about classroom expectations as a springboard for students to talk about their differing background experiences in school, and specifically the expectation of student talk in the classroom.

Methodology

This study builds on two earlier studies (Boyd, 1996; Miller, 1996) that examined discourse in this classroom. One study examined the amount of student and teacher talk and the use of five types of intertextual links in the class discussion. The other study identified the teacher's participant roles and patterns of word use in the class discussion. This study found that the teacher used the roles of clarifier, affirmer, and questioner most often and in these roles, the teacher adopted two student-initiated word choices: isolation and power. Building on these earlier findings we examine the same data with two questions: (a) What types of intertextual links were proposed by the students in this class, and (b) How does the teacher build on and incorporate the proposed student intertextual links?

Participants

Nine Asian students between the ages of 22 and 40 took this class, and all of them indicated that they did so to improve their spoken English. Six of the students were PhD students taking it for undergraduate credit, two were special status students, and one was an undergraduate (see Table 8.1 for a profile of the students).

Six of the nine students self-reported no exposure or very little exposure to the expectation of student talk in the classroom. Previously, class participation for these students had meant attending to the teacher and doing homework. Seven of the nine students had been in the United States for less than a year, five of them for a matter of weeks.

TABLE 8.1
Student Profiles

Students	Program	Age	LOR at Beginning of Class	Reason for Selecting Class	Exposure to Class Participation
Korean male	PhD	29	5 weeks	Enlarge English	Not much
Korean female 1	Special status	24	10 days	Advance English	None
Korean female 2	PhD	30	Few weeks	Improve language skill	—
Chinese male 1	PhD	40	3 years	Improve spoken English	None
Chinese male 2	PhD	26	2 years	For English fluency	None
Thai male	PhD	27	Few days	Improve English skills	Yes
Thai female	PhD	24	7 days	Improve speaking and writing	Yes
Japanese male	Special status	25	3 months	Improve English skills	Yes
Japanese female	Undergraduate	22	10 months	Improve spoken English	Occasional

Data Collection

We used the same classroom discourse transcript that was used for the two previous studies. To capture the classroom discourse in the ESL class, we audiotaped a 90-minute class discussion on language and identity. The class discussion focused on three pieces of literature: "Theme for English B" by Langston Hughes, "Aria" by Richard Rodriguez, and "How to Tame a Wild Tongue" by Gloria Anzaldua.

For this study, only lesson talk was analyzed. *Lesson talk* is defined as talk related to the class lesson (in this case the literature pieces) as opposed to *classroom management talk*, defined as talk related to assignment deadlines, assignment clarifications, and classroom procedures. In this class, 82.5% of the talk was lesson talk.

Data Analysis

We based our methodology design on three guiding principles of classroom talk: (a) students make sense of things by relating them to what they know, (b) literature has the potential to engage students in talk, and (c) the teacher plays a significant role in providing opportunities for students to participate and talk. To best examine the various facets of our study, we utilized both qualitative and quantitative approaches and we followed a tiered process in which each finding led to a more detailed analysis of the questions. This tiered process enabled us to uncover what happened in the classroom talk and also how it happened by examining the more discrete aspects of the talk.

Question 1: What Types of Intertextual Links are Proposed by Students?

For Question 1, we identified the overall student talk but then looked more discretely at the content to identify types of student-proposed intertextual links and to uncover what connections the students had proposed to the literature, and what resources were accessed to make sense of the literature. To determine the types of intertextual links proposed by the students, we used constant comparative qualitative analysis (Lecompte & Preissle, 1993) to code the students' talk. By constant comparative qualitative analysis we mean uncovering pattern, recurring cooccurrences or exclusive occurrences among variables. We used an individual's turn at talk as the unit of analysis. Following the inductive categorization of intertextual links, we conducted a tally of the number and type of each intertextual link in each turn at talk. Finally we used descriptive statistics to tally the relation between the types of intertextual links and the specific literature piece discussed.

Question 2: How Does the Teacher Build on and Incorporate the Student-Proposed Intertextual Links?

For Question 2, we identified the overall teacher roles, but then honed in only on the roles that immediately followed the student-proposed links. To better understand what was happening in the teacher roles in response to the student-proposed links, we analyzed the content and lexicon. First, to determine how the teacher built on and incorporated the proposed student intertextual links, we used turns at talk as the unit of analysis and coded the role or roles assumed by the teacher in each turn at talk. We used descriptive statistics to identify how often the teacher assumed each role. Identifying the teacher roles framed the subsequent analysis.

Second, to uncover the relation between the student-proposed intertextual links and the teacher's assumed roles, we studied the sequence of the intertextual links and the roles by examining closely the teacher responses that occurred immediately following a student-proposed intertextual link. However, we did not examine the responses following literature-based links because literature-based connections were an explicit instructional focus and thus possibly more contrived. We tallied the kinds of roles assumed by the teacher following the student-proposed intertextual links.

Finally, to better understand what was happening in the sequence of responses between teacher and student, we examined qualitatively the use of two student-initiated words—*isolation* and *power*—by looking at when they were used and in what context. More specifically, we studied in which intertextual links and teacher roles the words were used.

Findings

Question 1: What Types of Intertextual Links Were Proposed by the Students in This Class? This literature-based, sheltered English class was characterized by a high percentage of student talk: 68% of lesson talk was student talk. This number is made more conservative by the fact that all the utterances made by one student were not figured in because his accent was so difficult to understand that none of his words could be transcribed.

We uncovered five categories of intertextual links:

1. Literature-based: These included facts, quotes, or questions about literary work; perceptions of authorial perspective or intent; opinions about the literary work; and links to other literary works.
2. Personal: These related to family, friends, self-experience, and identity.
3. Classroom community: These were utterances where the members of the class built on each other's comments inviting or creating solidarity among them.
4. Language and culture: These were connections made to native, target, and other languages and cultures.
5. Universal: These were connections relating to the universal qualities of man and general concepts accepted by all.

An example of each type of link is provided in Table 8.2.

The intertextual links were tallied and Table 8.3 presents the results of our findings. The number of student-proposed intertextual links is displayed in relation to intertextual link categories and the literature piece under discussion.

We can note the following findings in this table. Ninety-seven intertextual links were proposed by students in this 90-minute class. The category of literature-based links is most represented. It has the highest number of student-proposed intertextual links overall (28), during the discussions of "Theme for English B" and "How to Tame a Wild Tongue," and was the second most frequent for "Aria." On 26 occasions, student talk was about language and culture. This was the second most frequent category overall; it was

TABLE 8.2
An Example of Each Category of Intertextual Link

Literature-based links

Fact, quote, or question about literary work
Perceptions of authorial perspective or intent
Opinions about the literary work

Lines 207–210
Um, I feel that way with your idea a little bit so, um, . . . I did not think he want to be a part of white society because here he says um . . "it is better to be white or black." But to me . . . I think he really feels that he . . um, I think . . .

Personal links

Relating to self-experience
Relating to self-identity

Lines 279–282
I remember first time, um, I went into the ( ) I plan to live in the dormitory and I the first time I went into the dorm, I feel that I am different from . . . , than all people because they are all Americans and I think I am the only Asian there.

Classroom community links

Inviting connection among members of class

Lines 166–168
I wonder if like any of you find that or what do you think or what did you wonder? Or why did he write them?

Language and culture links

Relating to experiences in U.S. culture
Relating to native or other languages

Lines 474–479
I want to talk to many American. But first they . . they . . . talk with me first. But I . . . my speaking is very slow, and he, he hears sometimes up to one minutes or up to two minutes and she go away from me. Why? Why? I . . I don't know. I'm not ready . . . I don't know. Many American people just have no patience.

Universal links

Relating of universal qualities of man
Relating of concepts

Lines 291–294
I do not like ( ) at this view from the society. When I was in Korea, I didn't have any power and have not much money so I have some isolation from the, the from the power, man who have power. I think, uh . . .

---

the most frequent category for "Aria" and "How to Tame a Wild Tongue." Personal-based links were represented 22 times. They were the second most frequent category in "Theme for English B" and "Aria" and third in "How to Tame a Wild Tongue." These three categories make up 78% (76 of 97) of the student-proposed intertextual links. The categories of classroom community and universal were less frequent (12 and 9, respectively).

TABLE 8.3
Frequency of Student-Proposed Intertextual Links Across Literature

Intertextual Links	Theme	Aria	Tame	Total
Literature-based	13	8	7	28
Personal	9	8	5	22
Classroom community	2	5	5	12
Language and culture	7	12	7	26
Universal	4	4	1	9
				97

Question 2: How Does the Teacher Build on and Incorporate the Proposed Student Intertextual Links? In this class the teacher assumed the following roles: questioner, affirmer, clarifier, summarizer, reflector, sharer of personal experience, and answerer. The definitions of these roles are stated in Table 8.4.

The teacher assumed the role of questioner most often, followed by the roles of affirmer and clarifier. The teacher assumed one of these three roles in 70% of the situations (see Table 8.5).

The teacher assumed these same three roles in 71% of the responses to a student-proposed intertextual link throughout the class (see Table 8.6). The teacher employed the affirmer role 17 times, followed by the questioner and clarifier roles 12 times each. The other four roles were assumed less than 7 times each.

A closer examination of the sequenced talk uncovers two specific ways in which the teacher built on the student-proposed intertextual links: (a) adopting and incorporating the student-initiated word choices, and (b) extending and building on student-generated word choices. One example of the adoption of student-initiated word choices includes the use of the words

TABLE 8.4
Teacher Role Categories

Title	Role
Affirmer	Explicitly acknowledges students' contributions
Answerer	Responds to students' questions
Clarifier	Confirms topics and ideas through restatement or further questioning
Questioner	Asks questions
Reflector	Provides opinions and draws conclusions
Sharer of experience	Relates personal experience
Summarizer	Synthesizes previous discussion points

TABLE 8.5
Total Teacher Roles

Role	Instances
Questioner	37
Affirmer	25
Clarifier	20
Summarizer	13
Reflector	12
Sharer of experience	5
Answerer	5

TABLE 8.6
Teacher Roles After Intertextual Links

Role	Instances
Affirmer	17
Questioner	12
Clarifier	12
Summarizer	7
Reflector	7
Sharer of experience	2
Answerer	1

isolation and *power* (see Excerpt A). After students initially proposed these words in the literature discussion, the teacher employed these words in her talk. The first student proposed the word *isolation* and the second student proposed the word *power*. However, the teacher adopted both of the student word choices immediately following the second student's turn at talk.

Excerpt A: Adoption/Incorporation of Student-Initiated Word Choices[1]

Lines 196–201

   E: We, yes, we can feel there is some kind of *isolation* every time. And the students in the . . in the . . in the poem and he really describes is very . . is very frankly for me . .

---

[1]The following is a key of symbols used in the transcriptions of both excerpts and adapted from Gumperz and Berenz (1993).

. . .	Pauses of less than 5 seconds
¼	Pauses of more than 5 seconds
( )	Unintelligible speech
[ ]	Nonlexical phenomenon, both vocal and nonvocal, that interrupt the lexical stretch (e.g., text [laugh] text)

this feeling about this desire to be member and to uh, to share his kind of identity with the dominant culture.

Lines 308–324

C: I think it is it is not a mark over certain black people. All of the people . . . all the people have a same feeling, who . . who don't have the *power* and money.

T: Another important one . . *power*. So maybe part . . you've identified a sense of *isolation*, is that what we're saying within the poem? And part of that means identifying race as being significant in that sense of *isolation* the color of your skin. C. was saying it's economic

C: Yeah.

T: Opportunities that you have based on that or that you do or do not have. *Power.* We talked about I think when we talked about the dominant culture . . M. talked about so . . what else is there? I'd like to read the poem again. Just think about what you said and then pull it together. I, I think it's lovely. It's a very *powerful* poem . . .

Another example (Excerpt B) shows how the teacher acknowledged and extended one student-generated phrase. The student speaking, TR, had been assigned to lead a class discussion on "Aria." When he used the metaphor "cultural shadow" in his talk, the teacher interrupted to identify the source of this metaphor and to draw class attention to his use of it. In the process she acknowledged and affirmed his selection of this phrase, making it socially significant by incorporating it into the classroom discourse. However, she changed it from a "cultural shadow" to "sociocultural shadow." The teacher then used this phrase as the focus for a lesson comparing metaphor and simile.

Excerpt B: How Teacher Extends and Builds on Student-Generated Word Phrase

Lines 594–627

TR: so I think this is because the . . the sociocultural influence and it could be viewed as a *cultural shadow* I think of.

T: I love that, where did you get that phrase? That's beautiful. *Sociocultural shadow.* Does he use that phrase?

TR: Yeah.

T: Oh, I missed that when I read that. That is beautiful.

TR: Oh no, I . . . .

T: You made that.

TR: Yeah . . . it's not in . . in the . . in the paper.

T: I might borrow that. I like that.

K: We might fight over it. [laughing]

T: Lovely. What does it mean to you, TR? I'm sorry I'm going off on a tangent, but I'm I'm I'm . . . that's what's hitting me . . that phrase.

TR: Shadowing that, um, during his earlier experience. He has a pretty wrongful perception about Spanish. He's not think that, uh, Spanish is, uh, equal language as he have English because of the people that speak it. So, the shadow means that, he's uh, speaking the language that is mostly spoken by the discriminated people. So, I think that's a shadow. So he thinks he one of the discriminated people too.

T: But what TR has done is created a metaphor for the experience of Richard Rodriguez in "Aria." And it's . . it's lovely. I mean it's lovely. But does someone know what a metaphor is? Creating or constructing a relationship between two things that would further illuminate, or help give some new insight into the experience or concept. He's talking about the *sociocultural shadow*. You may know the word simile often when we're teaching we talk about simile or metaphor. Simile uses the word like or as. A metaphor does not.

DISCUSSION

These Asian students, although new to the American classroom and the notion of active student participation in the classroom discourse, contributed 68% of the classroom talk. Because such a high level of student talk is not typical of ESL classrooms (Ernst, 1994; Johnson, 1995) it is of interest to examine the content of this student talk and the ways the teacher promoted such talk.

The assignment given for this class session was to read three pieces of literature and come to class prepared to contribute to a class discussion about them. It is therefore not very surprising that literature-based links were the most frequent type of intertextual link proposed by students. The students were explicitly directed to talk about the literature they had read for homework. Furthermore, the teacher selected this literature as part of a unit on language and identity and so one would expect that personal links and language and culture links would be the next frequent type of intertextual link proposed by students.

However, the degree to which the literature generated these intertextual links is most surprising. The students were making sense of the text by relating it to what they knew. Not counting the 28 literature-based links, 50% of student-proposed links were personal links or language and culture links. The other intertextual links proposed by students involved inviting connections to members of the classroom community and making generalizations beyond their experience. This affirms the potential of literature to engender opportunities for exploratory epistemic talk. The number of connections proposed by the students and the amount of overall student talk (68%) suggest that the literature engaged these students. Literature can provide a context for reflection and stimulate personal connections. These personal connections suggest that the students were indeed cognitively and actively engaged in the discussion. Students not only made personal connections but also invited comments from others providing evidence for active interaction about meaningful content. This talk among the students exemplifies Britton's (1969/1990) notion of talk as the action component of interaction.

The participant roles and the discourse of the teacher can restrict or encourage the student participation described here and the kinds of connections made (Bruner, 1986; Nystrand, 1997). In this study, the roles the teacher assumed most often were questioner, affirmer, and clarifier. In playing such roles the teacher encouraged students to extend their utterances and in doing so gave value to the connections the students proposed and the ideas they shared. The teacher privileged students' talk by questioning, affirming, and clarifying what they had said. Indeed, these three teacher discourse roles of affirmer, questioner, and clarifier constituted 70% of the teacher talk. Furthermore, after student-proposed intertextual links, the most frequent teacher discourse role was affirmer. As an affirmer, the teacher appeared to support and encourage student contributions to the classroom discourse. Furthermore, as affirmer the teacher was honoring different interpretations and validating more than one meaning. This connection between the affirmer role of the teacher and the student-proposed intertextual links reflects the potential importance of the teacher in encouraging students to use their personal resources to make meaning. By recognizing and building on the connections made by the students, the teacher, together with the students, coconstructs a range of meanings.

The example of the use of *power* and *isolation* illustrates how the teacher built on students' language, thus making socially significant their contributions. In the example of the phrase "sociocultural shadow" we have an example of how the teacher used student contributions as a vehicle for her teaching agenda. The teacher promoted language awareness in the context of what was being discussed. The student TR had created a metaphor; the teacher identified his phrase as a metaphor, explained the characteristics of a metaphor, and used the student-generated phrase as an example to teach and compare metaphor and simile, a concept important for one of the next day's readings in this unit. In this process the teacher not only fulfilled her predetermined teaching agenda; she affirmed the student's use of language. In effect, the teacher did more than affirm, she extended (or changed) the student's phrase from "cultural shadow" to "sociocultural shadow."

IMPLICATIONS

This literature-based class on language and culture provides evidence of the potential of literature to provide a springboard for student talk. This potential is best realized when the students are engaged (Nystrand & Gamoran, 1991); the public act of literary response in the classroom allows for more than one meaning and focuses on reflection and activating intertextual links (Britton, 1969/1990; Bruner, 1986; Langer, 1995; Rosenblatt, 1938/1995, 1978/1994). However, the role of the teacher is consequential to enhancing or defeating this potential for student talk. Specifically, the teacher can orchestrate opportunities for student talk by providing a stimulus such as literature that is linguistically appropriate and substantively engaging. The teacher can then support student utterances by selectively acknowledging and incorporating student-proposed intertextual links and student-initiated words into the classroom discourse. The teacher roles of affirmer, clarifier, and questioner were key to supporting student utterances in this class.

By selectively affirming and incorporating student utterances, the teacher can negotiate class objectives while also allowing students the opportunity to direct and elaborate on the topic and scope of discussion. This epistemic mode of engagement (Wells, 1990)—when students are motivated to articulate connections between new information and their experiences and home culture—engenders the kind of extended talk that promotes communicative competence. Such exploratory transformative talk, when students are composing at the point of utterance, and applying and transforming information from one schema to another, is cognitively challenging (Cazden, 1988). Speech unites the cognitive and the social, and talk that relates to what is personal is the type of coherent meaningful interaction that is called for in ESL classes. These meaning-focused interactions (Johnson, 1995) engender "a broad range of interactional and conversational roles and relationships" (Gutierrez, 1994, p. 362) as students make sense together. However, before students can be expected to perform various discourse roles (such as reflector, questioner, responder, and affirmer), these roles must be first modeled in the classroom by the teacher. The teacher in turn must then orchestrate varied and frequent opportunities for student talk and support student utterances through teacher roles such as affirmer, clarifier, summarizer, and questioner. Teacher talk can model, probe, and extend student utterances. By selectively building on student utterances, teachers indicate what counts and what is expected in the classroom.

CONCLUSION

In this study of a classroom with a high amount of student talk we showed how there were a large number of student-proposed intertextual links—97 in a 90-minute class. There were five types of student-proposed intertextual links: literature based, language and culture, personal, universal, and classroom community. These links were acknowledged through the teacher roles of affirmer, questioner, and clarifier. In these roles the teacher incorporated the student-proposed intertextual links through adopting student-initiated words and building on a student-generated phrase and using it as a teaching tool.

Teacher talk can engender or defeat the potential for student talk in the classroom. By selectively acknowledging, incorporating, and building on student-initiated words or student-proposed intertextual links, the teacher privileges student knowledge and ways of talking. In doing so, she encourages students to relate what is being studied to what is known and by promoting this epistemic mode of engagement (Wells, 1990) motivates them to use their resources to communicate. The teacher thus shapes the classroom discourse and consequently the type of language learning that will occur.

This study examined classroom talk and the connections between the students' use of intertextual links and the teacher's particular roles in the class discussion. There is, however, a need to look further at these intertextual links. For example, although we have indicated that 68% of the classroom talk was student talk, it would be interesting to focus on the length and mode—narrative or paradigmatic (Bruner, 1986)—of student utterances. Turns of talk were lengthy and many were narratives that told stories of students' own experiences. In the case of one student, all of her intertextual links were told in the form of a story about a third person—"I have a friend who. . . ." We noted that in many cases when the students were relating an anecdote, the turns of talk were not only longer, but conducted in what Bruner (1986) would call the narrative mode; that is, they were storytelling or entextualizing—making connections to the literature by telling a related anecdote.

A further examination of student talk could uncover any patterns that may exist as the teacher selectively acknowledges, incorporates, and builds on student utterances. For example, is there a specific type or particular student privileged? This study looked at one 90-minute class; there is a need to conduct a longitudinal study and examine changes across teacher–student interactions or uncover patterns across time.

It is important to focus attention on the growing competencies of language learners and instructional practices that promote exemplary student performance. An examination of the classroom discourse of an ESL class with a high amount of student talk may reveal those discourse conditions that engender active student talk. This research uncovered the types of student connections to the discourse and the ways the teacher plays a role. This study adds to the literature on classroom talk by reminding us that classroom instruction is more than providing a thorough comprehensive lesson; it also entails conscious planning regarding how the teacher will promote student talk, especially in a second language class where active student talk leads to second language learning.

REFERENCES

Almasi, J. (1996). A new view of discussion. In L. Gambrell & J. Almassi (Eds.), *Lively discussions: Fostering engaged reading* (pp. 2–24). Newark, DE: International Reading Association.

Barnes, D. (1990). Language in the secondary classroom. In D. Barnes, J. Britton, & M. Torbe (Eds.), *Language, the learner and the school* (pp. 11–87). Portsmouth, NH: Boynton/Cook. (Original work published 1969)

Bloome, D., & Egan-Robertson, A. (1993). The social construction of intertextuality in classroom reading and writing lessons. *Reading Research Quarterly, 28*, 305–333.

Boyd, M. (1996). *Building class participation: Intertextual links in an international ESL classroom*. Unpublished manuscript. University of Georgia.

Britton, J. (1990). Talking to learn. In D. Barnes, J. Britton, & M. Torbe (Eds.), *Language, the learner and the school* (pp. 91–130). Portsmouth, NH: Boynton/Cook. (Original work published 1969)

Bruner, J. (1986). *Actual minds, possible worlds*. Cambridge, MA: Harvard University Press.

Canale, M., & Swain, M. (1980). Theoretical bases of communicative approaches to second language teaching and testing. *Applied Linguistics, 1*, 1–47.

Carrell, P. (1982). Cohesion is not coherence. *TESOL Quarterly, 16*, 479–488.

Carrell, P. (1984). Schema theory and ESL reading: Classroom implications and applications. *The Modern Language Journal, 68*, 332–343.

Carrell, P. (1987). Content and formal schemata in ESL reading. *TESOL Quarterly, 21*, 461–477.

Cazden, C. (1988). *Classroom discourse: The language of teaching and learning*. Portsmouth, NH: Heinemann.

Celce-Murcia, M., Dornyei, Z., & Thurell, T. (1995). Communicative competence: A pedagogically motivated model with content specifications. *Issues in Applied Linguistics, 6*, 25–35.

Eeds, M., & Wells, D. (1989). Grand conversations: An exploration of meaning construction in literature study groups. *Research in the Teaching of English, 23*, 4–29.

Ernst, G. (1994). "Talking circles": Conversation and negotiation in the ESL classroom. *TESOL Quarterly, 28*, 293–322.

Gambrell, L. (1996). What research reveals about discussion. In L. Gambrell & J. Almasi (Eds.), *Lively discussions: Fostering engaged reading* (pp. 25–38). Newark, DE: International Reading Association.

Gambrell, L., & Almassi, J. (Eds.). (1996). *Lively discussions: Fostering engaged reading.* Newark, DE: International Reading Association.

Gee, J., & Green, J. (1998). Discourse analysis, learning, and social practice: A methodological study. *Review of Research in Education, 23,* 119–169.

Goldenberg, C. (1992–1993). Instructional conversations: Promoting comprehension through discussion. *The Reading Teacher, 46,* 316–326.

Gumperz, J., & Berenz, N. (1993). Transcribing conversational exchanges. In J. Edwards & M. Lampert (Eds.), *Talking data: Transcription and coding in discourse research* (pp. 91–121). Hillsdale, NJ: Lawrence Erlbaum Associates.

Gutierrez, K. (1994). How talk, context, and script shape contexts for learning: A cross-case comparison of journal sharing. *Linguistics and Education, 5,* 335–365.

Hymes, D. (1972). On communicative competence. In J. Pride & J. Holmes (Eds.), *Sociolinguistics: Selected readings* (pp. 269–293). Harmondsworth, UK: Penguin.

Johnson, K. (1995). *Understanding communication in second language classrooms.* New York: Cambridge University Press.

Langer, J. (1995). *Envisioning literature.* New York: Teachers College Press.

Lantolf, J. (1994). Sociocultural theory and second language learning: Introduction to the special issue. *The Modern Language Journal, 78,* 418–420.

Lecompte, M., & Preissle, J. (1993). *Ethnography and qualitative design in educational research.* Portsmouth, NH: Boynton/Cook.

McGinley, W., Kamberelis, G., Mahoney, T., Madigan, D., Rybicki, V., & Oliver, J. (1997). Re-visioning reading and teaching literature through the lens of narrative theory. In T. Rogers & A. Soter (Eds.), *Reading across cultures: Teaching literature in a diverse society* (pp.). New York: Teachers College Press.

McMahon, S., & Raphael, T. (1997). The book club program: Theoretical and research foundations. In S. McMahon & T. Raphael (Eds.), *The book club connection* (pp. 3–25). New York: Teachers College Press.

Mehan, H. (1979). "What time is it, Denise?": Asking known information questions in classroom discourse. *Theory Into Practice, 18,* 285–294.

Miller, V. (1996). *Establishing patterns of word use and participant roles in a class discussion on language and identity.* Unpublished manuscript. University of Georgia.

Moll, L. (1992). Funds of knowledge for teaching: Using a qualitative approach to connect homes and classrooms: *Theory Into Practice, 18*(4), 285–294.

Mosenthal, P. (1984). The effect of classroom ideology on children's production of narrative text. *American Educational Research Journal, 21,* 679–689.

Nystrand, M. (1997). *Opening dialogue: Understanding the dynamics of language and learning in the English classroom.* New York: Teachers College Press.

Nystrand, M., & Gamoran, A. (1991). Instructional discourse, student engagement, and literature achievement. *Research in the Teaching of English, 25,* 261–290.

Nystrand, M., Gamoran, A., & Heck, M. (1993). Using small groups for response to and thinking about literature. *English Journal, 83,* 14–22.

Palinscar, A. (1986). The role of dialogue in providing scaffolded instruction. *Educational Psychologist, 21*(1&2), 73–98.

Pica, T. (1987). The impact of interaction on comprehension. *TESOL Quarterly, 21*(4), 737–757.

Pica, T. (1991). Classroom interaction, negotiation, and comprehension: Redefining relationships. *System, 19*(4), 437–452.

Pica, T. (1994). The language learner's environment as a resource for linguistic input? A review of theory and research. *ITL, 105–106*, 69–116.

Platt, E., & Brooks, F. (1994). The "acquisition-rich environment" revisited. *The Modern Language Journal, 78*, 497–511.

Rosenblatt, L. (1995). *Literature as exploration.* New York: The Modern Language Association. (Original work published 1938)

Rosenblatt, T. (1994). *The reader, the text, the poem: The transactional theory of the literary work.* Southern Illinois University Press. (Original work published in 1978)

Rubin, D. (1990). Introduction: Ways of talking about talking and learning. In S. Hynds & D. Rubin (Eds.), *Perspectives on talk and learning* (pp. 1–20). Urbana, IL: National Council of Teachers of English.

Scholes, R. (1989). *Protocols of reading.* New Haven, CT: Yale University Press.

Short, K. (1992). Researching intertextuality within collaborative classroom learning environments. *Linguistics and Education, 4*, 313–333.

Smagorinsky, P., & Fly, P. (1993). The social environment of the classroom: A Vygotskian perspective on small group process. *Communication Education, 42*, 159–171.

Swain, M. (1994, October). *Three functions of output in second language learning.* Plenary presentation at Second Language Research Forum, Montréal, Canada.

Vygotsky, L. (1986). *Thought and language.* Cambridge, MA: MIT Press.

Wells, G. (1990). Talk about text: Where literacy is learned and taught. *Curriculum Inquiry, 20*, 369–405.

Wells, G. (1993). Reevaluating the IRF sequence: A proposal for the articulation of theories of activity and discourse for analysis of teaching and learning in the classroom. *Linguistics and Education, 5*, 1–37.

9

Teacher Questions as Scaffolded Assistance in an ESL Classroom

Dawn E. McCormick
Richard Donato

How teachers use questions during whole-class instruction has generated myriad discussions on the nature and role of this fundamental discursive tool for engaging learners in instructional interactions, checking comprehension, and building understandings of complex concepts (Cazden, 1988; Chaudron, 1988; Hatch, 1992; Long, 1981; Mehan, 1979; Tharp & Gallimore, 1988; Wells, 1996). Previous classroom-based studies have identified various question types, for example, closed- and open-ended questions (Barnes, 1969), display and referential questions (Long & Sato, 1983), forced-choice questions (Long, 1981), assisting and assessing questions (Tharp & Gallimore, 1988), and clarification requests (Chaudron, 1988; Gass, 1997; Pica, 1987). If, as Postman (1979) stated, "all our knowledge results from questions, . . . [and] question-asking is our most important intellectual tool" (p. 140), then continued research into this tool can potentially improve instruction.

While providing insight into the nature of questions itself, much second language (L2) research has focused on identifying question types and taxonomies (cf. Chaudron, 1988). More recently, based on input-oriented theories of second language acquisition (SLA), questions in the form of clarification requests have been investigated from the perspective of how they might promote the modification of interaction (Long, 1981) and negotiation of meaning. Thus, it is claimed that through the process of asking for clarification, greater levels of comprehensible input to learners is achieved (Gass, 1997; Pica, 1987). The question remains, however: Do these descriptions and theoretical investigations provide us with a comprehensive understanding of the functions of questions in classroom discourse?

In this chapter, we argue that a framework to study classroom questions must reflect their mediational quality; that is, their ability to assist learning. To achieve this, we explore a new perspective on the functions of teacher questions and their link to expressed instructional goals of the teacher. Our analysis reveals how one teacher's questions function in the context of classroom tasks and her expressed course goals. To this end, we conducted a sociocultural case study in which the concept of scaffolding (Wood, Bruner, & Ross, 1976) was used as a theoretical framework for investigating teacher questions. As we demonstrate, the analytical framework of this case study provided a lens through which to view teacher questions, their function as instructional tools, and their links to expressed instructional goals.

SOCIOCULTURAL THEORY

The theoretical base for this study was sociocultural theory. Three concepts of sociocultural theory in particular supported this investigation of teacher questions. First, learning occurs in highly contextualized activities that often take place during collaboration (Swain, 1995). Second, collaboration with a more knowledgeable individual during problem solving often results in cognitive development in the novice (Anton & DiCamilla, 1998; Donato, 1994; Rogoff, 1990; Rogoff & Lave, 1984; Wells, 1996, 1998). Third, speaking is the primary semiotic tool used to guide novices to perform what they cannot perform unassisted (Vygotsky, 1978; Wertsch, 1991, 1997). According to Vygotsky (1978), questions are one example of symbolic linguistic tools that semiotically mediate, assist, and scaffold mental activity during both formal and informal instructional activity. In this study, therefore, questions were viewed as one form of verbal assistance that arise in dialogue between experts and novices in the context of the language classroom.

The Concept of Scaffolding

To investigate teacher questions as mediational tools within the dialogue between the teacher and students, the concept of scaffolding was chosen. Over the past years, scaffolding has been introduced into the SLA literature by several researchers (cf. Anton & DiCamilla, 1998; Ellis, 1998; Hatch, 1992; Larsen-Freeman & Long, 1991; Oxford, 1997; Scarcella & Oxford, 1992; Slobin, 1982). In many of these discussions, particularly among L2 research studies not situated within a sociocultural framework (cf. Larsen-Freeman & Long, 1991; Oxford, 1997), the original concept of scaffolding, as operationalized by Wood et al. (1976), has been simplified and invoked to represent, in a general sense, interlocutor collaboration, graduated assistance, or cued help.

Although not entirely inaccurate, these reduced and simplified definitions of scaffolding often neglect or fail to capture the various moves and functions of discourse, including questions, as verbal assistance unfolds across time during learning interactions. Additionally, as Wells (1998) argued, scaffolding requires explicitly or implicitly acknowledging the transfer of responsibility from an expert to a novice for carrying out various parts of the task. Thus, not all forms of assistance qualify as scaffolded interactions. Finally, underlying the concept itself is the metaphor of learning as participation—one that contrasts sharply with the more common metaphor of learning as acquisition and the accumulation of knowledge in the individual (Sfard, 1998). We base our study of questions, therefore, on the flagship article of Wood et al. (1976) in which they introduce the metaphor and identify several well-defined functions and requirements of scaffolded interactions.

Scaffolding is the process by which experts assist novices to achieve a goal or solve a problem that the novice could not achieve or solve alone (Wood et al., 1976). Six functions constitute this process and are deployed dynamically as experts negotiate task definitions with novices (Wertsch, 1985), assess their level of competence, and determine what type of assistance they need to accomplish a particular part of the task:[1]

1. Recruitment (R)—Drawing the novice's attention to the task.
2. Reduction in degrees of freedom (RDF)—Simplifying or limiting the task demands.
3. Direction maintenance (DM)—Maintaining motivation and progress toward the goals of the task.

---

[1]In terms of L2 learning, *task* refers to any interaction during a class whereby students are expected to participate in speech or writing, generate a solution or answer, or derive an understanding from new material. Specifically, a task can take the form of expressing one's opinion in a group discussion about a video or text, engaging in form-focused exercises or problem-solving activity, or arriving at generalizations about the L2, target language cultural information, or the meaning of new vocabulary.

4. Marking critical features (MCF)—Calling the novice's attention to important aspects of the task.

5. Frustration control (FC)—Decreasing the novice's stress.

6. Demonstration (D)—Modeling the preferred procedures to achieve the goals. (Wood et al., 1976, p. 98)

Limitations of the metaphor of scaffolding have been identified in the literature and the debate continues concerning the usefulness of this construct (cf. Stone, 1993). For example, a persistent problem has been the lack of specification of the communicative and linguistic mechanisms that constitute the various functions of the scaffolding process. In this study, we attempt to address this limitation by examining closely one communicative mechanism during scaffolded interactions, namely the use of questions by the teacher. Specifically, we examine how one discursive feature of classroom life, teacher questions, develops class participation, learner comprehension, and comprehensibility.

Teacher Goals

To identify the scaffolding functions of questions in classroom events, the goals of the teacher cannot be overlooked. Wells (1996) contended that "classroom events are best understood as [goal-directed] actions" (p. 76). He suggested two different goal processes: (a) goals can be preestablished, a priori, and constant (i.e., no change over time) throughout instruction; and (b) unplanned and spontaneous goals may emerge and be negotiated and renegotiated during classroom tasks as a result of the coconstruction process. If instruction is understood as goal-directed actions, and teacher questions are a common part of instruction, then to understand the role of questions requires knowledge of the goals they are trying to achieve.

Woods (1996) described the conceptual structure of a course by identifying four levels of goals and units: (a) overall conceptual goals (course goals), (b) global conceptual units (skill and subskill goals), (c) intermediate conceptual units (task goals), and (d) local conceptual units. During scaffolded, teacher-fronted activities, teachers select and maintain course goals until the learner adopts the goals of the teacher or the learner pursues self-selected goals. Attention to a priori teacher goals is in keeping with Wood et al. (1976), in that the teachers must attend to the "theory of the task or problem and how it may be completed" (p. 97). A teacher's a priori instructional goals are, therefore, an integral component of the theory of the task or problem and may drive the selection of instructional tools, in this case the use of questions, needed to complete the task.

THE STUDY

Research Questions

The research questions of this study ask how an English as a second language (ESL) teacher's questions serve to scaffold learning during teacher-fronted activities and how these questions reflect the six specific functions of scaffolding already discussed. Imbedded in these research questions is the need to connect the teacher's use of questions and her expressed instructional goals as previously discussed. For the purpose of this chapter, we limit the discussion to teacher questions related to her expressed a priori course goals of ensuring student comprehension, student comprehensibility when speaking in class, and student ongoing participation in the social setting of the classroom.

Methodology

Context. The data were collected from a semester-long integrated skills ESL class in a university setting.[2] The course, offered two evenings a week for 2-hour class meetings, is designed to meet the needs of students who want to improve global English skills, but cannot attend an intensive English program or who have daytime obligations. Students must have a minimum score of 450 on the Test of English as a Foreign Language or 70 on the Michigan Test of English Proficiency. In some cases, students with scores lower than the minimum attend the class, but only with permission from the academic advisor and the instructor. The participants were the ESL teacher and the seven students enrolled in her class.

Class Materials. The text for the course was *Time: Reaching for Tomorrow* (Schinke-Llano, 1994), which is a collection of *Time* magazine articles, analogous listening texts, and activities. To supplement the text and add variety to the materials used in class, the teacher introduced materials that she created based on listening segments from National Public Radio programs and written texts from the local newspaper. In choosing

---

[2]Data and analysis for this study were taken from a larger study by McCormick (1997).

the additional material, the teacher selected topics that related to those in the commercial text, were requested by the students, and were culturally pertinent to the students' interests and experiences.

Participants. The instructor, a native English-speaking female, had earned a bachelor's degree in English/Creative Writing and a Master's degree in linguistics with a certificate in Teaching English to Speakers of Other Languages (TESOL). At the time of the study, she had taught English as a foreign language (EFL) in Africa and ESL in the United States for a total of 11.5 years. The teacher had previously taught the evening class before the semester during which the data were collected for this study. She did not share the native languages spoken by the students and only used English during the class studied.

Her seven students, the other participants in this study, spoke Chinese or Japanese. All seven ranged in age from 25 to 40 and had studied English in their home countries before coming to the United States. All seven were working at the time of the research and had less than 1 year of English study in the United States before the research began. Five were female and two were male. Each pseudonym used in this chapter was chosen by the participant.

Data Collection Techniques. A variety of data collection techniques was used in this study. The researcher audiotaped one interview with the teacher before and one interview after the period of in-class data collection. Each interview followed a semistructured interview format. The interview questions focused on the teacher's expressed goals for the course, skill and subskill goals (i.e., reading comprehension, writing, listening comprehension, speaking, grammar, pronunciation, vocabulary, and culture), and her instructional techniques for achieving these goals. In addition to interviews with the teacher, 20 of the 24 2-hour classes were videotaped. During the taping, field notes were taken to record all occurrences of teacher-fronted activities and when in the lesson they occurred, information written on the board, speakers, and occasions of specific teacher–student questioning segments and when in the lesson they occurred. After each of the 20 videotaped classes, the teacher wrote journal comments about her goals for that particular class, whether she had achieved these goals during instruction, and, if so, how, and any additional comments she chose to make. Five times over the course of videotaping, and no more than 24 hours after the actual class had occurred, the teacher and researcher viewed and discussed their reactions to a videotape of the class. Questions about the teacher's goals and how she tried to achieve them, as well as questions about why specific instructional practices were chosen, were asked. The teacher was not told that the focus of the research was teacher questions; however, she was aware of the researchers' interest in her goals because of the researchers' questions in the interviews and the guidelines for the journal comments. Each discussion was audiotaped and notes were made. The final data collection technique used was the collection of existing written documents that included information about the teacher, the students, the course, and the institute.

In sum, the data collection techniques employed in this study were interviews, verbal reports, teacher journals, videotaping, field notes, and the collection of existing information. The interviews, verbal reports, and journal comments were the sources of data on the teacher's expressed goals. The videotapes provided data of the teacher's use of questions and the field notes provided the researchers with information on the context of the teacher's questions.

The Teacher's Expressed Goals. A *course goal* was defined as a goal that spanned the semester and motivated the choice of classroom activities. The data sources for the teacher's course goals were her interviews, her journal notes, and the verbal reports. Teacher goals were noted by the researcher only if they were included in two or more of the data sources. Using multiple sources of data addressed the issue of the validity of the teacher's account of her goals and decreased the chance that the researcher would misrepresent the teacher's self-reports. Each of the three course goals discussed in this chapter—student comprehension, student comprehensibility, and student participation—was mentioned in the initial interview, the final interview, the journal notes, and the verbal reports, thus increasing the likelihood that the self-report data on goals were credible (Creswell, 1994, 1998; Silverman, 1993).

Classroom Data. After viewing the 20 videotapes, Videotapes 4, 9, 12, 16, and 20 were selected for analysis because they were accompanied by the teacher's verbal reports and they were found to be the most representative of the recurring routines for the course. They also contained an adequate number of teacher-fronted presentations for analysis. From the five videotapes, the classroom data were reduced to teacher-fronted activities, or only those "interactions controlled and directed by the teacher" (p. 182) as defined by Rulon and McCreary (1986). These segments were then displayed (i.e., transcribed) and indexed. Teacher-fronted activities, rather

than tutorial sessions or small group work, were chosen as a context bound-
ary for examining teacher questions because it has been documented that
teachers use questions frequently as an instructional tool when interacting
with the entire class (cf. Chaudron, 1988; Mehan, 1979; Mollica, 1994;
Nunan, 1991). A total of 15 teacher-fronted segments were identified.
Indexing the data included noting information about the context and content of each activity. Transcription methodology included identifying
speakers, indicating overlapping and latched utterances, briefly describing
nonverbal behavior, marking falling and rising intonation, and indicating
syllable and word stress. All 15 teacher-fronted activity segments were
transcribed for a total of 15 protocols. Questions were functionally identified in the corpus as requests for verbal or nonverbal responses following
Tharp (1993) and Ervin-Tripp (1976, 1977), and structurally identified by
rising intonation, question syntax, or occurrences of *wh-* words (Forman,
McCormick, & Donato, 1993; Wong, 1991).

After the questions were identified, they were coded for a specific scaffolding function; that is, R, RDF, DM, MCF, FC, and D. A total of 829
questions in the data were coded. The coding was verified (Miles &
Huberman, 1994) by reviewing the field notes, the teacher's journal comments, the interviews, and the teacher's verbal reports. Three passes
through the data were made to verify the coding of scaffolding functions.
An additional rater coded the questions of five randomly selected protocols (out of the 15 protocols). The researchers and rater reached 88%
agreement across all question functions within the five protocols.

During the coding of the data, questions were identified that are commonly referred to in the foreign language or second language literature as
comprehension checks (e.g., Is everything clear?) and clarification
requests (e.g., Could you explain what you said in another way?; cf. Long
& Sato, 1983). Because the comprehension checks related specifically to
the teacher's expressed goal of comprehension building and the clarification requests related to the teacher's expressed goal of comprehensibility,
they were considered subfunctions of DM and were coded DM-CC and
DM-CR, respectively.

Findings

The findings are explained in reference to each scaffolding function and
the goals for the course. In some cases, discourse segments are included
in the explanation to illustrate the scaffolding functions of the teacher's
questions as they relate to the teacher's goals.

R Questions. The teacher used questions to recruit the students' attention to classroom tasks only three times in the data. In one case, the teacher asked, "Why don't you guys give one of your questions?" to encourage students to start asking each other questions that they had written about a reading text. In the two other cases, the teacher used R questions before any other discourse to start an activity and invite student participation in the activity ("Does anybody have any questions about the papers I gave you, returned to you?"; "Are you following the main story?"). Most often the teacher used directives to recruit students into the task.

DM Questions. DM-CC questions and DM-CR questions existed across text topics, skill areas, and the semester (i.e., time). During teacher-fronted activities, the teacher was responsible for orchestrating the classroom discourse. Her comprehension check and clarification request questions monitored and facilitated the students' comprehension and comprehensibility.

All instances of comprehension checks ($n = 248$) occurred as the teacher and student worked though classroom tasks. The teacher used comprehension checks to monitor student comprehension during the activities (i.e., checking "online" comprehension). Segment A is one example of the teacher's use of DM-CC questions. In Segment A, taken from a postreading discussion, the teacher used comprehension checks (Lines A4–A8) about vocabulary introduced during teacher–student interaction. Students had read an article in their textbook called "Living Happily Near a Nuclear Trash Heap" by Dick Thompson. The article presented information from research studies on the employees of the nuclear plants mentioned in the article. (Note: In all protocol examples presented in this document, scaffolding function codes are in capital letters in parentheses):

Segment A

A1.	T:	(*7-second wait*) In other words, I guess what Sally is trying
A2.		to ask is what were some of the flaws with the studies? (DM)
A3.	SA:	Yeah.
A4.	T:	Can I say that? (DM-CC) What were some of the flaws? (DM-CC)
A5.		(*teacher looks at students, moves toward board*) Flaws? (DM-CC)
A6.		(*writes the word flaw on board—Snufkin enters class*) Singular,
A7.		flaw. Hi Snufkin. Does everybody know this word? (DM-CC)
A8.		Flaw? (DM-CC)

As we see in Lines A4, A5, A7, and A8, the teacher uses a series of DM-CC questions to ascertain whether her students understood the word *flaw*. In addition, by checking comprehension, the teacher is working to maintain student involvement in the task. Throughout the semester, the teacher used DM-CC questions to establish the students' comprehension of task demands, other–student discourse, teacher discourse, and vocabulary used in texts or during class discussions.

In addition to DM-CC questions, the teacher used DM-CR questions to increase comprehensibility by encouraging students to clarify, expand, elaborate, or reiterate some aspect of their discourse ($n = 130$). Examples of teacher DM-CR questions can be found in Segment B (also taken from the previous postreading activity).

Segment B

B1.	T:	Let's just go with the questions that we have.
B2.	SA:	I want to, I want to see the, this study's statistics, statistics,
B3.		scientific statistics, that is, is good study, like that.
B4.	T:	You mean you want to ask if the studies were scientific? (DM-CR)
B5.	SA:	Yeah, scientific, and the statistics, like that.
B6.	T:	And if the statistics were accurate? (DM-CR)
B7.	SA:	Yeah.
B8.	T:	Yeah.
B9.	SA:	I want to ask.

In Segment B, the teacher directs clarification request questions in Lines B4 and B6 to Sally's (SA) question. In this case, the teacher scaffolds the comprehensibility of Sally's questions ("you want to ask if . . . ?"; "if the statistics were accurate?"), the teacher's comprehension of Sally's questions, and it could be argued, potentially the other students' comprehension of Sally's questions.

DM-CC questions and DM-CR questions were present and robust throughout the transcripts. DM-CC questions accounted for 30% of the teacher questions coded and DM-CR questions accounted for 16% (percentages have been rounded to the nearest whole number). The frequency of DM-CC and DM-CR questions in this study attests to the teacher's efforts to realize her course goals of comprehension and comprehensibility.

As the preceding segments illustrate, DM questions were a pervasive discursive tool for building student participation, comprehension, and comprehensibility. With regard to course goals, the teacher used DM questions to invite students to participate and to express their ideas clearly in a way that was comprehensible to the group ($n = 322$). DM questions also helped the teacher work toward and achieve her goal of comprehension building during reading and listening activities. Segment C, which occurred immediately after Segment A in the same postreading discussion, contains examples of DM questions tied to comprehension and comprehensibility goals.

Segment C

C1.	T:	Anything else that was a problem with these studies? (DM)
C2.	RO:	Question is this number three?
C3.	T:	Ah-
C4.	RO:	Similar question?
C5.	T:	Yeah, that's a very similar question.
C6.	RO:	Yeah. [So-]
C7.	GE:	So I believe this, this contribution is true but is not scientific.
C8.	T:	It's not scientific, it's not accurate.
C9.	GE:	Yeah.
C10.	T:	Right, OK. Were there any other problems? (DM)

In Lines C1 and C10, the teacher asks the students to comment on problems with the research studies mentioned in the reading text. The students' responses to her questions allow the teacher to assess the students' comprehension of the text. We can see that in Line C7 Gemma (GE) provides a correct and appropriate answer that demonstrates her comprehension of the text and the teacher's question. In addition to maintaining direction toward her course goal of comprehension, the teacher's DM questions also encourage more students to participate, also a course goal. Because her questions invite a response, they provide students with an entryway to participation.

RDF Questions.   The teacher's use of RDF questions ($n = 64$) was based on her notion of the progress of the task, or usually, the lack of progress. When students could not answer a DM question, the teacher changed or modified her questions until the students could more actively participate in the discussion. The manner in which the teacher reduced the degrees of freedom of the task at hand (i.e., simplified the task demands) included asking a more specific question or a forced-choice question, changing vocabulary in the question, or focusing on a subpart of the question.

The following example is taken from a postlistening activity in which the teacher used RDF questions to help students understand a new vocabulary item encountered in a cloze activity.

Segment D

D1.	JE:	In, in- In number eight. I don't understand what is the global
D2.		explan- explanation.
D3.	T:	Mhm. OK.
D4.	JE:	Explanation.
D5.	T:	In this, in this way- Well, how is the global being used here? (RDF)
D6.		(RDF) What part of speech is it?
D7.	JE:	It's a adjective.
D8.	T:	It's an adjective. And what is it describing? (RDF)
D9.	JE:	(*very quietly*) What is it-
D10.	T:	What word is it describing? (RDF) What word is it modifying? (RDF)
D11.	JE:	Ex- explanation.
D12.	T:	Explanation. OK. And what is the meaning of global? (DM)
D13.	GW:	Worldwide.

During the review of the cloze text vocabulary, Jenni (JE) asks about the phrase "global explanation" in Lines D1 and D2. Beginning in Line D5, the teacher scaffolded the task of understanding new vocabulary, in this case "global explanation," by simplifying the task. The first subtask is for Jenni to identify the part of speech of global (Line D6), and the second subtask is to identify the word it describes (Lines D8 and D10). The teacher then returns to the original task of defining *global* in Line D12. Gwen (GW) provides the definition in Line D13 for the benefit of the class comprehension. In addition, later in the activity, Jenni indicates to the teacher her comprehension of *worldwide* as a synonym for *global* and her comprehension of the meaning of the word *worldwide*. Most often, the data revealed that RDF questions function in two ways. First, they help the teacher realize the goal of comprehension; second, they facilitate participation by making questions easier for students to answer. Jenni had an opportunity to participate in the construction of the meaning of the vocabulary item because the teacher's use of RDF questions provided her with manageable subtasks to perform. The completion of these subtasks contributed to the full solution of the task. In this way, we see how a question aimed at redefining and restructuring the problem space for the learner provides a venue for the learner to participate in the social setting of the classroom and build new knowledge.

MCF Questions.   Similar to RDF questions, MCF questions allowed the teacher to mark critical features of a task when problems arose during tasks. MCF questions (*n* = 46) called attention to text information, vocabulary, errors, and semantic and linguistic features when students were challenged by tasks or were not working toward the preferred responses and the teacher's goals. For example, in the following segment, the teacher uses an MCF question to focus the students' attention on a characteristic of a vocabulary word, *palace*, during a review of vocabulary they would encounter in a movie.

Segment E

    E1. T: Palace? (DM)

    E2. SN: Like castle.

    E3. JE: Special place, very good.

    E4. SA: Very nice.

    E5. T: Castle, special place, very nice. Who usually lives in palaces? (MCF)

    E6. SS: Kings.

    E7. T: Kings, and queens, princes and princesses.

    E8. Ss: Yeah.

    E9. GE: Maybe beautiful house?

  E10. T: Big, beautiful house, yeah, really big.

In this example, the teacher's marking of a characteristic of the word *palace* in Line E5 calls attention to a feature of the word that facilitates comprehension. Collectively, prior to the teacher's MCF question, the students demonstrated that they understand that a palace is like a castle (Line E2), or is a special, good (Line E3), and a very nice place (Line E4). After the teacher's question, they added that a palace is where kings live (Line E6). Throughout the course, the teacher used MCF questions to realize her expressed goal of comprehension. When breakdowns in language learning and communication occurred, both RDF and MCF questions acted as scaffolding repair tools.

D and FC Questions.   In contrast to other scaffolding functions of questions, D questions and FC questions were limited in the data. D questions, which occurred 12 times in the data, were used to model appropriate question forms, thus facilitating the teacher's goal of comprehensibility. For example, in Segment F, the teacher demonstrates an accurately formed question.

Segment F

  F1. JE: What means pontoons?

  F2. T: What does pontoons mean? (D) Repeat.

F3. JE: Pontoons.
F4. T: Yeah, what does, what does = (D)
F5. JE: = what does pontoons mean?

After the teacher models the accurate question form (Line F2), she tells the student to repeat the model (Line F2). When the student does not repeat the complete model, the teacher demonstrates the part of the appropriate form omitted by the student (Line F4). Modeling question forms specifically related to the teacher's course goal of improving student comprehensibility. Additionally, in this particular class, requests for direct repetition of an accurate sentence occurred rarely. Teacher recasts and follow-up questions asking for a direct repetition were not frequent feedback moves in this classroom (see Lyster, 1998, for a similar finding).

FC questions, which only occurred four times in the data, were located at times when the teacher asked if students needed help ("Do you want some help, Gemma?") or if repetition was needed for the purpose of comprehension ("Do you want the question to be repeated?"). On one occasion the teacher invited a student to participate in a class activity by asking him to comment on a topic that was in his field ("How's your computer there, Stan?").

CONCLUSION

Based on this analysis, scaffolding is a viable framework for investigating teacher questions. The concept of scaffolding originated by Wood et al. (1976), including the six scaffolding functions, demonstrates how teacher questions function as symbolic linguistic tools to achieve goals. In turn, the teacher's use of questions in this study reflects characteristics and functions of scaffolding as described by Greenfield (1984) and Wood et al. (1976). Her questions created supportive conditions for comprehension, comprehensibility, and participation of the students in the language lesson.

Specifically, in this study the teacher's questioning process expanded the students' learning during difficulties with text comprehension. For example, RDF and MCF questions assisted students during difficulties with complex classroom tasks, and DM questions maintained focus on the task and guided students through the comprehension of texts. The teacher's (expert) questions, when effectively used, enabled the students (novices) to achieve tasks they were not able to achieve alone. For example, understanding a vocabulary item occurred, in some cases, through the scaffolded assistance that the teacher's questions provided. When students struggled to express themselves, the teacher's questions served to increase the comprehensibility of their utterances by asking for clarification, expansion, and elaboration. When breakdowns occurred, MCF and RDF questions operated as repair tools. Finally, the teacher selectively chose questions to build participation. DM questions were frequently used as a means to keep discussions alive. Thus, the scaffolding functions of her questions appear to match her planned tasks and her self-reported goals for the course.

Further, when understood as semiotic tools that function in myriad ways to assist thinking, speaking, and learning (Brooks, Donato, & McGlone, 1997), the social and cognitive value of a question becomes apparent. Questions, as we have tried to show, are more than elicitation techniques. Additionally, they need to be understood as tools for shared cognitive functioning in the social context of tasks, courses, and goals (McCormick, 1997; Resnick, Levine, & Teasley, 1991) rather than restricted to the clarification and elaboration of linguistically encoded messages that are sent and received (Brooks & Donato, 1994; Brooks et al., 1997; Platt & Brooks, 1994; Reddy, 1979). Questions play a much broader role in L2 learning than has been acknowledged in previous research. They function as dynamic discursive tools to build collaboration and to scaffold comprehension and comprehensibility (Donato, 1994; McCormick, 1997; Swain, 1997) during language lessons. Rather than simply assigning a static function to a question type (e.g., display information, express new information, assess knowledge, provide a choice for an answer in a question, etc.), we have shown that a more valid understanding of a teacher's question can be achieved by anchoring them within the framework of scaffolding and in reference to a teacher's goals. This approach is consistent with sociocultural theory, which emphasizes that learning is a collaborative achievement situated in the discursive interactions that take place in communities of practice (Forman, Minick, & Stone, 1993; Haneda, 1997; Lantolf & Pavlenko, 1995; Lave & Wenger, 1991). That is, knowledge is a coconstructed process uniting social and individual processes mediated through semiotic systems, notably language. Questions are one highly productive and frequently invoked semiotic tool at the teacher's disposal for uniting these individual and social processes and for scaffolding L2 learning.

The genetic method (Vygotsky, 1978; Wertsch, 1990) of investigating the scaffolding process of teacher questions, starting outside the classroom with goals and working our way into classroom tasks, highlighted the role of teacher goals as explanations for how she used questions. One implication for teacher education, consistent with sociocultural theory, is to make teachers aware of the critical role goals play in and across all aspects of instruction—planning, presentations, and postlesson evaluation. It has long been recognized that goals can drive instruction and that accomplished teaching is dependent on the teacher's ability to be aware of, articulate, and enact her goals. Although teachers may be operating in their classroom based on unconscious and automatic goals (Leontiev, 1981), they must raise these goals to a level of conscious and controlled action to act as a reflective practitioner (Wallace, 1991). Further, by understanding one's instructional goals more clearly, a teacher's pedagogical choices become more transparent and amenable to control (Nunan & Lamb, 1996). In particular, the work with this teacher for this longitudinal case study made her more aware of her goals for instruction by articulating them. She was better able to understand her use of questions when matched with her expressed goals.

Investigating teacher questions within a scaffolding framework has provided insight into one communicative mechanism during scaffolded instruction (Stone, 1993). In this study, teacher questions scaffolded her overall course goals of participation, comprehension, and comprehensibility. Investigating question functions in this way moves beyond the literature on question types and taxonomies and enables us to better understand how questions operate as semiotic tools for achieving goal-directed instructional actions within the context of teacher–student classroom interaction.

REFERENCES

Anton, M., & DiCamilla, F. (1998). Socio-cognitive functions of L1 collaborative interaction in the L2 classroom. *The Canadian Modern Language Review, 54*, 314–342.

Barnes, D. (1969). Language in the secondary classroom. In D. Barnes, J. Britton, & H. Rosen (Eds.), *Language, the learner, and the school* (pp. 11–77). Harmondsworth, UK: Penguin.

Brooks, F. B., & Donato, R. (1994). Vygotskyan approaches to understanding foreign language learner discourse during communicative tasks. *Hispania, 77*, 262–274.

Brooks, F. B., Donato, R., & McGlone, J. V. (1997). When are they going to say "it" right? Understanding learner talk during pair-work tasks. *Foreign Language Annals, 30*, 524–541.

Cazden, C. B. (1988). *Classroom discourse: The language of teaching and learning.* Portsmouth, NH: Heineman.

Chaudron, C. (1988). *Second language classrooms: Research on teaching and learning.* New York: Cambridge University Press.

Creswell, J. W. (1994). *Research design: Qualitative and quantitative approaches.* Thousand Oaks, CA: Sage.

Creswell, J. W. (1998). *Qualitative inquiry and research design: Choosing among five traditions.* Thousand Oaks, CA: Sage.

Donato, R. (1994). Collective scaffolding in second language learning. In J. P. Lantolf & G. Appel (Eds.), *Vygotskian approaches to second language research* (pp. 33–56). Norwood, NJ: Ablex.

Ellis, R. (1998). Teaching and research: Options in grammar teaching. *TESOL Quarterly, 32,* 39–60.

Ervin-Tripp, S. (1976). Is Sybil there? The structure of some American English directives. *Language and Society, 5,* 25–66.

Ervin-Tripp, S. (1977). Wait for me, roller skate! In S. Ervin-Tripp & C. Mitchell-Kernan (Eds.), *Child discourse* (pp. 165–188). New York: Academic Press.

Forman, E. A., McCormick, D. E., & Donato, R. (1993, March). *The social and institutional context of learning mathematics: An ethnography study of classroom discourse.* Paper presented at the meeting of the Society for Research in Child Development, New Orleans, LA.

Forman, E. A., Minick, N., & Stone, C. A. (1993). *Contexts for learning: Sociocultural dynamics in children's development.* New York: Oxford University Press.

Gass, S. M. (1997). *Input, interaction and the second language learner.* Mahwah, NJ: Lawrence Erlbaum Associates.

Greenfield, P. M. (1984). Theory of the teacher in learning activities. In B. Rogoff & J. Lave (Eds.), *Everyday cognition: Its development in social context* (pp. 117–138). Cambridge, MA: Harvard University Press.

Haneda, M. (1997). Second language learning in a "community of practice:" A case study of adult Japanese learners. *Canadian Modern Language Review, 54,* 11–27.

Hatch, E. (1992). *Discourse and language education.* New York: Cambridge University Press.

Lantolf, J. P., & Pavlenko, A. (1995). Sociocultural theory and second language acquisition. *Annual Review of Applied Linguistics, 15,* 108–124.

Larsen-Freeman, D., & Long, M. H. (1991). *An introduction to second language acquisition research.* New York: Longman.

Lave, J., & Wenger, E. (1991). *Situated learning: Legitimate peripheral participation.* Cambridge, UK: Cambridge University Press.

Leontiev, A. N. (1981). The problem of activity in psychology. In J. V. Wertsch (Ed.), *The concept of activity in Soviet psychology* (pp. 37–71). Armonk, NY: M. E. Sharpe.

Long, M. H. (1981). Questions in foreigner talk discourse. *Language Learning, 31,* 135–157.

Long, M. H., & Sato, C. J. (1983). Classroom foreigner talk discourse: Forms and functions of teachers' questions. In H. W. Selinger & M. H. Long (Eds.), *Classroom-oriented research in second language acquisition* (pp. 268–285). Rowley, MA: Newbury House.

Lyster, R. (1998). Negotiation of form, recasts, and explicit correction in relation to error types and learner repair in immersion classrooms. *Language Learning, 48,* 183–218.

McCormick, D. E. (1997). *Using questions to scaffold language learning in an ESL classroom: A sociocultural case study.* Unpublished doctoral dissertation, University of Pittsburgh, Pittsburgh, PA.

Mehan, H. (1979). *Learning lessons.* Cambridge MA: Harvard University Press.

Miles, M. B., & Huberman, A. M. (1994). *Qualitative data analysis.* Thousand Oaks, CA: Sage.

Mollica, A. (1994). Planning for successful teaching: Questioning strategies. *Mosaic, 1*(4), 18–20.

Nunan, D. (1991). *Language teaching methodology: A textbook for teachers.* London: Prentice-Hall.

Nunan, D., & Lamb, C. (1996). *The self-directed teacher: Managing the learning process.* Cambridge, UK: Cambridge University Press.

Oxford, R. L. (1997). Cooperative learning, collaborative learning, and interaction: Three communicative strands in the language classroom. *The Modern Language Journal, 81*, 443–456.

Pica, T. (1987). Second language acquisition, social interaction, and the classroom. *Applied Linguistics, 8*, 3–21.

Platt, E., & Brooks, F. B. (1994). The "acquisition rich environment" revisited. *The Modern Language Journal, 78*, 497–511.

Postman, N. (1979). *Teaching as a conservative activity.* New York: Laurel Press.

Reddy, M. J. (1979). The conduit metaphor: A case of frame conflict in our language about language. In A. Ortony (Ed.), *Metaphor and thought* (pp. 284–324). Cambridge, UK: Cambridge University Press.

Resnick, L. B., Levine, J. M., & Teasley, S. D. (1991). *Perspectives on socially shared cognition.* Washington, DC: American Psychological Association.

Rogoff, B. (1990). *Apprenticeship in thinking: Cognitive development in social context.* New York: Oxford University Press.

Rogoff, B., & Lave, J. (1984) *Everyday cognition.* Cambridge, MA: Harvard University Press.

Rulon, K. A., & McCreary, J. (1986). Negotiation of context: Teacher-fronted and small group interaction. In R. Day (Ed.), *Talking to learn: Conversation in second language acquisition* (pp. 182–199). Rowley, MA: Newbury House.

Scarcella, R., & Oxford, R. L. (1992). *The tapestry of language learning.* Boston: Heinle & Heinle.

Schink-Llano, L. (1994). *Time: Reaching tomorrow.* Chicago: National Textbook Company.

Sfard, A. (1998). On two metaphors for learning and the dangers of choosing just one. *Educational Researcher, 27*(2), 4–12.

Silverman, D. (1993). *Interpreting qualitative data: Methods for analyzing talk, text, and interaction.* Thousand Oaks, CA: Sage.

Slobin, D. (1982). Universal and particular in the acquisition of language. In E. Wanner & L. Gleitman (Eds.), *Language acquisition: State of the art* (pp. 128–170). Cambridge, UK: Cambridge University Press.

Stone, C. A. (1993). What is missing in the metaphor of scaffolding? In E. A. Forman, N. Minick, & C. A. Stone (Eds.), *Contexts for learning: Sociocultural dynamics in children's development* (pp. 169–183). New York: Oxford University Press.

Swain, M. (1995). Three functions of output in second language learning. In G. Cook & B. Seidlhofer (Eds.), *Principle and practice in applied linguistics* (pp. 125–144). Oxford, UK: Oxford University Press.

Swain, M. (1997). Collaborative dialogue: Its contribution to second language learning. *Revista Canaria de Estudios Ingleses, 34*, 115–132.

Tharp, R. G. (1993). Institutional and social context of educational practice in reform. In E. A. Forman, N. Minick, & C. A. Stone (Eds.), *Contexts for learning: Sociocultural dynamics in children's development* (pp. 269–282). New York: Oxford University Press.

Tharp, R. G., & Gallimore, R. (1988). *Rousing minds to life: Teaching, learning, and schooling in social context*. New York: Cambridge University Press.

Vygotsky, L. S. (1978). *Mind in society: The development of higher psychological processes*. Cambridge, MA: Harvard University Press.

Wallace, M. J. (1991). *Training foreign language teachers: A reflective approach*. Cambridge, UK: Cambridge University Press.

Wells, G. (1996). Using the tool-kit of discourse in the activity of learning and teaching. *Mind, Culture, and Activity, 3*(2), 74–101.

Wells, G. (1998). Using L1 to master L2: A response to Anton and DiCamilla's socio-cognitive functions of L1 collaborative interaction in the L2 classroom. *The Canadian Modern Language Review, 54*, 343–353.

Wertsch, J. V. (1985). *Vygotsky and the social formation of mind*. Cambridge, MA: Harvard University Press.

Wertsch, J. V. (1990). The voice of rationality in a sociocultural approach to mind. In L. Moll (Ed.), *Vygotsky and education: Instructional implications and applications of sociohistorical psychology* (pp. 111–126). New York: Cambridge University Press.

Wertsch, J. V. (1991). *Voices of the mind: A sociocultural approach to mediated action*. Cambridge, MA: Harvard University Press.

Wertsch, J. V. (1997). *Mind as action*. New York: Oxford University Press.

Wong, E. D. (1991). Beyond the question/nonquestion alternative in classroom discourse. *Journal of Educational Psychology, 83*(1), 159–162.

Wood, D., Bruner, J. S., & Ross, G. (1976). The role of tutoring in problem solving. *Journal of Child Psychology and Psychiatry, 25*, 45–62.

Woods, D. (1996). *Teacher cognition in language teaching: Beliefs, decision-making, and classroom practice*. Cambridge, UK: Cambridge University Press.

10

Identity and Ideology: Culture and Pragmatics in Content-Based ESL

Diana Boxer
Florencia Cortés-Conde

The creation of membership in classroom discourse communities has important consequences for second language (L2) learners in formal settings. Different dialogic formats, group configurations, and task types can either encourage or prevent learners from building important relational identities (RIDs; Boxer & Cortés-Conde, 1997) that impact on their interactions, with consequences for their linguistic and pragmatic development.

We consider RID as distinct from individual and social identity. It is the bonding between interlocutors that is formed by the group and for the group. It exists only as a group identity; it does not belong to any of the individuals, but to the total group. One objective of L2 learning is to validate learners as interlocutors in a new speech community. RID can develop only when individuals perceive each other as valid interlocutors. For many learners, the first place they can receive such validation in their L2 is in the language classroom.

This study investigates the development of RID in adult and university intensive English as a second language (ESL) content-based courses. We draw on two important strands of thinking for applied linguistics: interest and research on content-based language learning (CBLL; e.g., Brinton, Snow, & Wesche, 1989; Chamot & O'Malley, 1986; Crandall, 1987; Leaver & Stryker, 1989), and interest in identity and identity development in the social sciences generally (e.g., Le Page & Tabouret-Keller, 1985; Wiley, 1994) and in applied linguistics specifically (e.g., McKay & Wong, 1996; Norton, 1997;

Peirce, 1995). Because RID exists only between interlocutors, the study of its development is particularly important in L2 classrooms. Where the focus is on content inquiry in L2, with active participation of learners in group task dialogue, we can clearly track RID to see precisely how it impacts on L2 use.

Classroom interaction at the microlevel creates group identities and these identities have the potential to facilitate language development. Literature in discourse analysis has dealt with such concepts as identity display (Goffman, 1959), performed social identity (Erickson & Schultz, 1982), realignment, and alignment (Gumperz, 1982). Hall (1995, 1998) demonstrated that teachers create and impose identities on learners, affecting their ability and motivation to learn. We expand on her research by seeking to ascertain the following:

1. In what ways do the interactional practices of students with their peers (or lack thereof) play a role in creating different types of learning communities?
2. How are valid interlocutor relationships constructed in L2 classroom discourse?

We contend that identities are generated at many different levels: teachers create and develop identities for their learners, learners create and develop identities for teachers, and learners develop and create identities for each other. Thus, there is the possibility of a community of practice (Lave & Wenger, 1991; Walters, 1996) that is not fixed, but that is important in the successful (or unsuccessful) learning of language and pragmatic rules of interaction. What can be learned in the classroom is how to develop an interactional identity that allows learners to know when to talk, what others want to talk about, and how generally to participate in conversational practices. The language classroom has the potential to become a temporary community of practice where the sociohistorical factors inscribed in language, the social identity individuals bring, and the social context in which all these variables interact (Hall, 1995) create for each type of class an identity that is beyond the sum of its parts.

BACKGROUND AND GENERAL OVERVIEW

CBLL

It is now widely believed that language learning is often most successful when accomplished through the study of content rather than focusing on language alone as the object of analysis (Brinton et al., 1989; Chamot &

O'Malley, 1986; Crandall, 1987; Leaver & Stryker, 1989). Indeed, the profession has witnessed a considerable degree of success in teaching language through the use of subject matter as the springboard for analysis of language data and forms.

In the realm of CBLL the expectation is that learners "own" their own inquiry. Thus, negotiated, interactive tasks are the norm on all levels. Where language itself is not the focus of the inquiry but some content knowledge to be discovered, discussed, and made a project of, negotiated interaction ensues. The ideal scenario is one in which small groups of students attack a project through a task approach, negotiating roles, assigning subtasks to each other, and sharing information, where such information is held by certain group members who can then impart their discoveries to the others. In such a manner, real-life information gap tasks occur. Because these tasks are not contrived by the teacher but emanate naturally out of content inquiry, students must not only stretch their linguistic abilities but use all areas of their developing communicative competence: discourse, sociocultural and strategic skills, and grammatical skills (Canale & Swain, 1980). Pragmatic competence incorporates both discourse and sociocultural competence: knowledge of rules of appropriate speech behavior (e.g., speech act usage, topics), turn taking, and such conversational phenomena as interrupting. We posit that the CBLL course that focuses on content inquiry will create dialogue on sociocultural matters, thereby having the possibility of naturally fostering pragmatic competence. We also posit that such competence is developed out of group relationships that are built among the students in language courses that take into account issues of identity and ideology in course design, thereby providing language students with possibilities for sociocultural dialogue and pragmatic development.

Identity and Language Learning

In the past several years there has been a developing interest among applied linguists in the relation of identity to L2 learning. According to McKay and Wong (1996), "learners are extremely complex social beings with a multitude of fluctuating, at times conflicting needs and desires" (p. 603). In their emphasis on agency enhancement and identity enhancement, McKay and Wong highlighted the importance of fluid and changing individual and social identities and their relation to multiple discourses (e.g., immigrant, minority, academic, gender). In this view, the learner's identity is an extremely important consideration for language learning, affecting *agency*, a concept that differs from the traditional view of motivation. Agency enhancement derives from identities that afford learners a sense of power over their environment and thereby their learning.

In a somewhat different but parallel view, Peirce (1995) and Norton (1997) highlighted the importance of investment enhancement in the discussion of identity and its relation to language learning. This perspective emphasizes the importance of social identity for successful language learning: "An investment in the target language is also an investment in a learner's own social identity, which changes across time and space" (Norton, 1997, p. 411). Peirce (1995) described *investment* as the relationship of social identity to power differences between learners and target language speakers. Thus investment has to do with access to resources that were previously unavailable to the learner. We contend that the first and foremost resource is interactional and that this availability for interaction creates opportunities for language learners to further their language acquisition.

We have proposed this new notion of RID that incorporates both investment and agency. This identity is intermediary between the individual identity and the social identity. Although RID changes across time and space, it belongs to the individual only within a specifically confined group interaction. It is not a part of an individual's fixed identity, but varies with interactions and with specific interlocutors and groups. Garrison (1999) probed the development of such identities among his ESL students. They described their perspectives on how RID develops:

> Student A: At first the people in my office we only spoke "where are you from?" and things like that. But now we can speak about our problems and make jokes.

> Student B: Over time you not only know the person better, he also know you better, in which case you feel more comfortable to talk and he feel more comfortable to listen. You may also develop a unique understanding.

> Student C: Because we understand each other more than other people. For example, I know what she doesn't want to talk about, so I avoid that to make us comfortable. What's more, I feel there is no barrier in conversation. For example, we won't feel uncomfortable to say I don't like something while the other like. (p. 15)

We see in these examples that as learners become proficient, not only in the language per se but in how to interact with particular individuals, they build a RID that is the foundation for further interactions.

RID differs from the prevailing conceptualization of social identity. We consider social identity to be based on a set of fixed attributes assigned to individuals by biological or sociopolitical circumstances that are in many cases beyond their control. RID, on the other hand, reflects a moment-to-moment possibility of shift in frames, footings, or alignments. Thus RID mediates between individual identity and social identity. It is the RID within and among groups in language classrooms that can create community. By affording the learner power over educational resources, RID has important consequences not only for identity enhancement but also for agency enhancement and investment enhancement. Through the community building that is inherent in RID, learners can become invested in their own community of learners and become active agents in the interactional practices necessary for successful L2 acquisition.

We posit a direct relation between the building of classroom community and the freedom to negotiate interaction, thus stretching the learners' linguistic and pragmatic abilities. When traditional teacher and student social roles prevail, there is decreased possibility for RID and therefore decreased possibility for negotiated interaction among peers. It is now widely agreed that negotiated interaction, between native speakers and non-native speakers and non-native speakers and non-native speakers, leads to linguistic leaps (e.g., Gass & Varonis, 1985; Long, 1983; Pica, 1988; Pica & Doughty, 1985). We posit that the same is true for pragmatic leaps. There is a need for sequential interaction (Boxer, 1993) before one can have negotiated interaction in which learners freely negotiate their linguistic and pragmatic use. Sequential interaction is based on a rapport that is built between interlocutors, leading to RID. Indeed, the security to negotiate comes through feeling membership. Thus, the notion of RID formation for language learners is an important first step in language development.

Based on these beliefs, this study seeks to explore the following issues:

1. To what extent does classroom ideology (e.g., configuration, content, and tasks) influence the amount of dialogue that goes on in L2 classrooms?

2. What is the relation between an open forum for dialogue focusing on identity and ideology and RID development?

3. What is the relation of RID to linguistic and pragmatic development in L2?

THE STUDY

Methodology

We have employed interactional sociolinguistic (microethnographic) analysis for this study. Such techniques allow for a focus on the various features of discourse, including paralinguistic phenomena such as intonation and extralinguistic phenomena such as body posture, gaze, and configuration of the setting. This type of analysis shows the moment-to-moment shifts in footings, alignments, and realignments that reveal emerging participant structures (Phillips, 1972), indicating rights and responsibilities of classroom community members to speak or be silent. An illustration of this concept has to do with setting. For example, in some of the activities the interactions remain teacher-fronted in nature despite the semicircular seating formation. It is clear in such instances that neither teacher nor students are ready to relinquish the traditional hierarchical roles. In other classes, despite seating in rows, time is spent allowing the students to present themselves. This freedom for identity display is evident in these classes regardless of whether paired work, group work, or whole-class discussion ensues.

The data for this study are ethnographic in nature and triangulated. They consist of videotaped natural classroom data from two ESL classes over two college semesters. We chose to analyze the discursive practices of these courses because they are theme-based course offerings for students at the upper levels of proficiency in all skills. This specific course focused on U.S. culture through literature and film. Having been instrumental in designing the curriculum for this course, we knew that these classes, offered as one section each semester, would provide an opportunity for analysis of task-based, dialogic language interaction. Running for 2-hour periods daily, the classes were videotaped approximately 10 times over the course of each semester, for a total of approximately 20 hours of data for each of the two semesters.

Microethnographic analysis of the videotaped classes focused on student–teacher and student–student interactions, types of tasks assigned, quantity and quality of language used, and negotiated interaction that indicated linguistic and pragmatic "stretching." Samples of some of the data were shown to the teachers and student consultants during the course of four ethnographic interviews each (one with each teacher and one with a student from each class) lasting for approximately 1.5 hours each. During the interviews, these consultants shed light on the interactional practices visible in the videotapes. Following Erickson and Schultz (1982), we asked the consultants to give us their analysis of segments of the videotaped classes of which they were part. By comparing perceptions with practices, we were able to ascertain how pedagogical theories were translated into classroom activities.

Given the research questions noted earlier, we explore here the repercussions of community identity formation for the development of sociocultural knowledge and pragmatic ability in L2 contexts. As in most adult intensive ESL programs in U.S. colleges and universities, students come from a variety of linguistic and cultural backgrounds. Heterogeneous ESL classes do not have the possibility of utilizing a shared cultural schema among the students. This constraint may affect how identity is displayed and developed at the microlevel. Nonetheless, this limitation is ameliorated by the students' experience of "being in the same boat;" that is, by the fact that they share the same sense of potential alienation. Thus, sociocultural awareness and pragmatic development in their L2 can be coconstructed by members of the group overtly sharing experiences of cultural conflict.

One important way that teachers and learners can construct a community is by displaying their individual cultural and ethnic identities. From prior observations of this course on U.S. culture during previous semesters, we knew that there was much potential for sharing of first language (L1) cultural information. This kind of discussion has the potential to create a new community based on the shared perception of a "threatening other" that is inherent in the immersion experience. The community of practice can allow for a safe haven where students build on their prior schemas their developing understanding of the new set of norms. If successful, the language classroom can become a *transitional space* in which one negotiates the meaning of the new culture vis-à-vis the old culture (Grinberg & Grinberg,1989).

As in all immersion L2 classes, the space is transitional; hence, it can provide language learners with a safe forum for acculturation where they are encouraged to act an identity that is breaking the L2 rules. This breaking of boundaries, when it is allowed to occur, is not seen as inappropriate but as a matter for dialogue. Because of the nature of immersion of ESL, the development of pragmatic and sociocultural competence occurs in two different arenas, the larger world and the classroom. The teacher is usually aware of the pitfalls that students face when leaving the classroom. The need for pragmatic competence is immediate; indeed, it is urgent.

Findings

In the first semester of data collection, there were 12 students in the class. Seven were female (one Lithuanian, two Japanese, three Korean, and one Swiss) and five were male (three Korean, one Japanese, and one

Omani). The instructor indicated that he encouraged relationship development over the semester in several ways: He organized parties at his apartment, he involved the students in extracurricular activities that had to do with U.S. culture (e.g., the group went to the theater to see a performance of *Dracula*), and he had them make a film about their experiences with U.S. culture.

These activities all had to do with exploring U.S. culture. Through carrying out the assigned group tasks, students were allowed, indeed encouraged, to explore many pragmatic issues. For example, in their excursions they needed to use invitations, greetings, and compliments, and they were encouraged to express opinions about what they saw. In participating in pot-luck dinners they practiced L2 norms for the sharing of food, inviting, greeting, complimenting, and leave-taking. In the planning of the movie there was a great deal of negotiation. The students assigned each other roles and worked earnestly on group tasks. They thus needed to make suggestions, offer requests and directives. They worked within an L2 paradigm of turn taking, interrupting, getting the floor, and holding the floor. They even dismissed the instructor, as we see in Excerpt 1.

Excerpt 1[1]

1. T: Okay, now in your groups I want you to work out the dividing the duties.
2. OM: We're doing it. Give us a chance.
3. SF: You can leave now!
4. SS: Yes, go. Leave us alone!

This mock "dismissal" in Lines 3 and 4 was no small achievement for those from many cultures that hold the teacher in a position of high social status; however, the mock nature[2] of the dismissal made it "safe."

In other data sequences from this class, we could clearly see how body posture, gaze, and interactional movements indicated involvement and RID developing between and among individual learners. For example, in another class from this course, this one focusing on the topic of world trade, six students formed a group for discussion of import and export

---

[1]T = teacher; OM = Omani male; SF = Swiss female; SS = Several students at once.

[2]The mere fact that students were able to perform the speech act in a "mock" form indicates that they had developed a certain degree of comfort in the class—in their interactions with each other and with the teacher. An RID had begun to develop; a community of practice was in place.

issues. This was one of two groups assigned to focus on this issue, with the teacher moving between groups to interact with them (see Excerpt 2).

Excerpt 2[3]

1. KM: Japan is too overprotection.
2. T: Oooh! Sounds bad! (all laugh)
3. LF: Everybody needs protection from the Americans!
4. T: Yeah, like superman!
5. KF: When we sell products we buy as much from America.
6. T: Really? So when you sell Hyundais you spend the money on Jurassic Park? So, Korea should put a tax on Jurassic Park!
7. KM: No, cause we need the movies! We all buy movies because we want to see them.

Throughout this interaction, the students exhibited a good-natured exchange. They freely expressed their own countries' frustrations regarding trade with the United States, but at the same time indicated their need for specific U.S. products. They clearly felt this classroom to be a safe arena for such expression. The teacher, rather than seriously defend the United States, made a joke out of the complaints about the trade balance situation. It was clear that a RID had developed over the course of the semester between students and teacher and among the students. They were actively engaged with each other, teased and joked with each other, and all were able to have a serious exchange on the subject while still smiling, laughing, and apparently having positive feelings about each other and the teacher. They practiced appropriate turn taking, interrupting, getting the floor, and interactional norms.

In the interview with this instructor, he asserted that group activities of this type mediated against the formation of cliques within the group; indeed, the group in its entirety became a clique. The students became very interested in each other's cultures as a backdrop for experiencing the new culture and in using the new pragmatic norms. They felt secure in sharing, contrasting, and acquiring these norms. The smooth sequential interaction (Boxer, 1993) that evolved naturally led to a great deal of negotiated interaction. What this means is that before a group can feel comfortable negotiating, which is vertical, they need to have the horizontal, which is the rapport that comes from building an RID.

---

[3]KM = Korean male; T = teacher; LF = Lithuanian female; KF = Korean female.

Negotiation and dialogue are extremely important for pragmatic and sociocultural competence as well as other levels of linguistic competence. In this class the teacher viewed himself as a facilitator: "People are there to learn and participate and it's the teacher's job to make sure they're learning something and then get out of the way." The focus on U.S. culture, to which they were all foreign, helped them generate a common goal. They shared parts of their own culture but came together as a cohesive group.

Our student consultant interviewed from this class (from Oman) corroborated how the interactional tasks in this course fostered a sense of community and RID. He indicated that he developed the ability to understand his classmates and use this understanding as a springboard for practicing linguistic forms and pragmatic norms. He stated:

> I was first uncomfortable with so many students from the Far East countries. But being in class with them changed my stereotypes I had of them. We were able to have a dialogue on many issues about our countries, the way we do things, that showed me I needed to see them and treat them differently from how I thought before. This course allowed us to think about issues in culture of many places and talk about important world problems.

In the next semester, a different instructor taught the same course. There were eight students, six male and two female. Among the male students, there were three Koreans, two Latin Americans, and one Japanese. The two female students were from Japan and Taiwan. This instructor also saw himself as facilitating community building; however, his classroom practices constituted frequent lecturing, indexing his role as purveyor of information. He did on some occasions bring students' experiences into the class discussion, but a large portion of classroom time was dedicated to teacher talk.

As in the fall course, many of the students (the six from Asian countries) came from cultures where the teacher typically conveys the knowledge. Teacher and students easily fell into traditional roles. Nevertheless, there were instances where, given the chance, the students were capable of a shift in paradigm. On the occasions when a shift occurred, pragmatic learning became possible. The common experience in this course, as in the other described earlier, was the contrast of pragmatic rules. When there was encouragement of face-to-face exchange, it became the pivotal factor in the acquisition of the norms of interaction of the L2. One example of how this was done, shown in Excerpt 3, occurred with a Japanese male student who had been reluctant to participate up to this point. The teacher encouraged him to speak up by asking him point blank to show him who he is.

Excerpt 3[4]

1. I: In Japan would you say to a teacher "sen sei?"
2. JM: Yes.
3. I: Do you want to do that here? I mean, do you have to force yourself not to do that or are you accustomed to that now and say "hey you" or "hey buddy?" (laughter)
4. JM: In Japan we have to say to the teacher "sen sei."
5. I: What happens if you don't? Do they ignore you?
6. JF: It never happens. It's so rude.
7. KM: Usually in Japan or Korea the teacher is much older than us. But here, like in ELI, the teacher about the same. In Japan and Korea it's a very different situation.
8. JM: It's basically the difference of culture, I think the class style is different, quite different.
9. TF: Teachers' social position is very high in Asia.
10. I: Really?
11. TF: (Leaning forward and with emphatic intonation) Really!!! You have to respect teachers very much.
12. I: Like a doctor or a lawyer?
13. SS: No, not that much.
14. KM: They say the teacher is like their parents
15. I: How about in Latin America?

Here the discussion continued with the contributions of two male students from Colombia and Ecuador. They took turns with each other, orienting themselves toward the Asian students. We noted that they shifted not only their bodies but even slightly moved their chairs to face their Japanese, Korean, and Taiwanese classmates. There was minimal participation of the instructor in this segment of the discussion. He set the stage and let them talk. They continued to do so until the end of class. The instructor positioned himself in that situation not as one of the interlocutors, but as hearer or audience.

---

[4]I = instructor; JM = Japanese male; JF = Japanese female; KM = Korean male; TF = Taiwanese female; SS = several students at once.

In initiating the preceding sequence about status differences in occupations, the instructor not only got the Japanese male student to interact (Line 8) but opened a dialogue in which all contributed animatedly and eventually without the instructor's overt participation. The teacher started out by doing much of the initiation–response–follow-up work typical of classroom discourse. However, the students' animated desire to share their norms resulted in their taking control of the discussion. At this point in the conversation, students saw themselves as valid interlocutors with a real need to exchange information. This became a natural conversation in which participants, including the instructor, were equal partners. On these occasions, pragmatic rules were naturally employed. For example, when the Taiwanese woman introduced herself in the discussion, offering her own perspective on status differences between teachers in Asia and the United States, the teacher engaged her further by using a normal conversational back-channel cue "really?" (Line 10). Because this showed interest, it encouraged the students to become more involved in the dialogue. As a response the Taiwanese student used the rejoinder "really!" (Line 11), building on the teacher's modeling. The teacher then engaged some of the others in his next turn by his question, "How about Latin Americans?" (Line 15). He positioned himself as a learner and thus encouraged not only active participation, but also the learning of some sociocultural information and pragmatic cues. He discussed them and at the same time modeled them. His questions were referential rather than display questions. This began as teacher-fronted negotiated interaction. Ultimately, the students ended up negotiating with each other. What was negotiated was the development of a meta-awareness of pragmatic norms—those of each other's societies. To develop a new schema, one must first become aware of one's own L1 schema. This is, for most nonexperts, below the level of consciousness.

In the next phase of this particular class, the instructor shifted the focus to U.S. terms of address. As we see in Excerpt 4 he began to explain to the students certain cultural differences by "telling them" who he is as a representative of U.S. culture.

Excerpt 4: Instructor Addressing the Two Females

1. I: Would you feel funny if someone called you "ma'am?"
2. SF: NO RESPONSE
3. I: Can you call (an older woman) Miss?
4. SF: NO RESPONSE

5. I: I mean, like in the office here, like (the receptionist), would you call her Miss plus name?

6. SS: No, just name.

This shift to discussion of norms of address terms for the host U.S. speech community elicited on the part of the students regression into a passive stance. As soon as the instructor started telling them to speak about U.S. culture, he lost them. They reverted back to a teacher-fronted hierarchical relationship that had not been the case when they were discussing each other's customs. The difference was salient in the microanalysis of body posture and gaze: The students shifted their bodies around, turning their eyes away from each other and toward the teacher. At this point, the instructor ceased to be a facilitator; indeed, he asserted himself as the purveyor of knowledge. Thus, rather than seeking to discover differences in terms of address through some task or project approach, the students were asked to absorb information conveyed in lecture format. Although the seating arrangement remained semicircular, the students oriented themselves toward the teacher rather than toward each other.

It was only when the instructor asked about their own norms and invited them to contrast and evaluate the differences in light of their L1 schemas that the students actively interacted, orienting themselves toward one another, leaning forward, and making eye contact with the others in the group as well as the instructor. Although the topic of U.S. regional terms of address seemed relevant at this transition point, the students were not yet ready to discuss them. It was the first part of the semester and many of them, although at a high level of language skills, were newly arrived. They could not yet discuss the nuances of difference between titles and first naming. They could only share their own norms and begin to contrast them. Affording the students the opportunity to tell who they are, to display their identities, gave them the opportunity to begin to build community.

The instructors in both semester courses indicated that they viewed themselves as facilitators; however, what this actually meant to each was somewhat different. In the course taught in the fall semester, the teacher allowed the students much freedom to interact with each other through well-planned tasks focusing on real inquiry (recall the project approach in which students needed to negotiate with each other). The second instructor took a more traditional role, with teacher-fronted activities and teacher talk predominating, even when discussion focused around the students' L1 cultures and pragmatic norms. The difference was in the first instructor's attitude of taking the students' cultural differences and using them as a springboard for content inquiry. Because pragmatic norms are not categorical rules, and largely below the level of consciousness for native speakers, teaching them overtly can give rise to severe problems of communication (Scollon & Scollon, 1995).

The immersion of heterogeneous groups in an L2 sociocultural context has great potential. This common immersion experience, when used appropriately, can become part of developing a communal identity that safely allows L2 learners to build a new schema of understanding. The evolution of a new identity involves incorporating new L2 norms of interaction through (a) a new awareness of their L1 norms, and (b) drawing contrasts between the two sets of norms. The very nature of immersion provides these opportunities, but they must be fully exploited to create RID development, sociocultural awareness, and linguistic and pragmatic leaps.

CONCLUSION

The ESL teacher is a bridge between the classroom community and the societies whose cultures the language represents. For ESL instructors the task is to facilitate a safe space in which cultural awareness can be mediated and discussed. Both teachers asserted that they saw their role as one of facilitator. However, what this meant for each of them was very different. Both indicated that their goal was to actively generate community among the students. However, one of the two consistently promoted interaction among students, thus promoting RID. When teachers fostered interactions and group discussions concerning cultural norms, they encouraged the emergence of a community of practice. However, when they took on the role of the information brokers, students became passive and accepted the hierarchy of traditional student–teacher exchanges. They either said what was expected of them or became silent. For the teacher to play the role of facilitator he or she must bring the culture into the classroom, at the same time not imposing the traditional hierarchical structure. It is a difficult task indeed to try to balance this authoritarian role with the need for a decentralized power structure when creating a community of practice.

Communicative teaching practices necessitate a certain threshold of interaction and dialogue. More efforts than a change of seating arrangements and attention to group tasks are required. To ignore issues of identity and ideology when researching classroom discourse and designing pedagogical approaches is to assume that space can be easily adapted to specific tasks. The view of facilitating as manipulating the classroom physical space does not take into account that it is also a psychological and ideological space.

Traditional teacher–student hierarchical roles are deeply ingrained. The power of this hierarchy is constructed relationally. We have observed many classes in which the teacher cedes the spatial position in front of the room. However, the symbolic power is still in place in the minds of the instructor and the students. If more than the space is to be relinquished, something must replace it, or both teacher and students will fall into the customary pattern of teacher-directed learning. We believe that what must occupy this vacuum is a *relational identity* actively constructed by the group. The change of room space can open the possibility to a less hierarchical communication, but it is not sufficient to change the classroom ideology. Microethnographic analysis reveals that RID development in language classrooms impacts directly on sociocultural and pragmatic competence.

Because it has the potential to question and dispel stereotypes, open dialogue is a crucial cultural concern basic to fostering pragmatic and sociocultural competence. We have seen in the preceding analysis how the ESL immersion context has the potential to foster a community of practice where the RID encourages a dialogic forum. CBLL is particularly suited to dialogue on content inquiry, if approached strategically. However, this requires that the instructor promote the status of the students to valid and equal interlocutors. Information exchanges must be based on real concerns; tasks must relate to the cultures in which the languages are spoken; students must be encouraged to enter into dialogues about their own perspectives. Group and paired work should be concerned with airing opinions, debating issues, and solving problems. In sum, for the dialogue to be worthwhile, we need to make the language classroom a safe space for expressing stereotypes, challenging them, and possibly transforming them.

The student informant from Ecuador (spring semester) indicated that he had gone out of his way to participate in a network that was not his own. First, he did this just by putting himself in the uncomfortable position of stepping into a new network. By electing a content-based course, he was asked to relate the course material to larger global issues. Confrontation with a different worldview is not created by the instructor but by the immersion context itself. Some students are willing to take such a risk and experience different norms; however, it should be the teacher's task to provide the forum for safe pragmatic exploration.

For ESL students in intensive programs, the culture is all around them. The teacher, therefore, need not be its representative. He or she is able to create a place of comfort and still encourage pragmatic awareness. This is accomplished through the creation of RIDs and a sense of community that is free flowing. In the study of pragmatics and language learning this creation of a sense of community, or, as we have termed it, RID, is paramount. The ESL students, if allowed to show who they are, will use this license to build community.

REFERENCES

Boxer, D. (1993). Complaints as positive strategies: What the learner needs to know. *TESOL Quarterly, 27*, 277–299.

Boxer, D., & Cortés-Conde, F. (1997). From bonding to biting: Conversational joking and identity display. *Journal of Pragmatics, 27*, 275–294.

Brinton, D., Snow, M., & Wesche, M. (1989). *Content-based second language instruction.* New York: HarperCollins.

Canale, M., & Swain, M. (1980). Theoretical bases of communicative approaches to second language teaching and testing. *Applied Linguistics, 1*, 1–47.

Chamot, A., & O'Malley, M. (1986). *A cognitive language learning approach: An ESL content-based curriculum.* Wheaton, MD: National Clearinghouse for Bilingual Education.

Crandall, J. (1987). *ESL through content-area instruction: Mathematics, science, social science.* Englewood Cliffs, NJ: Prentice-Hall.

Erickson, F., & Schultz, J. (1982). *The counselor as gatekeeper.* New York: Academic Press.

Garrison, D. (1999). *Relational identity and second language users.* Unpublished master's thesis, University of Florida.

Gass, S., & Varonis, E. (1985). Task variation and non-native/non-native negotiation of meaning. In S. Gass & C. Madden (Eds.), *Input in second language acquisition* (pp. 149–161). Rowley, MA: Newbury House.

Goffman, E. (1959). *The presentation of self in everyday life.* New York: Doubleday.

Grinberg, L., & Grinberg, R. (1989). *Psychoanalytic perspectives on migration and exile.* New Haven, CT: Yale University Press.

Gumperz, J. (1982). *Discourse strategies.* Cambridge, UK: Cambridge University Press.

Hall, J. K. (1995). (Re)creating our worlds with words: A sociohistorical perspective of face-to-face interaction. *Applied Linguistics, 16*, 206–232.

Hall, J. K. (1998). Differential teacher attention to student: The construction of different opportunities for learning in the IRF. *Linguistics and Education, 9*, 287–311.

Lave, J., & Wenger, E. (1991). *Situated learning: Legitimate peripheral participation.* Cambridge, UK: Cambridge University Press.

Leaver, B., & Stryker, S. (1989). Content-based instruction for foreign language classrooms. *Foreign Language Annals, 23*, 269–275.

Le Page, R. B., & Tabouret-Keller, A. (1985). *Acts of identity.* Cambridge, UK: Cambridge University Press.

Long, M. (1983). Linguistic and conversational adjustments to non-native speakers. *Studies in Second Language Acquisition, 5*, 177–193.

McKay, S. L., & Wong, S. D. (1996). Multiple discourses, multiple identities: Investment and agency in second language learning among Chinese adolescent immigrant students. *Harvard Education Review, 3*, 577–608.

Norton, B. (1997). Language, identity, and the ownership of English. *TESOL Quarterly, 31*, 409–429.

Peirce, B. N. (1995). Social identity, investment, and language learning. *TESOL Quarterly, 29*, 9–31.

Phillips, S. U. (1972). Participant structures and communicative competence: Warm Springs children in community and classroom. In C. Cazden, D. Hymes, & V. John (Eds.), *Functions of language in the classroom* (pp. 370–394). New York: Teachers College Press.

Pica, T. (1988). Interlanguage adjustments as an outcome of NS/NNS negotiated interactions. *Language Learning, 38*, 45–73.

Pica, T., & Doughty, C. (1985). The role of group work in classroom second language acquisition. *Studies in Second Language Acquisition, 7*, 233–248.

Scollon, R., & Scollon, S. W. (1995). *Intercultural communication.* Oxford, UK: Blackwell.

Walters, K. (1996). Gender, identity and the political economy of language: Anglophone wives in Tunisia. *Language in Society, 25*, 515–555.

Wiley, N. (1994). *The semiotic self.* Chicago: University of Chicago Press.

11

Mr. Wonder-ful: Portrait of a Dialogic Teacher

Lorrie Stoops Verplaetse

The role of classroom interaction has taken on increased importance in studies addressing both the linguistic development and academic development of students, especially linguistic minority students. This chapter describes the interaction pattern of one highly dialogic middle school science teacher in the United States. The teacher was one of three teachers I observed as part of a larger study looking at teacher input and interaction opportunities for mainstreamed limited English-proficient (LEP) students. All three teachers had been selected for the earlier study because of their reputations for being highly interactive, but this teacher's classes appeared to be exceptionally interactive. The students seemed actively engaged and curious, the teacher's questions seemed to be of high cognitive quality, and the topics appeared to be academically rigorous. I decided to look more closely (quantitatively and qualitatively) at the specific strategies used by this teacher to create what I thought to be exceptionally high-quality class involvement.

I have written about this instructor before, but from a different perspective (Verplaetse, 1995, 1998). At that time, I pointed out that native-speaking teachers unwittingly modify their input in ways that prohibit interaction opportunities for linguistic minority students. Although this teacher did, indeed, unwittingly modify his talk in some prohibitive ways for his linguistic minority students, his standard or norm for interaction appeared to be so much higher than was typical, that even with the prohibitive modifications, the linguistic minority students were participating at exceptional levels of frequency and cognition.

I present this analysis of this teacher's talk as a model for teacher training use for those who wish to improve interaction strategies in the classroom. By identifying the interactive strategies that this teacher employs, it is my intention to describe strategies that would be exemplary to be used with all students, but particularly with linguistic minority students.

THE IMPORTANCE OF INTERACTION: A REVIEW OF THE LITERATURE

To determine the importance of interaction for linguistic minority students in content classrooms, we must look to two bodies of literature: the role of interaction in student development and the role of interaction in second language (L2) development. The literature speaks to the importance of interaction for student development in the following four ways. First, through classroom interaction, a student simultaneously develops socially, communicatively, and academically. Green and Harker (1982) described the school curriculum as "tripartite in nature," and "composed of academic, social, and communicative needs" (p. 183). As Mehan (1978) pointed out, the social and communicative skills needed to gain access to the content are acquired simultaneously during the learning of the academic content. Second, although no claim is being made regarding the effect of interaction on academic achievement, interaction does allow the student the opportunity to share in the coconstruction of knowledge (Wertsch & Toma, 1990). Consequently, if a student is to partake in the coconstruction of the content knowledge, the student must partake in the classroom interaction. Third, interaction determines the level of comembership a student is to experience within the group (Zuengler, 1993). Consequently, limited interaction opportunities could lead to a student's marginalized social role within the classroom community. Fourth, interaction provides the learner with the repeated practice needed to develop communicative competency in higher level academic communicative skills (Hall, 1993; O'Connor & Michaels, 1993). As an example, Rosebery, Warren, and Conant (1992) found Haitian middle school students appropriating scientific discourse patterns through the ongoing interactive classroom practice called *collaborative inquiry*. This fourth point concerning higher level academic communication skills brings us to the second body of literature, that of the role of interaction in L2 development.

Second language acquisition literature discusses interaction in two ways: first, as a source of learner output, and second, as that point in the discourse where negotiated repair work takes place. As a source of output, interaction, according to Swain (1985), allows the learner to practice the target language, thus enhancing fluency; to notice or trigger a particular structural form that needs modifying; to test hypotheses about structural points; and to reflect metalinguistically. Similar to Swain's first function of output, Brown (1991) and McLaughlin (1987) pointed out that interaction provides the opportunity for the non-native speaker (NNS) to practice structural components, increasing the likelihood of automaticity of such components. In brief, interaction means practice opportunities, and practice leads to fluency.

From the perspective of interaction as negotiated repair work, interaction is credited with providing NNSs the opportunity to negotiate meaning. This negotiation provides the learner with increased chances for comprehension of the target language input (Gass & Varonis, 1985; Pica, 1994; Pica, Doughty, & Young, 1986).

Many studies have outlined the importance of interaction on L2 development, but most have not shown empirically a direct causal relation. Recent studies have attempted to draw closer and clearer connections between interaction and specific points of L2 development. In particular, Donato (1994), Ohta (1997), and Swain (1995) analyzed the collaborative dialogues of L2 students and found that through collaborative mediation the students accurately coconstructed a structural form of the target language. In all three cases, later production evidence indicated that the students had learned the new target structures. It should be noted that in each of these three studies, although the communicative task may not have been on the topic of linguistic structure, the negotiation itself was focused metalinguistic talk about language structure.

Several other studies in which the participants interact about topics other than a focus on linguistic form also provide empirical evidence of a causal connection between interaction and L2 development. Gass and Varonis (1994) showed that negotiated repair work in a dyad description task resulted in the learner's new usage of descriptive expressions after a brief delayed period of time. Interestingly, during the original interaction, the new expressions were spoken by the other interlocutor, not the language learner; that is, through the interaction the language learner appropriated the new expressions and used them in later production activities. Snow's (1990) study of elementary schoolchildren (native English speaking and NNS) giving formal definitions in English and in French as an L2 analyzed the importance of two factors in the resultant quality of the definitions. The two factors were the knowledge of the definition genre and its appropriate form and the opportunity to practice giving definitions.

Snow found that the academic communicative task of giving definitions in an L2 required practice over time, and through such practice, the skill improved. Snow claimed that both the opportunity to hear relevant models and to practice producing definitions were beneficial. Finally, Ballenger's (1997) analysis of middle school bilingual Haitian–English classroom talk reveals that students who are unfamiliar with the language and vocabulary of English science talk eventually can modify their talk and begin to appropriate the new discourse of academic science English. They accomplish this through the initial use of their own first language (L1) home pragmatic practices, which are mediated by clarification questions coming from the teacher and other students.

In this chapter, the term *interaction* means the opportunity to produce output, thus to practice extended discourse. Such opportunities may include negotiation, but negotiation can occur at the microlevel, such as in the previously mentioned studies, or it can occur at a macrolevel, as students and teacher collaboratively work through extended discourse to make sense of an idea. Through such interaction, students have the opportunity to practice extended talk and to move toward fluency. The teacher described in this study uses interaction expertly. In so doing, he provides students the opportunities to produce extended output and to negotiate meaning through repair work. As the literature suggests, through interaction his students may develop their social roles in the group, advance their knowledge of science, develop their skills in academic science talk, and in the case of the LEP students, develop their L2 linguistic competency.

THE STUDY

Research Questions and Methodology

The research question for this study is this: What particular discourse strategies does this teacher use to create such an interactive classroom during full-class, teacher-fronted discussions? To answer this question, I first conducted a quantitative analysis of this teacher's initiation and feedback moves, used in full-class discussions. Specifically, I conducted a frequency count of the following acts:

1. Number of teacher elicitations in the initiation move and in three scaffolding moves.
2. Number of high cognitive level elicitations in the initiation and scaffolding moves.

3. Number of open-ended elicitations in the initiation and scaffolding moves.

4. Number and distribution of feedback acts.

To establish a context for the frequency count, I conducted a similar count for the two other teachers in Verplaetse (1995) and used those counts for the purpose of comparison. As mentioned earlier, all three teachers had been recommended for the earlier study because of their interactive teaching styles, yet this particular teacher's full-class discussions had appeared, through personal observation, to be exceptionally interactive. If, through the comparison, a quantitative difference is found in this one teacher's discourse strategies, then it is safe to suggest that his identified distinctive strategies may be contributing to the high level of class engagement. Following the quantitative analysis, I conducted a qualitative analysis of selected text taken from this teacher's full-class discussions to provide additional insight.

The data for the description of this one highly interactive middle school science teacher, collected during the aforementioned earlier study, consist of 5 hours of transcribed classroom discussions, 6 additional hours of classroom observations, and three interviews with this teacher—two during the data collection and one after preliminary data analysis. Additional data used for the quantitative comparison come from the same earlier study and consist of 4 hours of transcribed classroom discussions for each of the two other teachers. Observations and videotapings were conducted during the middle of the school year (November and December). Class days for videotaping were selected based on scheduling availability for the researcher and the teacher, coupled with the intent to capture primarily class days when full-class discussions were planned. A brief description of each of the three teachers' classes is found in Table 11.1.

TABLE 11.1
Description of the Three Teachers and Their Classes

Teacher	Grade/ Class	Total No. Students	No. LEP Students	LEP's Native Languages	Class Hours Taped
A[a]	7/Biological Science	25	4	Russian	3
	8/Physical Science	21	4	Russian	2
B	10–12/Integrated Science	17	3	Vietnamese, Cambodian	4
C	7,8/Biological Science	21	3	Haitian	4

[a]Teacher A = Mr. Wonder-ful.

A full explanation for the coding of the utterances can be found in Verplaetse (1995). But a brief explanation is warranted at this time to account for the various types of scaffolding moves discussed in this chapter. The tapes of the class discussions are coded in a modified version of the Sinclair and Coulthard (1975) system designed for English-speaking classrooms (see Table 11.2). Teacher utterances are coded for move type and act type. Modifications were made to the Sinclair and Coulthard system to accommodate coding for entire teacher–student transactions rather than single three-part exchanges and to design a way to identify various teacher scaffolding strategies.

Teacher utterances are coded for one of four move types: the initiation move, the response move, the feedback move, and a scaffold/initiation move. Unlike Sinclair and Coulthard's system, this study identifies two initiation moves: the initiation move and the scaffold/initiation move. Both initiate teacher–student exchanges. However, the initiation move initiates an entire teacher–student transaction rather than a single interactional

TABLE 11.2
Coding for Moves and Acts

Move	Act
Initiation	Elicitation
	Check
	Directive
Scaffold/initiation	Elicitation
	Check
	Directive
Response	Reply (answers, accepts, clues, comments)
	Prompt
	Elicitation
	Check
	Directive
Feedback	Accept (repetition, paraphrasing, backchannels)
	Evaluate (explicit or exaggerated tonal)
	Comment (answer, clue, rhetorical and tag questions, expand, inform)
	Prompt
	Elicitation
	Check
	Directive
	Cue

Note. Types of scaffolding elicitations: feedback = to reformulate a student answer that is either incorrect or insufficient; response = to reverse direction of inquiry by responding to a student question with a question; scaffold/initiation = to further challenge a student after a successfully completed exchange.

exchange. The scaffold/initiation move initiates additional, challenging, contiguous exchanges within the same teacher–student transaction at a point where the exchange could have satisfactorily ended. This scaffold/initiation move identifies one of three scaffolding options.

This study identifies three distinct scaffolding events, recognizing that the types of teacher questioning may differ depending on the purpose of the scaffold. As just described, the first type, the scaffold/initiation move, further challenges a student at the point of a successful completion of an exchange. The other two scaffolding events are coded as elicitations in both the response move and the feedback move. The feedback elicitation scaffolds by offering a question to a student answer that was either incorrect or insufficient. The purpose of this second scaffolding event is to redirect or reformulate the student's thinking. The third scaffolding event, the response elicitation, reverses the direction of inquiry by responding to a student question with another question. The three scaffolding types are listed at the bottom of Table 11.2.

As previously mentioned, in addition to coding each teacher utterance as a move type, the utterances are also coded for act type. To answer the specific research question, this chapter focuses on the teacher's use of the elicitation act in all four moves and on the distribution of acts found in the feedback move.

Findings

This interactive teacher's full-class discussions consisted of two distinct participant structures; that is, through the use of conventional discourse configurations such as pace, pitch, verbal routines, and verbal patterns, this teacher marked two distinctive speech events within his full-class discussions (Erickson & Shultz, 1981). The first of these participant structures can be called the *inquiry phase*. During this discussion phase, the teacher engaged students through the use of questions. Students discussed the raised question by speculating, wondering, hypothesizing, and attempting explanations. Students' hands were always in the air during this phase. The inquiry phase occurred frequently. It preceded the introduction of new information and occurred after content information had been presented to students in the form of a minilecture or by students accessing resources (texts, films) for information. Additionally, it occurred before and after small group labwork was conducted.

The second full-class participant structure can be called *rapid-fire review*. This teacher-fronted phase was employed during the review of homework problems. Students bid for turns; additionally, the teacher drafted nonvolunteering students to take turns. After being identified to participate, this student gave an answer to a homework problem (either orally or by going up to the board). The teacher then followed up with a rapid evaluation act, indicating the accuracy or inaccuracy of the answer and quickly designating another student to give a new answer to the same problem if the previous answer had been incorrect or to move to the next problem.

A third participant structure was regularly used in this teacher's classroom, *small group labwork*. During this time students worked in teams and the teacher walked about the room interacting with the teams. Given that the research question for this study focuses on full-class discussions, this particular participant structure is not investigated in this chapter.

To begin the findings of the quantitative analysis, Tables 11.3 and 11.4 indicate the nature of this teacher's use of elicitation. In this section of the analysis, our dialogic teacher is labeled Teacher A.

Turning to Table 11.3, the first interesting point to notice is that Teacher A talked less than Teachers B and C. Teacher A issued almost half as many spoken acts as the other two teachers did, as indicated in column 3. Columns 4 and 5 of Table 11.3 refer to the total number of elicitations issued by the teacher, but because we are concerned only with full-class, teacher-fronted discussions, we attend to the last two columns to determine the number of teacher-fronted elicitations and the cognitive nature of those elicitations. From column 6 we see that it is not necessarily the number of elicitations that creates the high level of engagement in the classroom, for Teacher A issued more than Teacher C but less than Teacher B. Note, however, the ratio of high to low cognitive level questions as indicated in column 7. Here we see that 50% of all questions issued by Teacher

TABLE 11.3
Number and Cognitive Levels of Teacher Elicitations
in All Taped Classes and in Teacher-Fronted Classes Only

Teacher	Class Hours Taped	Total Acts	Total Elicitations	Cognitive Levels of Total Elicitations High:Low	Elicitations in Teacher-Fronted Classes Only	Cognitive Levels in Teacher-Fronted Classes High:Low
A	5	676	164	79 : 85	127	62 : 65
B	4	1,046	224	28 : 196	162	16 : 146
C	4	1,105	130	53 : 77	46	30 : 16

A in full-class, teacher-fronted discussions were of a high cognitive level. Still, this does not yet distinguish Teacher A, for we see that Teacher C used high cognitive questions more frequently.

The distinction becomes clearer as we turn to Table 11.4, which breaks down the teacher-fronted elicitations into initiation elicitations, scaffolding elicitations, and the three categories for the three scaffolding moves.

From Table 11.4, columns 2 and 3, we can determine that the high level of engaged curiosity exhibited in Teacher A's classes is not due to the number of initiation elicitations, for there is little difference between Teacher A or Teacher C both in the number of questions and in the cognitive level of questions. Notice, however, in columns 4 and 5 the difference in the use of scaffolding elicitations. Teacher A used strikingly more elicitations in the scaffolding moves: 77 as compared to 45 for Teacher B and 5 for Teacher C. More important, notice the ratio of high to low cognitive level questions in this environment; fully 50% of Teacher A's scaffolding elicitations are of high cognitive levels.

A final look at columns 6, 7, and 8 reveals that Teacher A's relative use of high cognitive level scaffolding questions is used appropriately most frequently in the scaffold/initiation moves (column 8). Recall that these moves occur after a teacher–student exchange that has been satisfactorily completed; that is, the student has responded to an elicitation in a way that has accurately satisfied or answered the elicitation, but the teacher chooses to expand the interaction with the student, further challenging the student for additional information. Note also, as indicated in column 6, that Teacher A elected to use high cognitive questions during the feedback move, those times when the student answered incorrectly and the teacher

TABLE 11.4
Number and Cognitive Levels of Elicitations
in Teacher-Fronted, Full-Class Discussions

	Elicitations				Three Types of Scaffolding		
Teacher	Total Number, Initiation Move Only	Cognitive Levels, in Initiation Only High:Low	Total Number, in Scaffold Moves	Cognitive Levels, in Scaffold Moves High:Low	High:Low in Feedback Move	High:Low in Response Move	High:Low in Scaffold/ Initiation Move
A	50	23 : 27	77	39 : 38	17 : 24	2 : 0	20 : 14
B	117	11 : 106	45	5 : 40	3 : 29	0 : 0	2 : 11
C	41	28 : 13	5	2 : 3	0 : 1	0 : 0	2 : 2

was attempting to guide the student toward the correct answer. Examples of this type of correction elicitation include "So, are you questioning how accurate that is?," and "Show me a sperm and an egg meeting and how I can get two Ys."

Considering the use of open-ended questions versus closed questions, given what we have discovered about Teacher A's use of high cognitive level elicitations, it is not surprising to find a similar pattern of open-ended question use.

Table 11.5 indicates that Teacher A does not distinguish himself in the overall use of elicitations in teacher-fronted talk (columns 2, 3, & 4). Rather, the striking difference appears in the scaffolding moves shown in column 5. It is in the scaffolding move that both the frequency of open-ended questions and the proportionate use of open-ended questions is strikingly greater for Teacher A than for the other two teachers.

The quantitative findings regarding the nature of the feedback move also inform this study. Table 11.6 shows the breakdown of feedback act types for Teacher A, again in comparison to Teachers B and C. Because the final three act types at the bottom of the table (evaluation, prompt, and cue) comprised approximately only 4% of all feedback acts for each of the three teachers with no interesting distribution differences, I disregard them at this point. However, an interesting distribution differentiation can be found in the first five act types. I have divided these five act types into two groups: those that express listening without evaluation and those that guide error correction. The listening acts consist of comprehension checks and acceptance acts, to include repetitions, paraphrases, and backchannels (as summarized in Table 11.2). The error correction acts consist of elicitations, directives, and comments, to include answers to questions, clues, rhetorical or tag questions, and paraphrases expanded with new information. Teacher A used the listening acts in the feedback moves considerably

TABLE 11.5
Ratio of Open to Closed Elicitations

Teacher	Total Elicitations Open : Closed	Elicitations in Teacher-Fronted Open : Closed	Initiation Elicitations in Teacher-Fronted Open : Closed	Scaffold Elicitations in Teacher-Fronted Open : Closed
A	99 : 65	70 : 57	28 : 22	42 : 35
B	80 : 144	58 : 104	42 : 75	16 : 29
C	73 : 57	27 : 19	25 : 16	2 : 3

TABLE 11.6
Distribution of Feedback Acts

Acts in Feedback Move	Teacher A	Teacher B	Teacher C
Total feedback acts	470	678	452
Acceptance	175 (37%)	154 (22.7%)	59 (13%)
Check	21 (4.4%)	9 (1.3%)	8 (1.7%)
Subtotal: Listening without evaluation acts	41.4%	24%	14.7%
Comment	182 (39%)	380 (56%)	283 (62.6%)
Elicitation	55 (12%)	55 (8%)	26 (5.7%)
Directive	12 (2.5%)	52 (7.6%)	59 (13%)
Subtotal: Guiding error correction acts	53.5%	71.6%	81.3%
Evaluation	11 (2%)	21 (3%)	14 (3%)
Prompt	8 (1.7%)	6 (1%)	3 (0.6%)
Cue	6 (1%)	1 (0.1%)	0 (0%)
Subtotal: Other	4.7%	4.1%	3.6%

more often that the other two teachers, particularly in relation to the use of the error correction acts. Nearly 42% of Teacher A's feedback moves were acts indicating listening without evaluation, whereas Teacher B used this act type 24 % of the time and Teacher C used it 15%. It is fair to say that in the feedback move, Teacher A issued a listening act (42%) almost as often as he issued a corrective act (53%), unlike Teachers B and C, who issued considerably more corrective acts (72% and 81%, respectively) than listening acts. This proportionately high use of listening acts will be illustrated in detail as we analyze a piece of Teacher A's class discussion in the next section.

Quantitatively we have seen that Teacher A used more elicitations and higher cognitive level elicitations in two scaffolding moves, those that work to repair faulty student answers and particularly those that challenge or expand already satisfactory student answers. We have also seen a corresponding increased use of openended questions. Finally we have seen that Teacher A issued almost as many listening acts as corrective acts in his feedback moves. As compared to the other teachers, he used fewer corrective acts and more listening acts. However, the real picture of this teacher's interactive style is revealed when we see the context in which his questions and responses are issued. For this we need to take a look at one of his class discussions.

Consider the following text, which comes from a seventh-grade class on life sciences. The class was studying chromosomes, cell division, and reproduction. They had already been introduced to the processes of mitosis, meiosis, and fertilization resulting in a zygote. After considerable discussion in an inquiry phase, they had finally reached a level of agreement on these three processes. Now Teacher A wanted to introduce them to the concept of the female X and the male Y chromosomes. He wanted to point out further that the chromosome of the sperm (be it an X or Y chromosome) determines the sex of a zygote. The conversation consisted of 114 turns in 17 minutes of talk. Portions of that conversation follow.

Text 1[1]

   1. T: OK. If everybody understands this perfectly well, somebody from the other class brought up a question.

   2. Ss: Who?

   3. T: I don't remember but we talked about it for a long time. And that is, what determines whether your zygote is going to turn into a male or a female?

   4. Ss: {---------}

   5. T: Let's assume that it's controlled genetically somehow, so you can't use divine intervention.

   6. N: {Well, I sorta-------}

   7. T: Louder.

   8. N: {There's like a --------}

   9. T: Louder!

10. N: Ok. The woman has um, the egg is - a boy, at first, but then—the sperm—there's like a Y if it's a girl and X if it's a boy—and if you have a Y and X, it's a girl . . .

11. T: OK, hold on. (begins drawing on the board what Nancy is explaining) Y and X. What is this Y and X stuff?

12. N: Um if the egg is an X then that's a boy, then the Y is the sperm. Well, the sperm can be either a Y or an X. If it's an X and a Y, then that's a girl, but if it's two Xs, then it's a boy.

---

[1]The following transcription symbols are used in this and subsequent texts.

( )	Author's explanatory notes
{-----text---}	Unintelligible or partially intelligible utterances
text= =text	Latching; one speaker immediately speaks after another with no pause to indicate that first speaker had intentionally ended his or her turn.

13. T: OK. So egg has to be an X. Sperm can be an X or a Y, and Y equals a girl? (still illustrating on the board)

14. N: Yeah {-------}

15. T: OK. So, somehow these things combine=

16. S: =should we write this down?

17. T: Nope. And you can get a zygote that's an X and an X. Or you can get a zygote that's an X and a Y.

18. N: No, so if it's an X and a X then it's a boy, but if it's an X and a Y then it's a girl=

19. J: =if it's an X and a X, it's uh

20. T: This would be a boy (pointing to Nancy's claims, as he has written them on the board) and this would be a girl. Now, this is, don't write this. This is just a hypothesis. But that makes sense.

21. S: What if you have twins?

(Turns 22–32: Continued talk about X and Y chromosomes with two students and full class)

33. T: . . . Now, you guys seem to be talking about X and Y. And people seem to be talking about X and Y like they're these old friends, like you understand exactly what they are. Can somebody let me in on this? (Hands raise) Are we just choosing X and Y randomly?

34. Ss: Yes, Yeah, . . .

35. T: Could, why don't we choose G and B? (hands are raised) Liana.

36. L: Well, X and Y are in math. . .

37. T: X and Y are in math.

38. L: It's on a calculator?

39. T: Yeah?

40. L: And it has X and Y on it, and {---ee} use.

41. T: So we can=

42. L: =it's like people use a lot of it for examples, because they use it in math.

43. T: OK. So they're commonly used as variables, as unknowns. So that's why we're just using X and Y? Is that why you were, you guys were using X and Y? (Smiling)

(Turns 44–111: Continued conversation about X and Y chromosomes with eight particular students and full class. Teacher is now explaining homework assignment, to look up "sex chromosomes" in the book, read about it, and draw a picture, explaining what they have been talking about.)

112. T: . . . You're going to draw a picture explaining how you get boys and girls. Now we know that it has something to do with fertilization. We know that it has something to do with X and Y chromosomes.

113. L: Do you know?

114. T: (looking at Liana for a moment) No, uhm, yes I know. I want you to figure it out.

At the beginning of this interactional unit, Teacher A brought up the topic question by reporting what another student had wondered about. The teacher said in Turn 1, "Somebody from the other class brought up a question." In response to "Who?" he continued, "I don't remember but we talked about it for a long time. And that is, what determines whether your zygote is going to turn into a male or a female?" The teacher was not asking the question; rather he was reporting the wonderings of another student. It was as if he had become the voice of a student.

Another example of this wondering type of questioning can be found in the teacher's turn, Line 33. "Now you guys seem to be talking about X and Y. And people seem to be talking about X and Y like they're these old friends, like you understand exactly what they are. Can somebody let me in on this? Are we just choosing X and Y randomly?" In the first of the two questions he spoke as if he did not understand. Then in the second question, he spoke collectively through the use of plural *we*. Again, the teacher spoke as if he had become one of the students.

The teacher's wondering out loud was apparently so unusual for the students, as compared to their other teachers' talk, that twice during my observations, I found students responding by explicitly asking the teacher, "Don't you know?" We see an example of this at the end of Text 1, in Turns 113 and 114, where Liana asked, "Do you know?" and the teacher responded after a pause, "No, uhm, yes I know, I want you to figure it out."

So, the manner in which Teacher A modeled possible student questions or possible scientist questions is one of two salient strategies that mark his classroom as highly interactive. However, after observing this teacher, I am convinced that the students interacted as much as they did not only because of the nature of his elicitations, but possibly more important, because of the nature of his followup acts—those feedback moves to students' answers to these questions.

The strategy most striking to me was Teacher A's use of the acceptance act in response to student comments, particularly in the inquiry phase of discussions. The teacher repeated or paraphrased the student's answer, whether that answer was correct or incorrect. When incorrect, he frequently neither corrected the response nor indicated that the response was incorrect. Rather, he accepted the student response—by paraphrasing that response or signaling in some other way that he had heard the response.

Consider his talk beginning in Turn 13 of Text 1. In the previous turn, Nancy, the student, had given a partially incorrect and somewhat confusing answer. The teacher accepted with an "OK," then paraphrased two correct portions of Nancy's answer with "So egg has to be an X, sperm can be an X or a Y." He then scaffolded with a corrective elicitation, targeting an incorrect part of her answer, "And Y equals a girl?" Nancy again answered incorrectly, "Yeah." The teacher accepted this in Turn 15 with "OK," then issued three paraphrases in which he tried to focus on and bring clarity to the accurate portions of Nancy's answer, "So, somehow these things combine," and in Turn 17, "And you can get a zygote that's an X and an X, or you can get a zygote that's an X and a Y." For a third time in Turn 18, Nancy repeated her incorrect assertion, reversing the sex assignment, "No, so if it's an X and a X then it's a boy, but if it's an X and Y then it's a girl." In Turn 20, Teacher A simply accepted Nancy's answer through paraphrasing, "This would be a boy (pointing to Nancy's diagram) and this would be a girl." But then, given that the answer was still incorrect, he told the class, "Don't write this. This is just a hypothesis." In no way had he signaled to Nancy that her answer was wrong; in fact, he had brought dignity to her speculations even though incorrect, by defining the act scientifically, calling it a *hypothesis*. Finally he said, "But that makes sense," thus issuing one of the few evaluative acts found in his texts. The few times that he did issue an evaluation, the act judged the thought process, not the truth value of the answer.

Lines 35 to 43 of Text 1 illustrate the power of the teacher's acceptance act, when the student's response has been not inaccurate, but merely insufficient. In this excerpt we see how the student modified and expanded her own answer in reaction to the teacher's acceptance acts. Liana expressed a thought in Line 36 that was at first insufficiently detailed. In response to teacher paraphrases and acceptance acts, Liana issued a second (Line 38), third (Line 40), and finally fourth more detailed answer in Line 42. This answer the teacher once again paraphrased in Turn 43, this time modeling appropriate science terminology, "So, they're commonly used as variables, as unknowns."

At this point, we have identified two particular strategies used by Teacher A that create a highly dialogic speech environment: the wondering out loud questioning and the act of nonjudgmental, accepting paraphrasing. Both of these strategies were effective in encouraging interaction for all students, native English speakers and nonnative English speakers alike. However, there were also two distinct strategies that this instructor used specifically to encourage LEP student interaction in full-class discussions. I turn to those strategies next.

Every time an LEP student raised her hand to volunteer, he called on that student. The second strategy to engage LEP students was this: He drafted them. He called on them even though they had not volunteered for a turn. Each time he took this risk, however, he did so with built-in safety features. He checked with them first to see if they could answer the question, or he warned them ahead of time that he was going to call on them. For example, while the teacher was taking the students through a rapidfire review phase, in the middle of his discussion on one problem, he leaned over to one of the LEP students and whispered only for her, "I'm going to ask you the next one. Be ready." In a later interview, Teacher A told me that he had learned from this student's English as a second language teacher that she had completed her homework satisfactorily, so Teacher A knew that she had the answers she needed to take part. She needed the opportunity and the encouragement to take the floor.

An example of Teacher A's drafting approach is illustrated in Text 2, in which one very shy LEP student, Lillia, takes part in the full-class discussion. Her fellow LEP friend is at the board drawing a diagram to represent mitosis. Lillia noticed that her friend was drawing a compilation of two diagrams, one for mitosis and the other for meiosis. As the teacher walked about the room and approached the LEP students' table, Lillia got his attention. Notice how the teacher made use of drafting (Lines 4 & 6), back-channel acceptance (Line 2), and paraphrase acceptance (Lines 10 & 15) to draw Lillia into the full-class discussion.

Text 2 (One student has been called up to the board to draw a diagram of mitosis. Teacher is walking about the room at the moment. One LEP student draws his attention.)

1. L: This is just metosis.
2. T: mm-hmm
3. L: but she wrote that (pointing to her notes)
4. T: Well, you better point that out when we're done.
5. L: What?
6. T: You say that when we're done.
7. L: I don't know how to pronounce this word.
8. T: Meiosis. (Dianne finishes at the board and the teacher invites reactions) Oh, the hands are up. Somebody sees something they want to change perhaps or something to talk about. (Lillia's hand is raised). Lillia, nice and loud.

9. L: {--draw----}
10. T: I asked her to draw mitosis.
11. L: Mitosis, but she draw mi- (struggles with word) meiosis.
12. T: Meiosis . . . Isn't mitosis in here? (Referring to diagram.)
13. Ss: (approx. 3 students all answer at same time) Yes, in the bottom cells.
14. L: (also speaking simultaneously) {----23, 23-----}
15. T: 23, 23, 23 (pointing to bottom section of diagram) That's meiosis. So she did MORE than she had to. That's okay. This process is mitosis, and this process is meiosis. (pointing to board diagram)

DISCUSSION

This highly interactive teacher employed distinctive discourse strategies both in his use of elicitations and in the feedback move. He used more elicitations and higher cognitive level elicitations in two scaffolding events, those that repair faulty student answers and particularly those that expand satisfactory answers. Additionally, one particularly noticeable questioning strategy that this teacher used was to wonder out loud. Although many of his questions were indeed display questions, the answer to which he did know, they appeared to be referential (unknown answer questions). At times they were not questions at all; rather the teacher spoke aloud a curiosity as if it were a question inside the students' minds. It was as if he were modeling inner speech questions for the students.

The teacher's use of feedback acts was even more striking, particularly his frequent use of acceptance acts (i.e., repetitions, back-channels, and paraphrases), especially when issued after a student's incorrect or insufficient answer. This teacher frequently echoed his students' comments without adding information and without signaling an evaluation. It was as if the teacher were not responding to the student's utterance, but simply filtering the utterance through his louder, clearer voice, putting the student's utterance out there for the entire class to hear and react to.

The accomplishments of this type of paraphrasing are fourfold. First, students' answers are not corrected or evaluated for the truth value of the statement; therefore, students may feel motivated and free to engage in the act of wondering out loud, the exchange of ideas through language. The second accomplishment of such paraphrasing is that all students hear the student speaker's utterance. This is particularly important for LEP students. The consequences are that all students hear the expressed idea and can think about the idea. The third accomplishment of this paraphrasing strategy is that ultimately the student's response is presented in appropriate science talk. Thus, all students are able to hear the thought expressed in appropriate academic discourse.

In this teacher's classroom, this process of moving from a student's initial less than academically precise utterance to the final accurate and clearly stated utterance took a variety of paths. The process was sometimes just between one student and the teacher, and the final utterance would come from the expert model (as illustrated in Text 1, Lines 35–43 of Liana and the teacher). Other times the initial raw utterance found its way through a number of students' turns interspersed with teacher turns ultimately coconstructed by many. Whichever path was taken, in the end the students heard a precise, accurate expression of one or several students' earlier ideas.

The fourth and final accomplishment of the paraphrase strategy is that the teacher's voice becomes the voice of the students. Once spoken by the student and echoed by the teacher, the student's utterance is an expressed thought, an internal wonder turned into external speech. That expressed thought hangs out there in the classroom, available for all students to consider. The utterance remains out there waiting for the same student to further expand on it. The teacher may also signal that the response is available for other students to react to or expand on. Such a speech environment is ripe for interactive coconstruction, because the topic of wonder has become the possession of the students, not of the teacher, even though the teacher may have introduced the topic and even though the floor is still highly controlled by the teacher.

With respect to the LEP students, I must point out that extremely rarely have I seen LEP students volunteering in other teachers' mainstreamed, full-class discussions. Why did they do so in this teacher's class? I speculate the following. First, given the highly interactive practices of the teacher and students, particularly the nonjudgmental, listening nature of teacher responses, even the LEP students were drawn into the participation. Second, students could understand each other's ideas through the effective use of the teacher's paraphrasing. Third, after having been drafted enough times, LEP students gained confidence in their ability to speak in full-class discussions.

CONCLUSION

In summary, this chapter has argued the importance of interaction for LEP students mainstreamed in content classrooms, that interaction helps the development of students' academic L2 competency by providing students the opportunity to practice extended discourse leading to fluency and by providing students the opportunity to hear academic talk that they can later appropriate as their own. We examined the discourse strategies of a particularly dialogic teacher in full-class, teacherfronted discussions and found the teacher serving as the voice of the students by first, issuing elicitations by wondering out loud and hence modeling possible internal student questions and second, by responding to students' answers in accepting paraphrases, echoing the voice of the students. Finally, to engage LEP students in particular, this highly interactive instructor made a point to always call on them when they volunteered for the floor. Furthermore, he drafted them into turns, but always with preliminary built-in safety features.

In closing, let us consider two quotations on the importance of interaction and practice for students. The first comes from Lemke (1990), as he discussed the importance of variation, that students need to be able to express a scientific thought in a variety of ways:

> [Variation] not only leads to mastery of meanings, rather than memorization of wordings, it also gives students models of different, and so flexible, ways of constructing the thematic relations with words. Of course, just listening to the teacher do this is not enough; they need practice at doing it themselves, at putting things into "their own" or "different" words. (p. 113)

The second quote comes from one of Teacher A's LEP students, at the end of class on the day of our analyzed discussion. During that class period Dianne had volunteered twice in the full-class discussion, had drawn a figure of mitosis on the board, and later had engaged in a four-turn exchange about the chromosomes of twins. After the full-class discussion had ended, Dianne approached the teacher's desk and asked a question about her book. Upon receipt of an answer, she hesitated for a moment and then said to the teacher, "And thank you very much for letting me talk." The teacher responded, "Well, thank you for doing it."

ACKNOWLEDGMENTS

I express my deep appreciation to the three teachers who agreed to be part of this study. It takes great courage to subject oneself to such scrutiny. Each is a wonderful teacher, from whom I have learned much. I would also like to extend a very special thanks to my colleagues at Technical Education Research Centers, Inc. (TERC) of Cambridge, Massachusetts, in particular Dr. Ann Rosebery, Dr. Beth Warren, and Dr. Cindy Ballenger, who were so willing to share their knowledge, their contacts, their data, and their support. Finally, I wish to thank my advisors who gave me so much assistance during the original 1995 study, out of which this chapter grew: Dr. Mary Catherine O'Connor, Dr. Maria Estela Brisk, and Dr. Catherine Snow.

REFERENCES

Ballenger, C. (1997). Social identities, moral narratives, scientific argumentation: Science talk in a bilingual classroom. *Language and Education, 11*(1), 1–14.

Brown, R. (1991). Group work, task difference, and second language acquisition. *Applied Linguistics, 12*(1), 1–10.

Donato, R. (1994). Collective scaffolding in second language learning. In J. Lantolf & G. Appel (Eds.), *Vygotskian approaches to second language research* (pp. 33–57). Norwood, NJ: Ablex.

Erickson, F., & Shultz, J. (1981). When is a context? Some issues and methods in the analysis of social competence. In J. Green & C. Wallat (Eds.), *Ethnography and language in educational settings* (pp. 147–160). Norwood, NJ: Ablex.

Gass, S. M., & Varonis, E. M. (1985). Task variation and nonnative/nonnative negotiation of meaning. In S. Gass & C. Madden (Eds.), *Input in second language acquisition* (pp. 149–161). Rowley, MA: Newbury House.

Gass, S. M., & Varonis, E. M. (1994). Input, interaction, and second language production. *Studies in Second Language Acquisition, 16*, 283–302.

Green, J., & Harker, J. (1982). Gaining access to learning: Conversational, social, and cognitive demands of group participation. In L. Wilkinson (Ed.), *Communicating in the classroom* (pp. 183–221). New York: Academic Press.

Hall, J. K. (1993). The role of oral practices in the accomplishment of our everyday lives: The sociocultural dimension of interaction with implications for the learning of another language. *Applied Linguistics, 14*, 145–166.

Lemke, J. (1990). *Talking science: Language, learning, and values.* Norwood, NJ: Ablex.

McLaughlin, B. (1987). *Theories of second-language learning.* Baltimore: Edward Arnold.

Mehan, H. (1978). Structuring school structure. *Harvard Educational Review, 48*(1), 32–64.

O'Connor, M. C., & Michaels, S. (1993). Aligning academic task and participation status through revoicing: Analysis of a classroom discourse strategy. *Anthropology and Education Quarterly, 24*, 318–335.

Ohta, A. S. (1997, March). *Re-thinking interaction in SLA: A Vygotskian analysis of the role of collaborative classroom interaction in the acquisition of L2 grammar.* Paper presented at the American Association of Applied Linguistics Conference, Orlando, FL.

Pica, T. (1994). Research on negotiation: What does it reveal about second-language learning conditions, processes, and outcomes? *Language Learning, 44*, 493–527.

Pica, T., Doughty, C., & Young, R. (1986). Making input comprehensible: Do interactional modifications help? *I.T.L. Review of Applied Linguistics, 72*, 1–25.

Rosebery, A., Warren, B., & Conant, F. (1992). Appropriating scientific discourse: Findings from language minority classrooms. *The Journal of the Learning Sciences, 2*, 61–94.

Sinclair, J. M., & Coulthard, R. M. (1975). *Towards an analysis of discourse: The English used by teachers and pupils*. London: Oxford University Press.

Snow, C. (1990). The development of definitional skill. *Journal of Child Language, 17*, 697–710.

Swain, M. (1985). Communicative competence: Some roles of comprehensible input and comprehensible output in its development. In S. Gass & C. Madden (Eds.), *Input in second language acquisition* (pp. 235–257). Rowley, MA: Newbury House.

Swain, M. (1995, March). *Collaborative dialogue: Its contribution to second language learning*. Paper presented at the American Association of Applied Linguistics Conference, Long Beach, CA.

Verplaetse, L. (1995). *Discourse modifications in teacher interactions with limited English proficient students in content classrooms*. Unpublished doctoral dissertation, Boston University.

Verplaetse, L. (1998). How content teachers interact with English language learners. *TESOL Journal, 7*(5), 24–28.

Wertsch, J. A., & Toma, C. (1990, April). *Discourse and learning in the classroom: A sociocultural approach*. Paper presented at University of Georgia, Visiting Lecturer Series on Constructivism in Education, Athens, GA.

Zuengler, J. (1993). Encouraging learners' conversational participation: The effect of content knowledge. *Language Learning, 43*, 403–432.

12

A Different Teacher Role in Language Arts Education: Interaction in a Small Circle With Teacher

Resi Damhuis

Around the world, children of refugees and immigrant workers have to learn the educational language of their host country as a second language (L2). This learning must take place during regular school activities, which are primarily conducted in the L2. Therefore, L2 learning depends heavily on the interaction during these regular activities. Interaction in the L2 and self-initiated output in this interaction by the L2 learner are of crucial importance for second language acquisition (SLA). However, research has shown that interaction in traditional school activities is often rather poor with respect to enhancing SLA. In addition, non-native speaking (NNS) students do not get involved often in higher level thinking in classroom discourse, and hence they do not acquire the L2 well enough to succeed in school. Consequently, to improve classroom interaction, the teacher must adopt a new role.

In this chapter, I argue that higher level thinking and self-initiated output are necessary for SLA. I then describe an educational intervention focused on these two features and on the role of the teacher in realizing them. Finally, through a qualitative analysis of interactions, the effectiveness of the intervention is analyzed.

THE IMPORTANCE OF SELF-INITIATED OUTPUT
AND COMPLEX COGNITIVE LANGUAGE FUNCTIONS

Language acquisition depends on the interaction in which the language learner engages (Klein, 1986). Interaction must contain not only appropriate input by an interlocutor, as stated by the input hypothesis (Krashen, 1985), but also ample production by the language learner himself or herself as the comprehensible output hypothesis states (Swain, 1985, 1995). These hypotheses have to be considered not as rivals (Krashen, 1994, 1998), but as complements to each other (Swain, 1995).

On the one hand, interaction needs to offer learners the necessary input: What interlocutors say to learners serves as a model of the target language. The input has to be comprehensible and adjusted to learners at a level of linguistic difficulty just a little above their present level (Krashen, 1985). On the other hand, interaction needs to offer learners opportunities to use the language themselves. Obviously, output assists learners to become fluent in the actual use of the language. However, what is more important is that output serves accuracy by triggering further language learning:

> Output may stimulate learners to move from the semantic, open-ended, non-deterministic, strategic processing prevalent in comprehension to the complete grammatical processing needed for accurate production. Output, thus, would seem to have a potentially significant role in the development of syntax and morphology. (Swain, 1995, p. 128)

What kind of output is needed to optimally enhance SLA? Output has to be comprehensible (Swain, 1985, 1995) or even "pushed" (Van den Branden, 1997). The interlocutor has to grasp the meanings intended by the language learner, and if not, negotiation should take place to push the learner to more comprehensible or more accurate expression of intentions.

Yet another feature of output is linked to one of the requirements of the output hypothesis. This hypothesis requires that learners make full and flexible use of the target language to construct and build up their interlanguage system (Swain, 1985). From this requirement it can be inferred that optimal output is output that is initiated by the learner, as response output offers fewer opportunities to develop language fluency or accuracy. This proposition is corroborated by the following three areas of research.

First, research has found that initiating the discourse results in ampler and more diverse output. When students use new elements in their output, they usually have the initiative and are allowed to choose the topic themselves (Ellis, 1985).

> It is likely that learners' contributions will be more ample and syntactically complex if they have topic control (i.e., are not answering questions), . . . responses of any kind are likely to be sparser and leaner than speech acts that initiate discourse. (Ellis, 1990, p. 82)

In kindergarten SLA research, a wide variety of communicative acts and syntactic structures was found in NNS student output when NNSs initiated more than the teacher. On the other hand, when the teacher was the main initiator, NNSs produced single-word utterances, short phrases, and formulaic chunks (Cathcart, 1986). Swain, Allen, Harley, and Cummins (1989) found that extensive teacher-initiated talk in classrooms restricted student talk severely, allowing little opportunity for extended student talk at the length of a clause or more. In a study of French immersion classrooms, Allen, Swain, Harley, and Cummins (1990) found that extended student talk occurred more when students initiated interaction and had to find their own words.

Second, research has revealed that initiatives are important because they motivate the learner to use the L2. Ellis (1984) claimed that the need to communicate in the L2 is felt best when learners are free to express their own meanings; that is, choose the topic of conversation themselves. According to Zuengler and Bent (1991), initiations that are performed mainly by interlocutors may have negative effects on L2 learners because the learners constantly have to subordinate themselves while interacting.

Third, becoming a competent speaker of a language requires not just skills in responding, but also skills in actively contributing to a conversation. Activities in which the learner is allowed to express initiative in the areas of topic, self-selection, allocation, and sequence "are most likely to lead to the acquisition of skills in speaker change, interactional competence, and therefore to language development" (Van Lier, 1988, p. 133). In addition, an active, initiative-rich role in the interaction allows for a two-way negotiation. Being involved in negotiation (whether of meaning or of content) is found to improve immediate subsequent output by the L2 learner (Van den Branden, 1997). Taking part in the negotiation of meaning, moreover, helps to build the conversation (Pica, 1987; see also the review in Van den Branden, 1997) and enables language learners to receive adjusted input and to provide adjusted output when needed.

In sum, it is not response output but self-initiated output that allows learners to make full and flexible use of the target language (cf. Swain, 1995), which in turn triggers further language learning (cf. Swain, 1995). The term *self-initiated output* is used in this chapter to cover a broader concept than "speech act initiations." It refers to active, initiative-rich participation in the interaction that is not restricted by interlocutors but allows learners to initiate the discourse in one or several aspects, for example, wording, turn taking, and topic (Damhuis, 1995). Learners are allowed to decide when to speak and what to speak about, and how to convey their intended meanings in the target language.

An important aspect of language development in school is mastery of cognitive complex language functions, especially in the light of school tasks. School success requires cognitive academic language proficiency as opposed to basic interpersonal communicative skills that suffice for daily conversations outside of school (Cummins, 1984). Academic language proficiency requires the speaker to perform complex thought processes and to express these verbally, often in context reduced situations.

Complex language functions have been investigated in actual oral language use to find empirical evidence for the relation of such language functions with school success as in the Home School Study of Language and Literacy Development (e.g., Snow & Kurland, 1996). This long-term and large-scale study has revealed that the experience of children with talk containing complex cognitive language functions is related to several aspects of language proficiency that are good predictors of literacy, which in turn is a core element of school success.

Emphasis on self-initiated output and complex cognitive language functions fits into the innovative, educational perspective of active learning, that is, learning through transaction. The perspective of language pedagogy has changed markedly in the past decades (cf. Verhoeven, 1996). Instead of a transmission model, now a transactional model of schooling is employed, based on Vygotsky's (1934/1987) theory of learning through social interaction. Higher mental functions have a social origin; by means of social interaction mental processes move from interpsychological functioning to intrapsychological functioning.

Within the transactional model, learning as a social activity entails classroom discourse that differs from conventional classroom discourse. Talk functions at two levels: univocal and dialogic. At the univocal level the main purpose is to convey information. At the dialogic level talk is a thinking device, a generator of meaning (Lotman, 1988; cf. Wertsch & Toma, 1995). Whereas the transmission model of communication is solely concerned with the conveying of information (the univocal level), the constructivist view (Steffe & Gale, 1995) of social learning requires students to take an active stance toward anything that is said and to treat talk as a thinking device (the dialogic level).

In an interactive classroom the teacher crucially influences the patterns of participation (Cazden, 1988) by choosing to be a mentor instead of informant (Corder, 1977). In active learning, the teacher's new role is to coach the learning process and to scaffold the active learning of the students who coconstruct their knowledge through social interaction (Wertsch & Toma, 1995).

Qualitative research has been conducted to highlight these interaction patterns in authentic mathematics (Lampert, 1990) and science lessons (O'Connor & Michaels, 1996). These explorations reveal striking differences from conventional classroom interactions. In interactive classrooms, students learn the social skills and linguistic means to argue, to reason, to disagree, and to discuss (Lampert, 1990). The teacher is not the author of ideas, but the students are. The teacher plays a role in revoicing contributions by students in a way that leaves the authorship with the students (O'Connor & Michaels, 1996).

On the other hand, conventional classroom interactions, in which the teacher has taken no specific measures to promote SLA, allow for very little self-initiated output by L2 learning students. Classroom interactions are often dominated by the teacher (e.g., Cazden, 1988; House, 1986; Kramsch, 1981; Long, 1981; Scarcella, 1983; Van Lier, 1988). With the teacher in control, the L2 learner mainly produces responses, due to the predominance of initiation–response–evaluation (IRE) sequences (Mehan, 1979; Sinclair & Coulthard, 1975). American classrooms rely heavily on the univocal, transmission-like function of talk, with roughly 80% of classroom talk taken up by teacher speech (Wertsch & Toma, 1995). For the Dutch language area, findings are similar: Hajer (1996, chap. 13, this volume) reports that one third of the interaction in subject teaching in secondary school is one-way teacher communication, one third is interaction stemming from teacher-initiated elicitations and checks, and only one third stems from student initiatives.

Two final points must be made regarding self-initiated output and complex cognitive language. First, although the IRE pattern that predominates teacher-initiated interaction (Mehan, 1979) reflects an asymmetric relationship between teacher and students, Wells (1994) pointed out that IRE sequences need not be totally restrictive. The quality of IREs may differ, depending on the type of question that constitutes the initiation. With open, communicative, or referential questions the IRE may be less restricting than with the customary instructional questions.

Second, group composition and size are related to the quality of interaction. Interaction in heterogeneous groups yields gains in language performance for both low and high proficient students (Van den Branden, 1997). However, several levels and dimensions of analyses of turn taking and topic initiatives in kindergarten classrooms with NNS and native speaking (NS) students show that interaction in the full group contains relatively little self-initiated output by NNS students (Blok, Damhuis, Oostdam, in press; Damhuis, 1993, 1995). On the other hand, interaction between a teacher and a small circle of children shows much more self-initiated output.

The literature review presented here can be summarized in four conclusions:

1. The L2 learner needs to self-initiate output for optimal SLA and active, transactional learning.
2. Experience with complex cognitive language functions is required for the development of academic language proficiency and active learning.
3. When teachers choose to play the role of coach and adopt a student-centered approach, they allow L2 learners to produce more self-initiated output and more complex cognitive language functions.
4. Interaction in small, heterogeneous groups has greater potential for promoting SLA through more self-initiated output and the use of more varied and more complex cognitive language functions than interaction in the full group or interaction in a homogeneous group.

These conclusions constitute the basis for an educational intervention designated "small circle with teacher." The description of this intervention follows.

AN EDUCATIONAL INTERVENTION:
THE SMALL CIRCLE WITH TEACHER

In the Netherlands, Dutch is the language of instruction; however, the student population includes a significant portion of NNS children to whom Dutch is an L2. Innovations in language arts education in the Netherlands integrate Dutch as first language (L1) and Dutch as L2. The National Center for Language Education in the Netherlands conducts several projects for the first four grades of primary education (ages 4–8). In the project concerning oral language skills, one intervention that is currently being developed is the "small circle with teacher." It seeks to improve language acquisition by NNS and NS students by providing students ample opportunities for the use of complex cognitive language functions and self-initiated output.

The small circle with teacher (abbreviated to *small circle*) is organized several times per week for approximately 15 minutes per session. The participants in this activity are the teacher and four or five students. These students have different levels of language proficiency: Some are NNS students, and others are NSs. The teacher plays a distinct role in this small group activity, specifically with respect to selecting the stimulus for talking and with respect to creating rich interaction. The main features of the small circle with teacher are summarized in Table 12.1. Following is a description of the intended small circle interaction.

The interaction in the small circle should be adjusted in such a way that children initiate more output and use more complex and more varied cognitive language functions than in traditional classroom settings. Students are offered challenging materials or subjects that form a suitable base for eliciting more complex cognitive language functions. In addition, teachers change their role from the traditional source of knowledge to a coaching role: being stimulating without directing the conversation completely (cf. Wertsch & Toma, 1995).

TABLE 12.1
Overview of 10 Core Characteristics of the Small Circle With Teacher

Stimuli
Teacher selects appropriate materials or a suitable topic.
Students bring in a topic by themselves and teacher uses that in the small circle.
Participation in the interaction
Students think about phenomena, processes, or problems and put their thoughts into words.
Students play the role of speaker—with self-initiated output—not just of supplier of responses.
Students react to each other without continuously using the teacher as intermediary.
Teacher plays role of responsive listener, not merely of speaker and initiator.
Coaching development of students
Teacher stimulates use of complex cognitive language functions.
Teacher stimulates further thinking and talking of students.
Organizational prerequisites
Teacher organizes small circle as routine activity in curriculum; students are used to it.
Teacher and students build up a routine of independent working, allowing teacher to conduct small circle.

The coaching role of the teacher implies that she sustains thought process-es and the expression of thoughts, accepts all ideas and contributions from the children as valuable, and follows the children in their train of thought instead of imposing on them the adult, true, knowledgeable point of view (dialogic function of talk). After the introduction of a suitable topic the teacher should withdraw more or less from the content of the conversation: She is not the dispenser of knowledge on the topic but she employs her expert skills to elicit thought and talk. The teacher's approach must be very open and student centered. The teacher is as curious about the materials as the children are; she shows and verbalizes her curiosity, inviting the children to come up with questions, solutions, and suggestions (see Lampert, 1990; O'Connor & Michaels, 1996). The teacher may ask questions, but they must be very open, not heading toward a universal truth, but only eliciting the children to think aloud about the materials presented and their properties. The questions should not supply complete language frames, to which a response of *yes* or *no* or a one-word utterance is sufficient. Questions must leave open the con-tent and form of the response.

Complex Cognitive Language Functions in the Small Circle

A variety of ways to describe cognitive complex language functions have been developed. This study uses a taxonomy of cognitive language func-tions, designed by Verhallen and Walst (1996), that is closely related to educational practice and L2 learning, as illustrated in Table 12.2.

Self-Initiated Output in the Small Circle

Following research on self-initiated output of NNS students in the first two grades of primary education (Damhuis, 1995), the teacher training program described in this study was developed to support teachers in their attempts to increase opportunities for self-initiated output by students in classroom inter-actions (Damhuis, 1998). Self-initiated output is considered at three levels: amount of participation, initiatives with respect to turn taking, and initiatives with respect to topic. At each level teachers learn to observe student partici-pation. In addition, teachers are supplied with practical suggestions on how to alter their own interactional behavior to stimulate their students to produce more self-initiated output. These behaviors are listed in Table 12.3. The key notion underlying all suggestions is that the teacher does not play the central role in the conversation, but leaves much more opportunity to the students.

TABLE 12.2
Taxonomy of Language Functions Adjusted for Teacher Use

Social language functions
Self-preservation
Self-directing
Other-directing
Structuring
Cognitive language functions
Reporting
Nominate (labeling)
Describe

Simple cognitive functions

Complex cognitive functions

Compare
Reasoning
Order chronologically
Conclude
Express means–purpose relation
Express cause–effect relation
Problem solve
Projecting
Imagining
Reference
Contextualized (here and now)
Decontextualized (past, future)

Reprinted from Verhallen and Walst (1996).

TABLE 12.3
Interactional Skills to Promote Active Student Participation:
A Summary of Teacher Training Suggestions

Amount of talk
  Create a safe atmosphere, wait patiently, and be friendly for contributions.
  Adjust input to a little above the level of the student (not too low).
  Bring student into an interesting situation, in which he or she is highly motivated to partici-
    pate in conversation.
  Keep silent, offering students more time to plan their production.
  Do not speak immediately after the first short contribution of a student.
  Do not interrupt a student's turn (unless a case of comprehensibility problems).
  Talk less (not after each student's turn; make your own turns less long).
Initiatives in turn taking
  Supply listening responses, leaving floor open again for student immediately afterward:
    Agree with student.
    Short response to indicate comprehension ("Oh," "Uh," "Indeed").
    Admiring response ("Great," "Nice," "Good").

(Continued)

TABLE 12.3 *(Continued)*

Surprised response ("Is that so?," "Oh dear!").
Repeat what student said (if needed in more correct form: expansion).
Repeat what student said in question form.
Ask for clarification.
Keep silent (friendly and patiently), offering students more time to plan their contribution.
Use questions only as a starting point or a continuing device (remember, a question always limits turn-taking initiative of the student).
If needed, ask a simple but interesting question to get started; proceed with listening responses.
If needed, ask open referential question; proceed with listening responses.
State something improbable, to tempt student to contribute himself or herself.
Be aware that many question forms only allow for very restricted responses.
Initiatives in topic
Accept topic that student brings in (use listening responses).
Accept student's perspective on topic (instead of adhering to and steering toward the adult view).
Build out together the student's topic (add to it and let student add to it).
Use negotiation of meaning to comprehend student's topic better.
Give student room to add to any current topic.
Indicate that you are available for conversation.
Keep silent (friendly and patiently), offering students more time to plan their contribution.
Do not monopolize the right to introduce new topics.
If needed, introduce a possibly interesting subject, but in an open, unrestricting way.
Use questions only as a starting point or a continuing device (remember, a question always limits turn-taking initiative of the student).
If needed, use open questions (not limiting the content completely) instead of closed ones (only one possible answer).
If needed, use why and how questions of the open kind (allowing ample responses), followed by listening responses.
If needed, use questions about student's own experience (as a starting point), followed by listening responses.
Leave floor open to student after his or her first response to question (by keeping silent or giving a listening response).
Be aware that most questions restrict the topic of the response.

Derived from Damhuis (1998).

METHODOLOGY

Research Questions for This Study

In this study, preliminary results of the educational intervention of small circle with teacher are reported. Currently the intervention is conducted on a small scale and therefore has provided qualitative data only. The study investigates whether interaction in the small circle with teacher actually contains self-initiated output and use of complex cognitive language functions by NNS students. If small circle interaction indeed contains such student talk, it is worthwhile to continue and extend the educational intervention. The research questions are the following:

1. Do students use complex cognitive language functions?
2. Does the teacher provide appropriate opportunities to students for using complex cognitive language functions?
3. Do students produce self-initiated output?
4. Does the teacher provide appropriate opportunities to students for self-initiated output?

Setting

The intervention was started in one class of combined Grades 1 and 2, a mixed group of 4- and 5-year olds (i.e., the first 2 years of primary education in the Netherlands). The school is located in one of Amsterdam's fast-growing districts outside the city center. Its population consists mainly of lower class students with a smaller proportion of middle-class children. In the intervention class, almost 70% of the students are NNSs (NNSs constitute about 60% of the school population). Although these children were born in the Netherlands, they often speak the language of their country of origin as their L1 at home. They are acquiring Dutch as an L2. In general their Dutch language proficiency is considerably less advanced than that of their NS Dutch peers.

Procedures for Implementing the Intervention

The project started in the school year 1997–1998. The school adviser of the research group trained the regular teacher to organize the small circle in her regular class, between September and December 1997. In January 1998 the teacher actually began to perform the small circle, coached by the school adviser and the researcher.

Data and Participants

Recordings. Two video recordings were used to illustrate the actual interaction that took place in the small circle in March 1998: one with 4-year-olds, and one with 5-year-olds. These small circles were conducted outside the regular classroom to allow the teacher to concentrate fully on shaping the interaction as a phase in the teacher's learning process. The recordings were transcribed.

Students.   In the small circle with the 5-year olds, two girls and three boys, all NNSs, took part. One of the students, a Turkish girl, was highly proficient in Dutch. The other girl and one of the boys, both Dutch-Hindustan, were at an intermediate L2 level. A Moroccan and a Dutch-Surinam boy were low proficient.

In the small circle with 4-year-olds, five children took part: one girl (NNS) and four boys (one NS, three NNS). An Egyptian boy was highly Dutch proficient. The NS boy and the NNS girl (from mixed Dutch-Surinam origin) were at an intermediate level of proficiency in Dutch. Two Moroccan boys were low proficient.

Stimuli.   The two small circles were focused on several devices for measuring length: various measuring rods, a tape measure, a flexible steel rule, and a piece of string. With the older children, a black piece of paper with two footprints was added to the materials. One footprint was large and one was a small foot (an idea from Heesen, 1996). The paper was put down with its blank side up. With the younger children, a children's book that was read earlier was added. In the story a little princess wanted to grow taller and used her crown to stand on.

Analysis.   The qualitative analysis focuses on the actual participation of NNS students and the teacher behavior related to it. It looks for representative instances of student and teacher language behavior with respect to complex cognitive language functions and self-initiated output. It must be kept in mind that the small circle aims solely at rich and active use of more complex thoughts and expression thereof to enhance SLA (not necessarily leading to an instructional goal of acquiring specific content knowledge).

Findings: In-Depth Analysis of Actual Interaction

Transcript excerpts from the two videotapes show that the conversations led to a wide range of complex cognitive language functions and much self-initiated output produced by the students. The teacher's behavior stimulated students to use complex language functions and to initiate output themselves.

Small Circle With 5-Year-Olds.   The small circle with 5-year-olds starts with turning over the paper with the footprints. The teacher shows surprise at the sight of the footprints in Example 1, Turn 1. One of the children wants to put his foot on the large print in Turns 3 and 5. This is an example of self-initiated output. The latter turn expresses a means–purpose relation. In Turn 16, this boy concludes that he has small feet. These initiatives occur at moments when the teacher did not ask a question, when the speaking floor was freely available.

The teacher follows up the topic aspect that Sh introduced. In doing so, she takes care to involve other children in that topic, modeling students' thought processes with her questions. First she asks Su to describe what Sh is doing. Su reacts with an extensive response in Turn 9, which can be considered a means–purpose relation. Next the teacher invites Y to interpret that action. Y's Turn 11 is a comparison.

The teacher's questions in Turns 8 and 10 are not completely open, because they concern the action of Sh, but the form and the actual content of the response have to be chosen by the children. Therefore, these questions did not prescribe the form or the exact content of the response.

Example 1[1]

1.	T:	What is that then?
2.	D:	A footstep
3.	Sh:	Miss, may I just do it?
4.	T:	What do you want to do?
5.	Sh:	With my foot [points at his foot and the paper].
6.	T:	Well, just try. I don't know what you want.
7.	Sh:	[takes off one shoe and puts his foot on the paper.]
8.	T:	What is he doing now, Su?
9.	Su:	He is measuring how big that foot uh of his is.
10.	T:	And what can you see now, Y?
11.	Y:	He is bigger [points].

---

[1]All examples have been translated from the original Dutch to English for presentation in this chapter. For the most part, the less correct use of Dutch has been maintained in equivalent, less correct use of English. The following is a key to the transcription symbols and abbreviations used in this and subsequent examples.

xx	Unintelligible syllable
[text]	Situational note made by observer
(text)	Text between parentheses is not understood for certain
text	Text is spoken simultaneously with the nearest underlined utterance
T	Teacher
D	High L2 level NNS
Sh, Su	Low L2 level NNSs
Ss	All NNS students

12. T: Who?

13. Y: That [points].

14. T: The one on the paper is bigger? Is that what you mean?

15. Y: [nods]

16. Sh: Yes, since I have small feet.

In the next excerpt, Example 2, Turn 1, the teacher summarizes what has been discussed thus far. The Turkish girl, D, takes a very long turn in Turn 7 that contains several complex cognitive language functions (i.e., reasoning). Although this turn is a response, it is not totally restricted in content or form. The question in Turn 6 that elicited this response is open and referential.

The teacher revoices this contribution in Turn 8 in a way that fits the description of O'Connor and Michaels (1996): She keeps authorship with the student, reformulates this student's contribution in a way that may be more comprehensible for the other students, and invites the others to comment on it. Here the teacher clearly values the contribution of the student and proposes it as a worthwhile suggestion to be considered by all students.

The teacher responds in Turn 11 to the participation by D. This response is just a statement, not a question, which leaves the speaking floor open to the students. D uses this opportunity with a new turn-taking initiative in Turn 12. In this turn she first agrees with the teacher's statement (no topic initiative yet). Then, however, she continues with an extensive sentence containing a complex cognitive language function, that is, a means–purpose relation.

Example 2

1. T: You are saying that his foot is small. The other is big.

2. D: Yes, but . . .

3. T: Mustn't we measure that first then?

4. D: Y<u>es</u>!

5. Sh: <u>Yes!</u>

6. T: But how do you know that so well then?

7. D: Uh, be . . . because uh that uh small because the one is small, and the big one is bigger. Thus then we can see it which is bigger. But then we do have to measure it first.

8. T: Yes. Do you hear what D says? We can already see that it is bigger. So, must we actually still really measure it, do you think?

  9. Ss: No [shake heads]

10. D: No. But then you can . . .

11. T: It's not necessary. But it is nice of course.

12. D: Yes. But then you can measure how many centimeter it is.

13. T: That really is very smart. Then we can really go measuring it. Well, D, you just go and begin. With what could we measure it?

Later on, as seen in Example 3, Turn 1, the teacher poses a hypothesis that R (who is the smallest child in this class) may well be taller than D when he has grown up. This prompts the children to a whole series of reasoning contributions: Turns 6, 11, 15, 19, 30, and 32. The students produce extensive, unrestricted utterances. Such extended discourse offers them rich experiences with more academic language use and opportunities to use their language in a flexible way. The teacher creates free slots on the speaking floor by uttering a listening response ("Oh") or a short statement. Several of her questions are solely listening responses echoing the students' output and giving back the floor to them.

Example 3

  1. T: But when R is enrolled later in the senior classes at school, then he is as big a boy as G. Will he then also weigh somewhat more on the balance?

  2. D: [nods]

  3. Sh: [nods]

  4. Y: [nods] Yeah.

  5. T: Yes, I think so, isn't it?

  6. D: Yes. Since he gets then will be bigger too and then can . . . and all children cannot weigh the same altogether. And that also will not stay that way.

  7. T: No.

  8. D: Since I can maybe weigh a bit bigger too now.

  9. T: But it could easily be, if you are very big, maybe uh a mother yourself, and then you meet R and maybe R will have grown bigger than you have then. That would be funny. Or is that impossible?

10. D: Yes, indeed.

11. Sh: Yes. Since fathers are taller than uh m . . mothers.

12. T: Fathers are often taller than mothers.

13. Sh: [nods]

14. T: How might that happen?

15. Sh: Be . . . uh uh . . . because mothers are a bit fat and fathers a bit thin.

16. T: And that's why they are also tall?

17. Sh: Yes.

18. T: Oh.

19. D: Yes, but fathers cannot have babies.

20. T: No, that is true [to D]. Are there any small fathers also, Y?

21. Y: [nods]

22. D: [nods]

23. Sh: <u>No!</u>

24. R.   <u>No!</u>

25. T: yes [to Y]? Is your father small, or is your father a bit tall, Y?

26. Y: Bit tall.

27. T: A bit tall.

28. Y: [nods]

29. T: And your father, Su?

30. Su: Um uh taller, a bit taller than me mother.

31. T: A bit taller than your mother.

32. Su: Because me mother is a bit like this and then my father is like this [indicates two heights].

33. T: They are both not so very tall? But still your father is taller than your mother is. A <u>bit</u> taller.

34. Su: [nods]

35. T: [nods to Su]

Small Circle With 4-Year-Olds.   One might expect the 4-year-olds to be too young to engage in complex thought processes and to talk about them in the L2. However, the videotaped small circle proved otherwise. At some point in this small circle the teacher asks what other parts of the body grow. Students volunteer many suggestions. Then, in Example 4, Turn 1, the teacher asks a referential, quite open question that activates thinking. A series of complex reasoning contributions emerges. I offers a conclusion in Turn 2. The teacher reformulates this particular instance into a general principle in Turns 3 and 5. Children suggest prerequisites for growing (Turns 6 and 9) and a consequence in Turn 11. All these contributions consist of fairly extensive turns, for example, the complete if–then construction in Turn 9.

The teacher reacts mainly with listening responses (Turns 10, 14, 21, 28) and statements (Turns 3–5, 12, 16, 23, 32). In this part of the interaction she hardly poses any new questions at all. She follows the train of thought of the students and offers them ample opportunity to initiate output.

When the children divert to the kind of bed they have themselves (from Turn 22 onward), the teacher follows this aspect of the topic. Although the students do not use the most complex language functions (descriptions), they still use the L2 at a cognitively more demanding level, as decontextualized language, because the utterances do not concern the here and now, but objects in their own homes.

In the last part the teacher reintroduces the matter of how the children may notice that they have grown. In Turn 37, the boy Dw starts with naming a body part that gets bigger, and O and I readily add other parts that grow. The teacher reacts with simple statements, as in Turns 41, 43, 45, and 47. It is obvious that the students select the topical aspects in this fragment of the discourse. The teacher leaves control of the conversation entirely in their hands. She shows that she is listening and that she appreciates the contributions; afterward, she leaves the floor free again for students to initiate output themselves.

Example 4[2]

1. T: How do you know now if your body grows? How can you know that now?
2. I: Can I shower by myself? Shower alone.
3. T: If you have grown bigger, you can . . .
4. I: Yes.
5. T: . . . you can do more by yourself. That is true.
6. D: And if you go to eat fruit.
7. O: If you . . .
8. T: Wait a moment [touches D and points at O, to indicate that O is allowed to speak now.]
9. O: If you will go to sleep well, there you will grow bigger by.
10. T: That is true, isn't it? If you rest very well.
11. I: The . . . then then you go buy big bed.
12. T: That is good, since you don't fit into your bed then.
13. I: No!
14. T: Noho,
15. O: Can you also not out, you go do somersault, of your bed out.
16. T: Yes, that would be a bit strange.
17. I: Yes, turn like that.

---

[2]The following abbreviations are used in this example

T	Teacher
O	High L2 level NNS
D	Intermediate L2 level NNS
I,F	Low L2 level NNSs
Dw	NS child, intermediate level

18.	T:	<u>Do you . . .</u>
19.	T:	Do you actually have a big bed at home? [to I]
20.	I:	[nods]
21.	T:	Goodness.
22.	O:	I have a bunk bed at home.
23.	T:	Yes, that is also possible.
24.	F:	Me too.
25.	T:	Then you sleep very high, don't you? [to O]
26.	O:	Yes. I go . . [stops because he has to cough].
27.	I:	Since I sleep very high.
28.	T:	[nods]
29.	I:	My friend too.
30.	T:	Your friend below [to I]. [then to whole circle:] But still about your body.
31.	Dw:	My girlfriend has a bunk bed too.
32.	T:	Sleeping also very high.
33.	Dw:	[nods]
34.	O:	Of mine too.
35.	F:	My girlfriend not.
36.	T:	No. But how can you know now, about your body? [short pause] That it has grown?
37.	Dw:	If you leg is <u>a bit bigger</u>.
38.	T:	<u>Who then goes . . .</u>
39.	T:	Because your leg has got a bit longer. Yes, that is . . .
40.	O:	If you get very tall, then you have long legs, as long as this [gestures the length].
41.	T:	That is true.
42.	O:	And a big head.
43.	T:	Yes. Your head gets <u>bigger</u>.
44.	O:	<u>And a</u> big nose.
45.	T:	Everything gets bigger.
46.	I:	And your ears get bigger.
47.	T:	That too!
48.	I:	Yes.

CONCLUSIONS

The qualitative analysis shows that interaction in the small circle with teacher can indeed provide students with ample opportunities to use complex cognitive language functions (concluding, means–purpose, and chronological ordering) and self-initiated output. Teacher behavior that invites the students to think and argue and that does not mainly consist of questions made this possible. Features of this behavior are as follows.

1. The teacher acted inquisitively. She was not the expert who holds all answers. She treated all suggestions of the children as valuable and legitimate.
2. The teacher was a necessary partner in the interaction to keep the conversation going and to keep the activity a truly conversational one. However, the crucial role of the teacher was to coach the children in their process of learning, thinking, listening, and speaking.
3. When the teacher used questions and thus initiated IRE sequences, they were often questions that left open the form of the response and very much of the content too. Her feedback was often a listening response.

An important consequence of the small circle was that not only the more proficient NNS students were involved and participated with complex functions and self-initiated output, but the lower proficient NNS students participated as well. In the small circle they had ample opportunity to think about a challenging subject, express their thoughts, and initiate output themselves. This held true not only for 5-year-olds, but also for the 4-year-old children.

The educational intervention small circle with teacher is still in its developmental phase. The research group continues to explore possibilities and limitations of the small circle. Our hope that this kind of educational activity fosters the use of more complex cognitive language functions and stimulates self-initiated output by NNS (and NS) students seems well grounded. Interaction that is created along the lines of this small circle, in which the teacher plays the new role of coach, has the potential to enhance active learning in general, and—more specifically—to enhance complete and swift SLA.

ACKNOWLEDGMENTS

The teacher of this project deserves to be thanked: Marian Luyckx (primary school Bisschop Huibers, Amsterdam) enthusiastically puts into practice what the research group (including herself) comes up with. Her overall view of education and her practical insights keep our feet on the ground, but her resourcefulness and her ability to translate plans into actual behavior show us that the potential power of the project actually can be realized, legitimizing our high hopes. Another invaluable participant is the school adviser, Anneke Zielhorst of the School Advisory Service "ABC" in Amsterdam. Despite a very busy schedule she manages to amply support the teacher in her search for solutions, and to contribute to the development of the content of this part of the project. Last, but not least, I thank my colleague researcher, Piet Litjens. He started up the project, studied the literature to select the subjects in oral language teaching that deserved more attention, started the work on this project concerning the small circle with teacher, and invited me to join the project. His experience in working with schools, school boards, and local governments is irreplaceable, but most of all he is a stimulating partner in discussions, truly talk at the dialogic level.

REFERENCES

Allen, P., Swain, M., Harley, B., & Cummins, J. (1990). Aspects of classroom treatment: Toward a more comprehensive view of second language education. In B. Harley, P. Allen, J. Cummins, & M. Swain (Eds.), *The development of second language proficiency* (pp. 57–81). Cambridge, UK: Cambridge University Press.

Blok, H., Damhuis, R., & Oostdam, R. (in press). Participation in sequences of young immigrant students in classroom discourse. *Studies in Second Language Acquisition*.

Cathcart, R. (1986). Situational differences and the sampling of young children's school language. In R. Day (Ed.), *Talking to learn: Conversation in second language acquisition* (pp. 118–140). Rowley, MA: Newbury House.

Cazden, C. B. (1988). *Classroom discourse. The language of teaching and learning*. Portsmouth, NH: Heinemann.

Corder, P. (1977). Language teaching and learning: A social encounter. In D. Brown, C. Yorio, & D. Crymes (Eds.), *On TESOL '77* (pp. 21–33). Washington, DC: TESOL.

Cummins, J. (1984). *Bilingualism and special education: Issues in assessment and pedagogy*. Clevedon, UK: Multilingual Matters.

Damhuis, R. (1993). Immigrant children in infant-class interactions: Opportunities for second-language acquisition of young multilingual children in Dutch infant classes. *Studies in Second Language Acquisition, 15*, 305–331.

Damhuis, R. (1995). *Interaction and second language acquisition: Participation and control in classroom conversations with young multilingual children* (Studies in Language and Language Use, No. 19). Amsterdam: Institute for Functional Research Into Language and Language Use.

Damhuis, R. (1998). *Leerkracht-interactievaardigheden voor het stimuleren van taalverwerving*. [Teachers' interactional skills for stimulating language acquisition]. 's-Hertogenbosch, The Netherlands: KPC-groep.

Ellis, R. (1984). *Classroom second language development*. Oxford, UK: Pergamon.

Ellis, R. (1985). Teacher–pupil interaction in second language development. In S. M. Gass & C. G. Madden (Eds.), *Input in second language acquisition* (pp. 69–85). Rowley, MA: Newbury House.

Ellis, R. (1990). *Instructed second language acquisition: Learning in the classroom.* Oxford, UK: Basil Blackwell.

Hajer, M. (1996). *Leren in een tweede taal: Interactie in vakonderwijs aan een meertalige mavo-klas* [Learning through a second language: Interaction in content area instruction in a multilingual class]. Groningen, The Netherlands: Wolters-Noordhoff.

Heesen, B. (1996). *Klein maar dapper: Filosoferen met jongere kinderen* [Small but tough: Philosophizing with younger children]. Best, The Netherlands: Damon.

House, J. (1986). Learning to talk: Talking to learn: An investigation of learner performance in two types of discourse. In G. Kasper (Ed.), *Learning, teaching and communication in the foreign language classroom* (pp. 43–57). Aarhus: Aarhus University Press.

Klein, W. (1986). *Second language acquisition.* Cambridge, UK: Cambridge University Press.

Krashen, S. D. (1985). *The input hypotheses: Issues and implications.* London: Longman.

Krashen, S. (1994). The input hypothesis and its rivals. In N. C. Ellis (Ed.), *Implicit and explicit learning of languages* (pp. 45–78). London: Academic Press.

Krashen, S. (1998). Comprehensible output? *System, 26,* 175–182.

Kramsch, C. (1981). *Discourse analysis and second language teaching* (Language in education: Theory and practice, No. 37). Washington, DC: Center for Applied Linguistics.

Lampert, M. (1990). When the problem is not the question and the solution is not the answer: Mathematical knowing and teaching. *American Educational Research Journal, 27,* 29–63.

Long, M. H. (1981). Questions in foreigner talk discourse. *Language Learning, 31,* 135–157.

Lotman, Y. M. (1988). Text within a text. *Soviet Psychology, 24*(3), 32–51.

Mehan, H. (1979). *Learning lessons: Social organization in the classroom.* Cambridge, MA: Harvard University Press.

O'Connor, M. C., & Michaels, S. (1996). Shifting participant frameworks: Orchestrating thinking practices in group discussion. In D. Hicks (Ed.), *Discourse, learning, and schooling* (pp. 63–103). Cambridge, UK: Cambridge University Press.

Pica, T. (1987). Secondlanguage acquisition, social interaction, and the classroom, *Applied Linguistics, 8*(1), 3–21.

Scarcella, R. C. (1983). Discourse accent in second language performance. In S. Gass & L. Selinker (Eds.), *Language transfer in language learning* (pp. 306–326). Rowley, MA: Newbury House.

Sinclair, J. M., & Coulthard, M. (1975). *Towards an analysis of discourse: The English used by teachers and pupils.* London: Oxford University Press.

Snow, C. E., & Kurland, B. F. (1996). Sticking to the point: Talk about magnets as a context for engaging in scientific discourse. In D. Hicks (Ed.), *Discourse, learning, and schooling* (pp. 189–220). Cambridge, UK: Cambridge University Press.

Steffe, L. P., & Gale, J. (Eds.). (1995). *Constructivism in education.* Hillsdale, NJ: Lawrence Erlbaum Associates.

Swain, M. (1985). Communicative competence: Some roles of comprehensible input and comprehensible output in its development. In S. M. Gass & C. G. Madden (Eds.), *Input in second language acquisition* (pp. 235–253). Rowley, MA: Newbury House.

Swain, M. (1995). Three functions of output in second language learning. In G. Cook & B. Seidlhofer (Eds.), *Principle & practice in applied linguistics: Studies in honor of H. G. Widdowson* (pp. 125–144). Oxford, UK: Oxford University Press.

Swain, M., Allen, P., Harley, B., & Cummins, J. (1989). *The development of bilingual proficiency project.* Toronto: Ontario Institute of Educational Studies, University of Toronto.

Van den Branden, K. (1997). Effects of negotiation on language learners' output. *Language Learning, 47*, 589–636.

Van Lier, L. (1988). *The classroom and the language learner: Ethnography and second-language classroom research.* London: Longman.

Verhallen, M., & Walst, R. (1996). Taalfuncties [Language functions]. In R. Appel, F. Kuiken, & A. Vermeer (Eds.), *Nederlands als tweede taal in het basisonderwijs: Handboek voor leerkrachten in het basisonderwijs* (pp. 89–100). Amsterdam: Meulenhoff Educatief.

Verhoeven, L. (1996). Language in education. In F. Coulmas (Ed.), *Handbook of sociolinguistics* (pp. 389–404). London: Basil Blackwell.

Vygotsky, L. S. (1987). *Thought and language.* Cambridge, UK: Cambridge University Press. (Original work published in 1934)

Wells, G. (1994). Reevaluating the IRF sequence: A proposal for the articulation of theories of activity and discourse for the analysis of teaching and learning in the classroom. *Linguistics and Education, 5*, 1–37.

Wertsch, J. V., & Toma, C. (1995). Discourse and learning in the classroom: A sociocultural approach. In L. P. Steffe & J. Gale (Eds.), *Constructivism in education* (pp. 159–174). Hillsdale, NJ: Lawrence Erlbaum Associates.

Zuengler, J., & Bent, B. (1991). Relative knowledge of content domain: An influence on native–non-native conversation. *Applied Linguistics, 12*, 397–415.

13

Creating a Language-Promoting Classroom: Content-Area Teachers at Work

Maaike Hajer

For many second language (L2) learners it is not enough to acquire basic L2 skills; they need academic language skills that enable them to succeed in school and study. Special courses have been designed to prepare L2 pupils for a smooth transition from L2 classes to education in different content areas in which these skills are required. In theory, advanced L2 development can be promoted in these very content lessons by offering opportunities for meaningful interaction, thus providing comprehensible input, as well as opportunities for productive L2 use and feedback (see, e.g., Snow & Brinton, 1997). However, many pupils are placed in mainstream content classes that are not specially adjusted to their language level. In this situation it is a challenge to the content-area teacher to create L2 learning opportunities, at the same time conveying subject matter through the L2. It is unclear to what extent these teachers succeed in creating L2 learning opportunities in practice.

In this chapter, I give an inside view of a multilingual classroom and reveal profiles of two teachers who are considerably successful in teaching subject matter through an L2. Taken from a larger case study of five content teachers of the same multilingual middle school class in the Netherlands with pupils who speak advanced Dutch as an L2, this chapter characterizes the interaction climates of the two teachers (of biology and geography) who were observed to be more language sensitive than their colleagues. The description consists of both examples from classroom discourse and computerized analyses from the complete set of data.

STUDYING CLASSROOM INTERACTION IN CONTENT AREAS

Content-area teaching has become a focus for L2 researchers for two reasons: (a) to improve the transition of L2 learners to mainstream classes, this is a step that is problematic in a variety of contexts around the world (Cummins, 1992), and (b) to determine the role of classroom interaction between native speakers (NSs) and non-native speakers (NNSs) as it affects language development (Pica, 1994; Gass, Mackey, & Pica, 1998). In theory, Long (1981) argued that if comprehension promotes language acquisition and conversational modifications lead to better comprehension, this implies that conversational modifications contribute to language acquisition. Later, Swain (1985) underlined the role of L2 production and the opportunity to get feedback as important for L2 learners. By participating in interaction, NNSs are able to ask for clarification and, as a result, receive more usable input (Gass, 1997). Furthermore, feedback containing recasts and rephrases draws the learner's attention to incorrectness and functions as a trigger for further restructuring of the learner's interlanguage.

These theoretical assumptions have been affirmed in part by empirical studies. Ellis, Tanaka, and Yamazaki (1994) showed how Japanese students of English attained better comprehension and increased vocabulary acquisition when they could talk about a complex written text than when they read the text in a premodified version without interaction opportunities. A similar experiment, carried out by VandenBranden (1995, 1997) in upper primary school, studied the influence of four conditions on text comprehension: (a) reading the original (complex) text, (b) reading a premodified version, (c) reading the original text with opportunity to discuss the text with a peer, and (d) reading the original text in a group of pupils with the researcher present and opportunities for interaction. Both conditions in which interaction and negotiation of meaning were possible led to significantly better results on a test of text comprehension questions. Polio and Gass (1998) also showed how comprehension is improved in interactive conditions.

Apart from effects of negotiation of meaning on comprehension, the effects on L2 production have also been studied. VandenBranden (1995, 1997) compared pairs of pupils who discussed the content of a detective story consisting of several pictures. Both before and after this task they were asked to describe the pictures orally. Pairs that used more sequences of negotiating meaning while carrying out the task exhibited an increased amount of L2 production in the posttest, as well as a greater variety in vocabulary. Gass and Varonis (1994) also showed how prior negotiation can affect production later on; however, the effects are not always obvious directly after the "treatment."

In these and other studies, the active participation of all NNSs may not be necessary. In the Ellis et al. (1994) study, even students who could observe peers actively engaging in interaction gained a better understanding of the text. Mackey (1995), however, did not find positive effects of observing interaction without opportunities for production.

Drawing on these and other studies, quantitative and qualitative aspects of NNS students' participation are crucial in the description of conditions for L2 acquisition in content classes. It is doubtful, however, to what extent sequences of negotiating meaning occur in classroom settings, given the asymmetrical, unequal roles of teachers and students. The teacher is the one who knows and the student is the one who does not know. This dominance could well prohibit NNS active participation (Deen, 1995; Polio & Gass, 1998). VandenBranden's study (1995, 1997) justifies these doubts. Compared with the experimental conditions, negotiating meaning seldom took place in naturalistic classroom settings. He also found that the length of this type of sequence was shorter in whole-group settings than in one-on-one interaction between the NS teacher and NNS pupils. VandenBranden concluded that classrooms are not a fertile context for negotiation of meaning to take place because teachers consider this type of interaction to be inefficient in their lessons.

Building on the idea that conditions for L2 learning could well be built into content area-teaching (Grabe & Stoller, 1997), the content-based approach (CBA) of L2 learning inspired the practice of many teachers and schools as well as the development of teaching materials (Brinton, Snow, & Wesche, 1989; Snow & Brinton, 1997). However, the broad range of courses, the great variety of contexts and methods, and the lack of empirical studies make it difficult to judge the weak and strong points of the CBA. The need for classroom observations was illustrated by Dicker's (1995) study of the application of Chamot and O'Malley's Cognitive Academic Language Learning Approach (CALLA), one special branch of the CBA (Chamot & O'Malley, 1994; O'Malley & Chamot, 1990). In his study, Dicker showed how well-designed CALLA materials promoting higher order thinking skills in L2 were transformed by teachers into lower order tasks. If content-area teaching is to be utilized as a breeding ground for L2 development, a better understanding of the role of teachers in creating interactive L2-promoting conditions is needed.

Most interaction studies focus on language forms and functions and on the structures of participation. However, in content-area teaching the thematic content is not only a trigger for pupil participation, but a goal on its own. On a theoretical level, this relation between language and content in interaction has been discussed from different angles. Mohan (1986) suggested that the challenge of education is to lead students into theoretical knowledge and academic language, building on their daily communicative skills and daily knowledge. He described how linguistic analysis of academic tasks can be used in a curriculum in which content and language are integrated.

Van Lier (1988) underlined the value of interaction in the acquisition of academic language proficiency. He stated that the character of language use in schools depends on the interaction type and the task type. Academic tasks with low-level goals can have a fixed and well-controlled structure and fixed interaction patterns. Van Lier mentioned pattern drills from language classes as an example. Pupils know the frame related to different activities and they activate this as soon as they start carrying out a task. In this way, classroom interaction is, to a certain extent, preplanned and the history and routines of a class are resources that pupils use in fulfilling a task. In more complex academic tasks, however, the interaction itself becomes an important resource for learning. In that case, the participation structures become less predictable and the opportunities for participation increase. Learning tasks should be designed in such a way that both complexity (social and academic) and resources (internal and external, such as textbooks) should be taken into account (van Lier, 1988). This interrelatedness of task complexity, available resources, and social and academic aspects should be integrated in classroom research, van Lier argued. This would mean that content complexity should be included as an influencing factor in interaction studies.

Even from L2 acquisition studies the impact of content has been brought into the discussions. Zuengler (1993) found a relation between background knowledge of a topic and participation in NS–NNS pair interaction. A greater familiarity with the topic led to more active involvement in interaction and a higher number of confirmation requests, suggesting that learners are less hampered by limited L2 skills when they have more access to the topic of the conversation. Ehrlich, Avery, and Yorio (1989) studied the content aspect of L2 input by native speakers and distinguished two types of modifications in the content of NS input to NNS: "skeletonizing" the message to the absolute core matter, and "embroidering" the message with extra information and reformulations. In the experiment, the second strategy led to less comprehension, which could be explained by extra difficulties in the additional input.

In a case study, I (Hajer, 1996) provided a description of interaction patterns in content teaching in a multilingual middle school classroom. I followed one mainstream class with a large number of L2 learners in five subjects—biology, geography, chemistry, physics, and math—taught by five different subject teachers. I found systematic differences in interaction patterns within the five school subjects. These differences concern the moments of pupil participation, the initiative taken by pupils and teachers for interaction, the intensity of interaction (as measured by the number of moves following an initiative) and the function of teacher and pupil utterances. The two subjects in which pupils participated most, both in whole-group activities and in one-on-one teacher–pupil conversations, were biology and geography. Interestingly, the differences in interaction climates were connected not only to teacher interactive styles, but to different demands put on pupils on the assessment tests. In geography and biology, a larger number of concepts and a higher cognitive level were demanded. Given these findings, I proposed that studies of interaction in content lessons should always take into account the cognitive dimension and content learning that is taking place.

How the complexity of the task and the use of different resources are dealt with (van Lier, 1988), how familiarity with and access to the topic are influencing interaction patterns (Zuengler, 1993), or which strategies teachers use in conveying the content (Ehrlich et al., 1989) have only fragmentarily been studied. Dicker's (1995) study of the CALLA program, mentioned earlier, suggests that strategies of skeletonizing and lowering cognitive demands do occur. Hajer (1996) showed how different teachers might choose different approaches with the same multilingual group of pupils. In this chapter I focus on the interaction practices of two teachers from my study who succeeded relatively well in creating a positive interaction climate, involving pupils in classroom discussions and putting high demands on their content learning. Observations of their behavior provide insights into the question of how to create L2 learning conditions while conveying subject matter.

THE STUDY

Design of the Case Study: One Class, Five School Subjects

This research comes from a case study of one multilingual class in the third year of a lower general secondary school in Amsterdam, the Netherlands. The class consisted of 3 Dutch NSs and 23 ethnic minority pupils for whom Dutch was an L2. These Moroccan, Turkish, Italian, and Pakistan children were born in Holland or had arrived before their eighth birthday. The class was followed through a series of lessons in five different school subjects: biology, geography, chemistry, physics, and mathematics. Each subject was taught by a different teacher. The subjects reported on in this chapter are geography and biology.

The teacher of geography was a 33-year-old man who had taught geography and history for 8 years at lower secondary school level. The teacher of biology was a 48-year-old woman with 20 years of experience in teaching biology, physics, and chemistry in lower, intermediate, and higher secondary education. She was bilingual in Dutch and German herself. Both teachers had attended in-service sessions on developing reading strategies in multilingual classes.

Table 13.1 displays the data gathered for both subjects. For each subject, 10 50-minute lessons were observed and recorded on tape. During group work, teacher interaction with individual pupils was recorded. After parts that did not belong to the content lesson itself (e.g., resolving conflicts between pupils) were omitted, the number of teacher and pupil utterances was found to total 5,311 and 2,923, respectively. Additional data consisted of class tests (two from each subject), exercise books, and teaching materials. Furthermore, the pupils and teachers were questioned, orally and in writing, about their experiences and their opinions concerning the role of Dutch as L2 in the subject lessons.

The aim of the study was to provide a description of interaction patterns in content teaching in a multilingual classroom that promote L2 student participation. The research questions in this chapter are the following:

- To what extent and on whose initiative do pupils participate in content lessons that have been designated as interactive content lessons?
- How intense is their participation?
- Which strategies do language-sensitive teachers use that lead to intense interaction in content classes?

TABLE 13.1
Summary of the Observation Data

	Lessons Observed	Lessons Transcribed	Utterances	Assessment Tests
Geography	10	8	5,311	2
Biology	10	7	2,923	2

Answering these questions will provide a deepened understanding of the ways in which content teachers can contribute to L2 acquisition of advanced learners who need further development of subject-specific L2 skills while acquiring content knowledge.

Levels of Analysis

The goal of the analysis was to reveal the structural and functional aspects of classroom interaction (who is talking, when, how, how long) as well as its content aspects (about which concepts and themes), in relation to the achievement of pupils, as performed on the tests. Table 13.2 displays the levels of analyses. Complete lessons were segmented into lesson segments, or situation types (Lemke, 1982) such as overview over the lesson,

TABLE 13.2
Levels of Analysis

I. Lesson segments		
Overview over the lesson (whole group)		
Explanation of new content (whole group)		
Seated work (individually, pairs, small groups)		
Going over seated work (whole group)		
II. Interaction types		
Teacher monologue		
Triad dialogue (initiative–response–feedback)		
Dialogue teacher–pupil		
Dialogue pupil–pupil		
III. Level of exchange types		
Initiative	*Teacher*	*Pupil*
One-way communication		
Directive	*Teacher directive*	*Pupil directive*
Informing	*Teacher inform*	*Pupil inform*
Two-way communication		
Eliciting	*Teacher elicitation*	*Pupil elicitation*
Checking comprehension	*Teacher check*	*Pupil check*
IV. Level of moves		
Initiating move		
Response move		
Feedback move		
V. Level of single utterances		
Questioning		
Informing		
Managing the interaction		
Feedback		
Directives		

explanation of new content, seated work, and going over seated work. Within these lesson segments basic structures of communication were characterized using Lemke's interaction types, such as teacher monologue, triad dialogue, dialogue teacher/student, or dialogue pupil/pupil. For further analyses, the Sinclair and Coulthard (1975) system of discourse analysis was adapted. Exchanges were identified as belonging to different exchange types: teacher informs, teacher elicitations, teacher checks, teacher directives, pupil informs, pupil elicitations, and pupil checks. Exchange types consist of moves: initiatives, responses, and feedback. Finally these moves consist of separate utterances. For each utterance there is a specification of which tasks it fulfills in terms of five main functional categories: to question, to inform, to maintain interaction, to provide feedback, and to direct. The study of the coded transcripts was largely done with the help of computer analysis using the Child Language Data Exchange System (CHILDES) program (MacWhinney, 1995).

Results

General Picture of Participation

The class of pupils moved from one classroom to another every 50 minutes to meet the next teacher and subject. It was striking how the pupils—at the same time—had to change atmosphere and routines. All teachers had their own classroom routines, their personal approaches to pupils, and their own interaction practices, putting specific demands on pupil participation. It seemed as if pupils were well aware of these differences and adjusted their behavior quickly. They knew, for instance, when to ask for vocabulary explanation: during or after reading a text or during or after doing seated work. They knew when to listen attentively and when to relax and talk with peers.

Participation According to Lesson Segment Type. As might be expected, teachers did a lot more talking than pupils. Overall, the teachers contributed about 72% of the number of utterances. This general picture, however, is very different when lesson segments are taken into account. Figure 13.1 illustrates the differences in participation during three segment types in biology and geography.

Pupils participated relatively more frequently while doing seated work with the teacher walking around and during the plenary discussions going over seated work. Also, during seated work a wider range of pupils was involved in interaction.

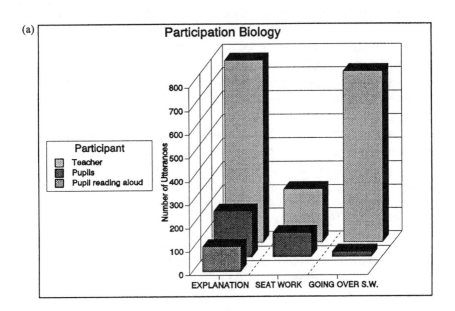

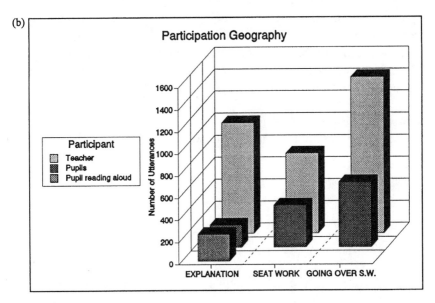

FIG. 13.1.   Participation of pupil and teacher within three lesson segments.

Participation According to Exchange Type. The analysis of exchange types provides insight into when and why pupils participate. On the whole, one third of all utterances stemmed from teacher informatives and teacher directives, constituting one-way communication. One third stemmed from teacher elicitations and comprehension checks, and one third from pupil initiatives. This general picture can be observed in both geography and biology, as shown in Fig. 13.2. The middle parts of the columns represent those utterances that stem from the teachers' efforts to establish two-way communication with the pupils. It is clear that the teacher established more communication during whole-group activities, whereas the floor seemed to be given to the pupils during seated work.

Examples of Teacher Efforts to Involve Pupils

In the following, I illustrate how teachers involved pupils in interaction with examples from three different lesson segments: an explanation of new subject matter, seated work, and going over seated work.

Explanation of New Subject Matter. During this lesson segment type, the main pupil participation took place in response to teacher-initiated comprehension checks. Both the geography and biology teachers used a text from the textbook as the main source, reading the text with the class and checking for unknown vocabulary. A typical example of their efforts to involve pupils is given in Example 1.

Example 1: Geography[1]
(Teacher interrupts a student, reading the text aloud)

Teacher:	What is sewerage?
Pupil:	It's a pipe under the ground.
Teacher:	Yes and what happens there?
Pupil:	Eh waste water in it . . .
Teacher:	Yes, waste water, waste water from houses, for instance from toilets, is drained off by the sewerage.

As this example illustrates, pupils were encouraged to express the meaning of academic concepts in everyday expressions. The teacher then gave feedback on their answers. This teacher strategy was frequently observed in geography and biology. Presumably, its value for L2 acquisi-

---

[1]These examples were all translated from the original Dutch into English for the purposes of presentation in this chapter.

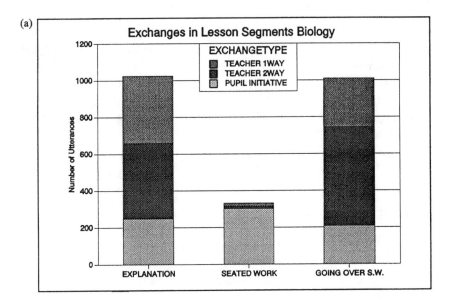

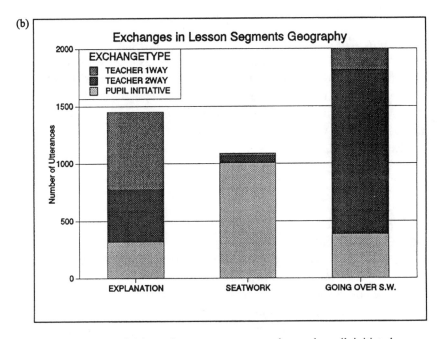

FIG. 13.2. Division of utterances over teacher and pupil initiated exchanges.

tion lies in its making the linguistic input from the textbook more comprehensible. The value for the development of productive skills is doubtful, as only short utterances were requested.

A less commonly used teacher strategy during this lesson segment was to ask pupils to signal unknown vocabulary and find the explanation by themselves. In this way, pupils were further stimulated to use learning strategies that they had been taught during language classes. In Example 2, the biology teacher uses this strategy after having read a part of the text.

Example 2: Biology

Teacher:	Any questions?
Pupil:	Excrement.
Teacher:	Let's read that part of the text again and see if you can find the meaning by yourself. "Some parts of the food cannot be digested. These leave the body as excrements". So, Mohammed, what would be the meaning of excrement?
Pupil:	Shit.
Teacher:	Exactly.

Seated Work.   After the introduction of new subject matter, pupils often did seated work with content teachers usually walking around, answering individual questions. Asking their own questions, pupils used more productive L2 skills, which led to more negotiation of meaning, as is shown in Example 3. In this example, Jermain asked a question of the Biology teacher, who was walking around while the pupils were working on text-related questions.

Example 3: Biology

Jermain:	How do you get sour teeth?
Teacher:	Sour teeth?
Jermain:	Yes.
Teacher:	That does not exist. Sour or acid in your mouth can be converted into, eh sugar can be converted into acid. That is it.
Jermain:	But ma'am
Teacher:	What do you mean by sour teeth then?
Jermain:	I don't know. Uh, your teeth hurt when you are going to eat something or when you are drinking
Teacher:	Oh, yes, yes, your gums are withdrawn, and so the necks of the teeth are open and very sensitive. That is what you mean.
Jermain:	Ma'am, if you eat something cold or hot you get a silly feeling.
Teacher:	Yes, that can happen when the neck of a tooth is open. It is painful.

The teacher took her time to understand and answer Jermain's question. This gave him the opportunity to reformulate his question several times and to relate his concept of sour teeth to the content knowledge and appropriate wording. It was remarkable to observe that several pupils only asked their questions during the moments of seated work. In particular, the Moroccan girls only raised their hands, whether in biology or geography, when a "private" discussion with a teacher was possible.

Going Over Seated Work. Going over seated work provided discussions of text-related questions that were well-structured moments, ideal for pupil participation. The initiative to involve students in interaction was often taken by the teacher. Example 4 is taken from a biology lesson in which the class was discussing text-related questions.

Example 4: Biology

Teacher: OK Sadik, next question.

Sadik: *[Sadik reads from the textbook.]* "Some people use their teeth to open bottles (crown caps). Why is that bad for their teeth?" Because the enamel can be damaged.

Teacher: An alternative. Aziz?

Aziz: Eh, how do you put it. Eh there comes cavities in those teeth and microbes can come in.

Teacher: That is a step ahead. How do you pick up those cavities?

Tolga: <Because your molars wear out. >

Aziz: <That those things that you don't make cavities>
[two pupils talking at the same time.]

Teacher: aha, so what Sadik said

Pupil: is right!

Teacher: And what Aziz said, if we compare those two answers, first happens what Sadik said and then it goes on until you get real cavities. First the enamel is damaged, and once it has been damaged, those microbes are going to harm the tooth and cause cavities that penetrate to the cement.

In this example the biology teacher stimulated pupils' L2 production by postponing her final evaluation of their answers. Before she gave feedback on Sadik's answer she transferred the turn to other pupils by asking for alternative or additional information. In her feedback she then connected the answers to each other. This way of working required the class to listen to each other and to add onto peer L2 production.

Not only teachers took initiatives during this lesson segment. A very frequent function of pupil initiatives was to check for correct answers.

Because it was in the interest of each pupil to write down answers correctly (knowing these notes will be a crucial source when preparing for the assessment tests), they often wanted to check if their alternative was correct, as in Example 5.

Example 5: Geography

Teacher: Question 6 is a difficult one. Abdeslam can you read that one please.

Ab: "What harmful effect does the discharge of cooling water into rivers have?" Uh, plants and fishes die out.

Teacher: And how?

Ab: The water is too warm.

Teacher: Yes, correct. So you can write down that because at a certain moment . . . uh . . . the cooling water gets warm, the word already tells you it is cooling something but then it gets warm itself. And that is being discharged to the rivers and ditches. So the temperature rises and that's not beneficial to the growth of plants in the first place and, what is more, oxygen is in one way or the other removed. So fish can die. So, to repeat, you can write down as follows. The water in rivers . . .
         [several pupils bid for a turn.]

Teacher: Saba.

Saba: I've got 'a threat to the life of plants and animals'.

Teacher: Yes that's also correct. Fine. But you should also say that it is because the water gets warmer. So to repeat . . . Mohammed.

Moham: The water temperature rises.

Teacher: Yes, that's correct and therefore it is a threat to plants and fishes. So write down the water in rivers gets too warm, water in rivers gets too warm, comma, bad for plants and fishes.

In this extract several pupils had the opportunity to give their answers. It is clear that they themselves took the initiative to check their alternatives. The teacher was open for questions and allowed pupils to take the floor. He then gave feedback and additional input. This suggests that pupils repeatedly heard the same subject matter explained. They also gave each other various wordings of the same concept, so that they could grasp the similarity between "the water gets warmer" and "the water temperature rises."

The Intensity of Interaction: The Level of Moves

Teacher and pupil initiatives seemed to be bound to different lesson segments. The exchanges varied in length, as measured in number of utterances following an initiative. They also varied in intensity, measured by the number of moves from teacher and pupils following one initiative. Example 3 (Jermain asking about the sour teeth) illustrates a longer exchange in which the pupil's initiative and bid for turn lead to several turn takings of both pupil and teacher. These moves together form one exchange type, namely a pupil elicitation (Sinclair & Coulthard, 1975). The more moves following an initiative, the higher the intensity of interaction.

A comparison was made with respect to the intensity of interaction during the three segment types. Figure 13.3 shows a clear distinction among these three segment types. The most intense interaction occurred during whole-class discussions where teacher elicitations form the starting point for interaction. In both biology and geography, the mean length of teacher elicitation exchanges was more than 10 moves. During seated work, pupil initiatives led to the most intense interactions with a mean length of 8 moves per exchange type.

The two teachers apparently used their means of interaction in a pronounced way; they used the floor themselves in plenary situations, but gave the floor to the pupils during seated work. The number of teacher initiatives and pupil initiatives and the intensity of the exchange types was complementary. During whole-class activities, teachers led the exchanges and allocated turns within one exchange to several pupils. Teachers tried to involve more pupils in the interaction. Negative feedback of a pupil's answer often led to transfer of the turn to another student. It should be noted that, as a result, pupils had fewer opportunities to reformulate their own answers.

A different pattern was found during seated work. In pupil-initiated exchanges, one or two pupils continued to talk with the teacher without losing the floor. They could not only formulate their questions but also reformulate them until they came to a better understanding of the content matter. During these moments, teachers took more time to negotiate meaning and were less hampered by their need to control and involve the whole group. In short, interaction during seated work with an ambulant teacher seemed to be more natural, resembling communication patterns in the real world outside school.

Interaction Climate and Cognitive Demands: Remarkable Links

Hajer (1996) found that the more interactive climates of the geography and biology classes were directly related to the thematic content of the lessons. Differences among the five teachers concerned the cognitive demands made on the pupils. In biology, for example, not only the number of central concepts exceeded that of the other four subjects, but the

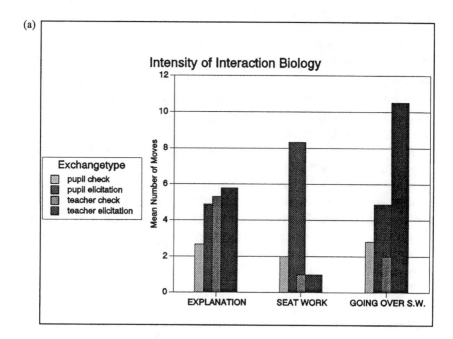

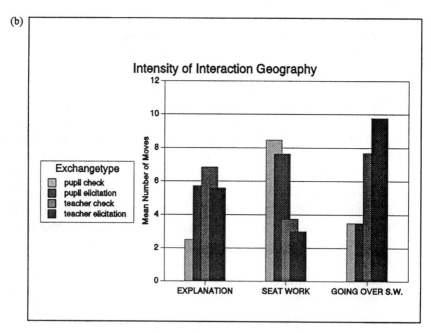

FIG. 13.3. Intensity of interaction within exchange types and lesson segments.

cognitive level of the questions on the assessment tests was also higher. Not only were definitions of isolated concepts addressed, but so were the relations between the different concepts and the variety of contexts in which they should be placed. These academic expectations were obvious in the lessons preceding the assessment tests.

Classroom interaction is one of many resources available for learning. Most central concepts appear both in textbook questions and frequently in classroom interaction. The two interactive teachers apparently used the strategy of explicitly making these resources accessible to the pupils. The geography teacher, for example, explicitly related his explanations to those in the textbooks, reading these texts together with the pupils in class. The biology teacher made the most demands on pupils by discussing texts in the classroom and looking for explicit signals that phrases from the text had been understood. This teacher was not satisfied with answers directly quoted from the textbooks. Instead she urged the pupils to rephrase them in their own wording. Rote learning was not enough to pass the tests. In general this instructional strategy could be characterized as putting cognitive and linguistic demands on pupils.

The comments made by teachers and pupils give additional information about the link between interaction climate and cognitive demands. The biology and geography teachers saw it as their duty to explain difficult texts and to check for comprehension; they deliberately gave the textbook a central place in their teaching. They consciously chose the approach of talking with the pupils about the content matter as a way of reaching the subject goals, as opposed to avoiding the often difficult communication and limiting the subject goals as a solution.

For the pupils, the routines of content classes were obvious. The pupils' assessment of teachers' behaviors corresponded to the teacher characteristics observed; for example, the opportunity to ask questions and the length of exchanges. The pupils' views reflected a quite calculating attitude; they just did what was necessary to pass the assessment tests. Whether that involved a good understanding of the subject matter or not was, in principle, not important to them.

CONCLUSION AND DISCUSSION:
DISTINGUISHING TEACHER PROFILES

This study aimed at illuminating interaction-promoting features used by two content-area teachers who had been found to be relatively interaction promoting compared to three colleagues teaching the same group of multilingual pupils. The interactive teachers made good use of clearly structured lessons with recognizable moments for active pupil participation. During the explanation of new subject matter, the teachers took the initiative to involve pupils in discussing new vocabulary and understanding written texts. During seated work they left room for the pupils' own initiatives to ask questions. At such times, the pupil initiatives led to intense interaction that would resemble natural communication more than whole-class interaction; more pupils were actively involved, more productive L2 use was registered, and there was more individual feedback from the teacher. It seems important for teachers to create fixed moments for these pupil–teacher dialogues.

While going over seated work, teachers took initiatives to get the pupils involved and lengthened exchanges by asking further questions and delaying final feedback, leading to a more intense interaction. Additionally, an important teacher strategy linked to efforts to actively involve pupils was putting high cognitive demands on content learning.

One way of characterizing the two teachers' strategies is by labeling the type of choices teachers can make while working in multilingual classes. Ehrlich et al. (1989) observed that teachers not only show modifications in their own speech and interaction patterns, but also adjust the content of the message, thus skeletonizing the message. Hajer (1996) illustrated this tendency in teacher behavior, where lowering demands on productive skills was connected with skeletonizing content. In such a context, interaction might simply not be necessary for achieving the goals of the lesson. Additionally, Teemant, Bernhardt, and Rodriguez-Munoz (1997) discussed the danger of compromising content in content-based L2 courses and argued in favor of appropriate elaborative techniques that would be beneficial for both NS and NNS students in a multilingual class. This interdependence seems to be highly influenced by the routines of an individual teacher and his or her views and beliefs. As a hypothesis, two different teacher profiles can be distinguished: the academic language-avoiding and the language-sensitive content teacher, whose practices differ on the dimensions mentioned in Table 13.3.

Some limitations in the two teachers' current practices should be mentioned. A few passages of more intense interaction were preplanned by the teacher and several central concepts were not explicitly discussed at all during the course. Also, feedback on linguistic form was seldom provided for, and pupils often relied on safe quotations from the textbook instead of using more productive L2 skills. It is obvious that even those subject teachers most inclined to intense interaction need the support of further

TABLE 13.3
Dimensions of Two Profiles of Content Teachers in Multilingual Classrooms

Content Teacher		
Academic Language-Avoiding		*Language-Sensitive*
–	Interaction Climate	+
	Fixed moments for pupil participation	
	Explicit prompts and elicitations	
	Length and intensity of exchanges	
	Demanding written and oral production in L2	
	Making metalinguistic comments	
	Explicit feedback on content and form	
	Content Aspects	
	Number of concepts taught	
	Skeletonizing or embroidering subject matter	
	Requiring higher level thinking skills	
	Correcting or assessing content learning	
	Relating oral to written explanations in textbooks	
	Views and Beliefs	
	Low versus high expectations of pupils' achievement	
	Views on and knowledge of the L2 acquisition process	
	Attitudes toward their role in language and content learning	

training and specially designed materials to promote interaction in pairs and in whole-class situations. A growing request for language-sensitive content instruction can be expected as more teachers encounter linguistic heterogeneity in their mainstream classrooms.

From this study's findings, implications for future research can be drawn. Considering the interrelation between the interaction climates and the level of content teaching in the subjects observed, research into linguistic aspects of subject teaching should not be isolated from the content aspects of interaction. Interaction seems to be necessary in content courses when pupils feel that a real understanding of course content will be needed to pass their assessment tests. As Doyle (1983) put it, "the evaluative climate connects academic tasks with a reward structure" (p. 182). Pupils who know that they will get a reward without understanding the content will not be stimulated to use the classroom interaction as a resource for learning. Thus, theory on cognitive academic language skills should take into account the influence teachers and pupils have on the problems of language use in classrooms. Their influence concerns both the cognitive dimension as well as the contextual dimension of basic interpersonal communicative skills and cognitive academic language proficiency (Cummins, 1992). It would be worthwhile researching whether active pupil participation in classroom interaction, as part of improving L2 learning conditions, could be triggered by a content curriculum, in which high demands are put on conceptual learning, with productive use of the concepts involved.

REFERENCES

Brinton, D., Snow, M., & Wesche, M. (1989). *Content-based second language instruction.* Boston: Heinle & Heinle.

Chamot, A. U., & O'Malley, J. M. (1994). *The CALLA handbook: Implementing the cognitive academic language learning approach.* Reading, MA: Addison-Wesley.

Cummins, J. (1992). Language proficiency, bilingualism, and academic achievement. In P. Richard-Amato & M. A. Snow (Eds.), The multicultural classroom. *Readings for content-area teachers* (pp. 16–26). Reading, MA: Addison-Wesley.

Deen, J. (1995). *Dealing with problems in intercultural communication: A study of negotiation of meaning in native–nonnative speaker interaction.* Unpublished doctoral dissertation, Tilburg University, Tilburg, The Netherlands.

Dicker, C. L. (1995). *The construction and maintenance of behavioral patterns in a content-based language instruction class.* Unpublished doctoral dissertation, Columbia University, New York.

Doyle, W. (1983). Academic work. *Review of Educational Research, 53,* 159–199.

Ehrlich, S., Avery, P., & Yorio, C. (1989). Discourse structure and the negotiation of comprehensible input. *Studies in Second Language Acquisition, 11,* 397–414.

Ellis, R., Tanaka,Y., & Yamazaki, A. (1994). Classroom interaction, comprehension, and the acquisition of L2 word meanings. *Language Learning, 44,* 449–491.

Gass, S. M. (1997). *Input, interaction and the second language learner.* Mahwah, NJ: Lawrence Erlbaum Associates.

Gass, S. M., Mackey, A., & Pica, T. (1998). The role of input and interaction in second language acquisition. *Modern Language Journal, 82,* 299–307.

Gass, S. M., & Varonis, E. M. (1994). Input, interaction, and second language production. *Studies in Second Language Acquisition, 16,* 283–302.

Grabe, W., & Stoller, F. (1997). Content-based instruction: Research foundations. In M. A. Snow & D. M. Brinton (Eds.), *The content-based classroom: Perspectives on integrating language and content* (pp. 5–21). White Plains, NY: Longman.

Hajer, M. (1996). *Leren in een tweede taal: Interactie in vakonderwijs aan een meertalige mavo-klas* [Learning through a second language: Interaction in content area lessons in a multilingual class]. (Doctoral dissertation, Catholic University of Brabant, Tilburg, The Netherlands). Groningen: Wolters-Noordhoff.

Lemke, J. L. (1982). *Classroom communication of science* (Final rep.). City University of New York, Brooklyn, NY.

Long, M. (1981). Input, interaction, and second language acquisition. In H. Winitz (Ed.), *Native language and foreign language acquisition* (pp. 259–278). New York: Annals of the New York Academy of Sciences.

Mackey, A. (1995). *Stepping up the pace: Input, interaction and interlanguage development. An empirical study of questions in ESL.* Unpublished doctoral dissertation, University of Sydney, Australia.

MacWhinney, B. (1995). *The CHILDES project: Tools for analyzing talk* (2nd ed.). Hillsdale, NJ: Lawrence Erlbaum Associates.

Mohan, B. (1986). *Language and content.* Reading, MA: Addison-Wesley.

O'Malley, M., & Chamot, A. U. (1990). *Learning strategies in second language learning.* Cambridge, UK: Cambridge University Press.

Pica, T. (1994). Research on negotiation: What does it reveal about second-language learning conditions, processes, and outcomes? *Language Learning, 44*, 493–527.

Polio, C., & Gass, S. M. (1998). The role of interaction in native speaker comprehension of nonnative speaker speech. *Modern Language Journal, 82*, 308–319.

Sinclair, J. M., & Coulthard, M. (1975). *Towards an analysis of discourse: The English of teachers and pupils.* Oxford, UK: Oxford University Press.

Snow, M. A., & Brinton, D. M. (Eds.). (1997). *The content-based classroom: Perspectives on integrating language and content.* White Plains, NY: Longman.

Swain, M. (1985). Communicative competence: Some roles of comprehensible input and comprehensible output in its development. In S. Gass & C. Madden (Eds.), *Input in second language acquisition* (pp. 235–253). Rowley, MA: Newbury House.

Teemant, A., Bernhardt, E., & Rodriguez-Munoz, M. (1997). Collaborating with content-area teachers: What we need to share. In M. A. Snow & D. M. Brinton (Eds.), *The content-based classroom: Perspectives on integrating language and content* (pp. 311–318). White Plains, NY: Longman.

VandenBranden, K. (1995). *Negotiation of meaning in second language acquisition: A study of primary school classes.* Leuven, Belgium: Proefschrift, K.U.

VandenBranden, K. (1997). Effects of negotiation on language learners' output. *Language Learning, 47*, 589–636.

van Lier, L. (1988). *The classroom and the language learner: Ethnography and second-language classroom research.* New York: Longman.

Zuengler, J. (1993). Encouraging learners' conversational participation: The effect of content knowledge. *Language Learning, 43*, 403–432.

Classroom Interaction and Additional Language Learning: Implications for Teaching and Research

Joan Kelly Hall

The issues investigated in the 12 studies of this volume are varied. They range from the role of teacher questions in scaffolding learning to the role of interpersonal interactions in the learning of particular forms for creating peer solidarity to learner appropriation of strategies for facilitating their own and each other's language learning. The specific language learning contexts are fairly varied as well. The sites range from elementary classrooms to adult intensive language courses, and the target languages include English, Japanese, Dutch, Hebrew, German, and French. These differences in research focus and language learning contexts notwithstanding, taken as a whole, the findings arising from these studies provide compelling evidence on particular practices for promoting the development of additional languages. Thus, they have important theoretical and pedagogical implications. My intent in this chapter is to summarize these findings and attempt to lay out a set of implications for identifying and sustaining effectual practices in classrooms serving second and foreign language students. I conclude with a discussion on implications for language teacher preparation and some suggested directions for future research on second and foreign language learning.

SUMMARY OF FINDINGS

Several interesting findings on classroom-based additional language development can be gleaned from individual studies, but taken as a whole, four particularly robust findings emerge. The first has to do with the role of repetition, revoicing, and recasting of members' contributions to the interactions. Several studies demonstrate that both teacher and student repetition, echoes, reformulations, and paraphrases of all or part of their own and each other's utterances not only provide cognitive benefits, but they engender positive social consequences as well. In terms of cognitive benefits, Duff (chap. 6, this volume), for example, found that in addition to helping to create topical connections among speakers' contributions, repetition and paraphrasing of terms by both teacher and students in large group classroom conversations served to validate the concepts and ideas initially raised by students in the interaction and to draw their attention to key concepts or linguistic forms. These findings corroborate those by Sullivan (chap. 4, this volume), Boyd and Maloof (chap. 8, this volume), Verplaetse (chap. 11, this volume), and Damhuis (chap. 12, this volume), who found that incorporating and extending word choices in the classroom interaction through repetition, revoicings, and recasts of classroom members' utterances facilitated the students' appropriation of new words and ideas. In the studies by Verplaetse, Damhuis, and Boyd and Maloof, it was the teacher who was primarily responsible for helping to create the connections. Each teacher used repetitions and recasts of student utterances in such a way as to affirm their contributions and make them available to the full class for their consideration. In this way, individual student utterances were linked together and woven into the larger classroom discourse, thereby creating a collective knowledge base on which all students could draw for subsequent contributions. In Sullivan's study, students and the teacher echoed or reformulated each other's utterances and in so doing helped to maintain topical coherence and build a base of shared knowledge. Ohta (chap. 3, this volume) reported similar findings on the benefits of repetition and recasts, at least in terms of focusing students' attention on particular linguistic forms. Of interest in her study is the fact that repetitions and recasts proved to be beneficial to individual learners even though they were not intended to be. That is, both teacher and student utterances functioned as incidental recasts for individual learners in that in their private turns—turns addressed to themselves—individual learners were able to compare their own responses to those they heard addressed to others in large group interaction and make changes accordingly.

Findings from several studies demonstrate that the use of repetition, revoicings, and recasts in classroom interaction served social purposes as well. Duff, Sullivan, and Verplaetse, in particular, found that the building of a shared base of knowledge through repetition and paraphrasing of classroom members' utterances helped to create a sense of community. In Duff and Sullivan's classrooms, it also lent a humorous, lighthearted side to learning in that classroom members could use their collectively constructed knowledge to play on each other's words and ideas. This use of humor, in turn, heightened learners' enjoyment in their classroom interactions and motivated them to continue their participation. Their continued engagement provided them with ample opportunities not only to become more affiliated with the subject but to build on and sustain their interpersonal relationships as a community of language learners and users as well. It should be noted that although there were numerous benefits reported for the use of repetition and paraphrasing in these studies, Duff highlights the fact that repetition may not always be helpful. As she shows in some of her data, persistent, intentional repetition to focus on form in classroom interaction can be mind-numbing and thus likely to counteract any possible developmental benefits.

Connected to the finding on the social purposes of repetition, revoicings, and recasts is the second key finding emerging from several studies. Social context and, more specifically, the interpersonal relationships formed as part of the context, are fundamental to the construction of shared sociocultural knowledge and interpersonal bonds, which in turn influence the process of additional language learning. Although undertaken in different language learning contexts, studies by Kinginger (chap. 2, this volume), Sullivan (chap. 4, this volume), Duff (chap. 6, this volume), Consolo (chap. 5, this volume), and Boxer and Cortés-Conde (chap. 10, this volume) all found that the interpersonal connections developed in classroom interactions nurtured student engagement in them, and thus provided multiple opportunities for language learners to use and extend their knowledge of the target language. In their interactions with each other they became acquainted, made their perspectives known, showed support for others, and increased group solidarity. In Kinginger's study it was the desire to make friends with their French-speaking peers that provided the impetus for the students of French to learn the appropriate forms for the expression of solidarity. In the sharing of personal stories and cultural norms, the English-language learners in the study by Boxer and Cortés-Conde fostered the development of group relationships, which in turn provided comfortable, safe contexts in which they were able to become better acquainted with each other and with the new culture in which they were living. Engaging in meaningful conversations on such motivating topics, the authors argue, helped learners invest in their community of learners and become active agents in the development of their sociocultural awareness and pragmatic competence, knowledge of which is essential to their success as English-language learners and users.

In the studies by Sullivan and Duff, the learners knew each other and thus were motivated by the rapport already established in these interpersonal relationships to use the target language to share their perspectives on a topic with which they were familiar, to engage in repartee with each other, and, more generally, to display the enjoyment they felt in each other's company. Through their active participation in discussions that mattered, these language learners saw themselves as valid interlocutors with a real need to interact with each other. The interpersonal relationships that were nurtured in their classroom communities engendered positive emotional energy and an active interest in learning. As Kinginger notes, it is in the "vagaries, perils, and delights of making sense in the company of other human beings who interest them" that the development of such essential everyday communicative skills and abilities is fostered.

A third finding to emerge across these studies has to do with the significance of the role of the teacher in fostering additional language learning. Across learning contexts it was found that teachers at all levels who acted inquisitively; asked intellectually weighty and socially relevant questions; provided multiple opportunities for the students to be full participants in the conversation; and in other ways displayed a genuine interest in learning, in the topic, in the students' expressed thoughts, and in the students themselves, helped to establish a dynamic, motivating learning environment. In the studies by Consolo (chap. 5, this volume), Verplaetse (chap. 11, this volume), Damhuis (chap. 12, this volume), and Hajer (chap. 13, this volume), for example, teachers identified as being highly interactive and thus facilitative of a motivating learning environment were characterized by their affirming reactions to students' participation. By and large they treated students' contributions as valuable and legitimate, regardless of whether they were "right." Moreover, they actively invited students to participate, to propose topics for discussion, and to offer their opinions on the topics at hand. They also actively attempted to understand the learners' expressed thoughts from the learners' particular perspectives rather than imposing their own views on what the students were attempting to say. Similarly, in McCormick and Donato's (chap. 9, this volume) study, the teacher actively orchestrated the classroom discourse, guiding the students' participation through her mindful, goal-directed use of questions. In the questions they posed to students, their responses to student-posed questions and comments, and their own reflections and musing on the topics, the teachers in these different studies maintained a cognitively and socially rich interactional environment and provided models of appropriate academic and social discourse for the students. They also stimulated the learners to attempt to express their own thoughts and opinions on the topics and thereby become fully participating members of their community of learners.

In addition to engendering individual student participation, teachers played a significant role in managing the interactions, incorporating students' voices into the conversation, and making connections among the various contributions. The teacher in Boyd and Maloof's (chap. 8, this volume) study, for example, affirmed student contributions, clarified and summarized the ongoing conversation, and participated as an equal interlocutor through the sharing of her own personal experiences with her students. In a similar manner, in eliciting and affirming learners' contributions in classroom discussions, the English-language teachers in the Boxer and Cortés-Conde (chap. 10, this volume) study acted as bridges between their classroom communities and the cultures of the language learners, validating the students as equal interlocutors. In so doing, they motivated the learners to continue to participate in the ongoing conversations. It is important to note that, regardless of the level of students' linguistic and intellectual abilities, the issue being addressed, or, as shown in Consolo's study, the native-speaking status of the teacher, in all cases the conversations nurtured by effective teachers were topically coherent, cognitively complex, and meaningful to the learners. Across contexts, we saw how such interactions provided opportunities for learners together to develop and build on such conversational skills as monitoring and assessing the relevance of the cues provided in each other's talk, detecting and correcting possible sources of misunderstanding, and redirecting the flow of interaction in rhetorically appropriate ways.

A last finding shared by several studies reveals the active role of language learners in the learning process. In looking at the use of private speech by individual learners, Ohta's study (chap. 3, this volume) most explicitly addresses this issue. Her findings demonstrate that learners not directly addressed by the teacher, a group she labels *auditors*, are as actively involved in making use of the teacher's assistance as are those learners who are the focus of the teacher's attention. Through observation and reflection on teacher-directed talk to other students, the learners in her study were able to make appropriate modifications to their own language use. This investigation demonstrates the ability of individual learners to attend to and make use of classroom practices in which their involvement is at best indirect. The students in Kinginger's study (chap. 2, this volume) were similarly involved in their own learning. In their interactions with peers and through their observations of language use by others in peer interactions, they noticed relevant cues for effecting interpersonal relationships. Using their own reflections, as well as some help from peers, they were ultimately able to modify their own language use in appropriate ways. The study by Takahashi, Austin, and Morimoto (chap. 7, this volume) provides equally impressive evidence on the resourcefulness of learners in the process of learning an additional language by revealing how young language learners appropriated and made active use of the teacher's strategies for monitoring their own learning. The authors argue that these appropriations indicate that in addition to learning the target language, the students were also learning how to learn.

Closely related to the finding on the role that learners play in their own learning is the finding on the role peers can play in assisting others in the process. French-speaking peers in Kinginger's study were shown to provide active and appropriate assistance in learning the relevant forms for the expression of peer solidarity to their French-learning counterparts. Likewise, students in the study of Takahashi et al. made active, enthusiastic use of the learning strategies they had appropriated from the teacher to assist their classmates in their own learning. Finally, in Sullivan's (chap. 4, this volume) study, we saw how, through their willingness and enthusiasm for engaging in repartee and word play with each other, learners collaborated in generating and sustaining a motivating learning environment.

In sum, the studies in this volume offer us several persuasive findings on classroom practices that help facilitate additional language learning. We have learned about the consequential role of repetition, paraphrasing, recasting, and revoicing by class participants of their own and each other's utterances in fostering cohesive and effectual communities of language learners and users. In making salient relevant communicative resources, in helping to build a shared foundation of knowledge, and in stimulating good-natured playfulness with language and with each other, such practices help to create intellectually and communicatively nourishing learning environments. Moreover, we have learned of the importance of establishing and maintaining prosocial interpersonal relationships among members of these communities to the construction of opportunities for learners to use and extend their knowledge of the target language. In fostering the establishment of somewhat secure interpersonal bonds among the members, these relationships help to create an environment within which learners feel safe to participate in their interactional explorations. Finally, we have confirmed the substantial roles that both teachers and students play in creating and sustaining effectual learning contexts in their classroom communities and learned of some specific characteristics of these roles. Teachers who display a genuine interest in and enthusiasm for the subject and their students, who model intentional, self-motivated learning, and who are respectful toward and nurture students' participation in ongoing interactions help their classrooms develop into effectual communities of language learners. Likewise, students who take responsibility for their own learning, who appropriate and use the learning strategies provided by the teacher and others who are more expert, and who are provided with opportunities to assist others in their learning are successful language learners.

Together, these findings have important implications for what we do in our language classrooms. They also raise some significant issues for teacher preparation programs and future research agendas. I address each of these in the next section.

IMPLICATIONS FOR CLASSROOM PRACTICES, TEACHER PREPARATION, AND FUTURE RESEARCH ON ADDITIONAL LANGUAGE DEVELOPMENT

Several implications for language pedagogy can be drawn from the findings of these 12 studies. First, they confirm the need for students to be provided with multiple and varied opportunities to engage in meaningful interactions in the target language. One of our tasks as language teachers, then, is to mindfully organize the interactional environment in our classrooms to make such opportunities readily available. As pointed out by Boxer and Cortés-Conde (chap. 10, this volume), this entails more than a change of seating arrangements. To make the interactions meaningful, we need to help learners make connections between the topical content of the interactions and their interests and background experiences. As we have seen in the studies presented here, substantive issues can be introduced in language classrooms through the sharing of literature, personal stories, and interpersonal experiences. In the questions we as teachers ask and the threads we help to weave among the various student contributions in the unfolding conversations, we can encourage learners to relate these issues to those personal experiences and social relationships that are real and thus of significance to them. Motivating learners to make connections between their own and others' background knowledge and experiences and to share these connections with each other promotes their extended engagement in the interactions. This, in turn, facilitates their development as both learners and users of the new language.

In content-based classrooms, we must connect the topics to what learners already know and guide their participation in interactions through modeling academic discourse appropriate to the subject matter and the grade level of the learners, asking cognitively challenging questions, expanding and assessing their involvement, helping them to reformulate their own and others' contributions, and providing direct instruction when necessary.

Second, in the opportunities for interaction that we make available, we must ensure that not only the cognitive but the affective dimensions are considered. That is, in any task or activity, regardless of whether the goal is academic or social, we must assist learners in appropriating the elements needed to complete the task and the discursive strategies needed to build and extend interpersonal bonds. As shown in these studies, making interpersonal connections with each other in their classroom interactions fostered a sense of community among the members, thereby helping to create a motivating learning environment. Thus, we need to view such genres of talk as storytelling, wordplay, interpersonal repartee, and even the activity of singing not as disruptions to the task of learning but as essential to its accomplishment and ultimately to learners' success as additional language users.

Third, language learners of all ages and levels need to be seen as active, creative participants in the learning process. As demonstrated in these studies, even the youngest learners were able to engage in, indeed, help to construct intellectually rich interactions. Moreover, they were able to mediate their own learning without the explicit help or directed attention of the teacher. Perhaps even more striking is the fact that they were able to aid each other in the process. Thus, in addition to providing opportunities for learners to use the target language, we need to create opportunities for them to demonstrate and further develop their ingenuity and skill at the very process of learning for both their benefit and the benefit of their peers.

Finally, as teachers of either language or content we must understand the inextricable link between our classroom practices and student development and, more specifically, the significant role we play in creating conditions that define both the substance and direction of student development, and use this knowledge to improve on our own practices. As these studies made clear, language learning is a locally based endeavor. Thus, effecting change in our classrooms will result not from imposing solutions from outside but from nurturing effectual practices that are indigenous to our particular contexts. Given this, as teachers we need to know well our environments. Such understanding can only come through our active involvement as researchers in our classrooms. Conducting investigations of our practices and reflecting on our findings will help us build a base of knowledge about the processes and outcomes of learning as they occur in our classrooms. The more knowledgeable and articulate we are about our goals as teachers and the more knowledgeable we are about what actually occurs in our classrooms, the more likely we will be able to create and sustain effectual classroom communities of language learners.

As for teacher preparation, findings from the studies suggest three general means for improving on our programs. First, given what we have learned here about additional language development, it is reasonable to suggest that the effectiveness of aspiring language teachers, particularly those who are non-native speakers of the target language, in creating facilitative language learning environments in their own classrooms depends in large part on the learning environments they experience as additional language learners. Thus, university language programs for teacher candidates must create the conditions for language learning and use in their own classrooms that will facilitate the learners' successful appropriation of the means needed for participation in a range of intellectual and practical activities in the target language.

Likewise, we must provide learning opportunities in language education courses that help develop language teacher candidates' understanding of and ability to create effectual learning communities of their own, to assume responsibility for their own learning, and ultimately, to maintain themselves as lifelong learners in their chosen profession. Such understanding requires in part knowledge of theoretical and empirical underpinnings of such concepts as communication, communicative competence, and interpersonal relationships. Teacher candidates also need to learn about the role of classroom discourse in learning, and in particular, of specific practices such as those we have learned about here that lead to additional language learning. Combining this knowledge with their own experiences and self-reflections, teacher candidates will be able to develop the expertise they need to create competent communities of additional language learners.

Third, because of the ubiquity of second language learners in mainstream classrooms, effective content-area teachers are as significant to the development of second language learners as language teachers are. Thus, they must be adequately prepared to work with second language learners in ways that actively promote learners' involvement in their classroom activities. All content-area teachers must become what Hajer (chap. 13, this volume) refers to as language sensitive.

Finally, in terms of future research on second and foreign language learning, several fruitful areas for possible study are suggested by these studies. Perhaps most important is the need for more empirical research on different learning contexts, particularly in foreign language learning classrooms. As we saw here, only two studies on foreign language learning (those by Duff and Takahashi et al.) examined foreign language classrooms outside of the university setting. This small representation was due not to a lack of interest on our part in including additional studies on foreign language learning in elementary, middle, and secondary grades, as we tried to solicit such studies from colleagues in the field. Rather, we believe that the small number is indicative of a lack of investigatory interest in these contexts. This is unfortunate, as the early years of language learning are of special significance to learners' development. For what they learn here, both in terms of what counts as language and as the process of learning, sets the foundation on which their subsequent development will be based. A full understanding of classroom-based foreign language learning then requires extensive investigation of these sites. Hopefully, for both theoretical and practical considerations, the few studies in ths volume will provide the impetus for future research on foreign language learning in contexts other than university classrooms.

Along with contributing to a stronger empirical understanding of foreign language learning, additional research on a variety of second and foreign language learning contexts will provide us with more robust data on which to ground theoretical discussions on the issue of foreign versus second language contexts of learning. As we noted in the introduction, in creating two different sections for the volume, we considered second language and foreign language learning classrooms to be distinct learning environments. However, looking across the 12 studies contained here, we have discovered that findings on effective practices for both second and foreign language learning are more similar than different. That is, what was shown to be useful in promoting language learning in foreign language classrooms was shown to be equally useful in second language learning contexts. Without question, further research is needed to help us compare the scope and consequences of contextual conditions not only across these two larger learning contexts but within them as well.

It is safe to state that the myriad issues connected to classroom interaction and additional language learning in all learning contexts require more extensive examination. However, three seem of special importance. First, given the significance of interpersonal relationships to language learning found in these studies, it would behoove us to examine more closely the various means by which such relationships are established. How, for example, do we create and sustain rapport among individuals who come from varied backgrounds or who are reticent to participate? Also, as pointed out by Kinginger (chap. 2, this volume), it would be beneficial to examine how social processes are enabled by new communications tools and resources such as the Internet, e-mail, and videoconferences, and how these relationships and processes interact with language learning.

A second but no less important concern is the need for more longitudinal data. Although all the studies in this volume link language development to the particular practices they examined, several do not actually document specific changes in learners' use of language in their data. Those that do, among them Kinginger (chap. 2, this volume) and Takahashi et al. (chap. 7, this volume), allow us to see the actual processes and outcomes of learning as they are occurring and thus provide a more solid basis for the claims made about language development. Because, as pointed out by Vygotsky (1978), the only way to truly understand a skill in its final form is by analyzing its development, a more complete understanding of both the processes and outcomes of additional language learning requires more long-term investigations.

A final area to consider for future research on additional language learning has to do with the actual methods used in the research. As we saw in these studies, the use of ethnographic and discourse-analytic methods, with their emphasis on the broader context in which the language learning takes places, allowed the investigators to see connections they might not otherwise have seen with methods traditionally used to study second and foreign language learning. Because of the richness of findings arising from data collected with methods such as participant observation, audio and video recordings, interviews, and field notes, we need to continue these methodological pursuits. Moreover, we ought to consider developing and using more innovative ways of collecting classroom learning data. Ohta's (chap. 3, this volume) use of individually miked learners to gather data on their private speech is exemplary in that it let us into a world that would otherwise have been invisible to the researcher using taped data of whole-classroom interactions.

In summary, these 12 studies have several important implications for language pedagogy, teacher preparation, and future research on additional language learning. Taken together, their findings have added valuable knowledge to our understanding of the links between classroom interaction and the accomplishment of additional language learning and thus are useful contributions to the construction of a more comprehensive theory of additional language learning. On a practical level, they provide empirical evidence that can be used in the transformation of our own classroom practices so that they facilitate the development of learners' additional language abilities in ways that are adequate and appropriate to their social, academic, and other needs.

REFERENCE

Vygotsky, L. S. (1978). *Mind in society: The development of higher psychological processes*. Cambridge, MA: Harvard University Press.

Authors' Biographies

Theresa Austin is Associate Professor in Language, Literacy and Culture at the University of Massachusetts, Amherst. Her research includes investigations at both micro- and macrolevels of second language and literacy, planning, and policy. Dr. Austin uses a sociocultural framework to examine the development of cross-cultural pragmatics and the impact of technology-aided instruction on language learning. Through several collaborative action research projects, she has conducted ethnographic research to examine how teachers' teaching practices can improve students' learning opportunities. Having designed and implemented curricula for teaching Japanese, Spanish, Chinese, and English as a second language at places such as the University of Massachusetts, Florida Atlantic University, New York University, the University of California (Los Angeles, Berkeley), and the City University of New York (Queens College), she serves as a consultant for elementary, secondary, and university programs in foreign languages. Currently she is analyzing the political and pedagogical implications of the standards movement in foreign language education.

Diana Boxer is Associate Professor in the Program in Linguistics at the University of Florida, where she has also been Associate Director of the English Language Institute (ELI) since 1992. At the ELI she has been responsible for overseeing the academic program, including design and implementation of content-based English as a second language courses. Her teaching and research focus on the discourse and pragmatics of face-to-face interaction, second language acquisition, sociolinguistics, and gender and language. She is author of *Complaining and Commiserating: A Speech Act View of Solidarity in Spoken American English* (1993, New York: Peter Lang) and she has published in such journals as *TESOL Quarterly, Journal of Pragmatics, Discourse and Society, Text, ELT Journal,* and *Women and Language.*

Maureen Boyd is currently a doctoral student in Teaching Additional Languages in the Department of Language Education at the University of Georgia. Her dissertation examines the role of literature in the elementary English as a second language (ESL) classroom as evidenced through the talk in the classroom. She has taught English literature and ESL for 12 years in international schools in the Middle East and Asia.

Douglas Altamiro Consolo holds a BA in Linguistics and an MA in Applied Linguistics from the State University of Campinas (UNICAMP) in Brazil and a PhD in the Teaching of English as a Foreign Language from the University of Reading, England. He has taught a variety of courses in English as a foreign language (EFL) in private language institutes and at the university level. He has also worked in teacher training at undergraduate and postgraduate levels. As a researcher in applied linguistics, his main interests are within the area of language teaching (teacher education) and language learning (foreign language acquisition), with a focus on spoken language and classroom interaction. He has presented papers in several conferences in the United States, Europe, and Latin America, and he has published in Brazil and abroad. At present he is an EFL teacher and lecturer for the MA program in Linguistic Studies at UNESP, in São José do Rio Preto, Brazil.

Florencia Cortés-Conde directs the Program of Communication at the Universidad de San Andrés in Buenos Aires, Argentina, were she also teaches courses in Theory of Communication and Linguistics. She has published in the *Journal of Pragmatics* and the *Bilingual Review/Revista Bilingüe.* She has also published "Is Bilingualism Possible in an Immigrational Setting?" in *Spanish in Contact* (Roca & Jensen, 1996), and "English Spanish Bilingualism: The Other Side of the Coin" in the *Texas Linguistic Forum,* Vol. 33 (1993).

Resi Damhuis graduated in General Linguistics at the University of Amsterdam, The Netherlands, in 1985. Since 1981 she has been engaged in educational research at the SCO-Kohnstamm Institute for Educational Research of the University of Amsterdam. Her activities and publications concentrate on second language acquisition of young multilingual children. These studies concern features of kindergarten conversations with multilingual children, the assessment of language proficiency of 6-year-old Dutch and immigrant children, and the construction of vocabulary tests. She published her dissertation in 1995: *Interaction and Second Language Acquisition: Participation and Control in Classroom Conversations With Young Multilingual Children* (Amsterdam: Institute for Functional Research into Language and Language Use). She has written a teacher training course on interaction skills for primary school teachers. Since 1998 she has worked for the National Center for Language Education at the University of Nijmegen, developing new approaches to language arts teaching in primary education, focusing on oral language skills.

Richard Donato is Associate Professor of Foreign Language Education in the Department of Instruction and Learning at the University of Pittsburgh with joint appointments in the Department of French and Italian, the Department of Spanish and Portuguese, and the Department of Linguistics. His responsibilities include coordinating the university's graduate programs in foreign language education and English as a second language. He serves on the editorial board of the *Modern Language Journal*. He was the recipient of the Pennsylvania State Modern Language Association Teacher of the Year Award for 1996 and in 1997 was the recipient (with his co-authors G. Richard Tucker and Janis L. Antonek) of the Modern Language Journal/ American Council on the Teaching of Foreign Languages Paul Pimsleur Award for excellence in foreign language learning research. His research focuses on sociocultural perspectives on classroom language learning, early language learning, and foreign language classroom discourse analysis.

Patricia A. Duff is Associate Professor of Language Education at the University of British Columbia in Vancouver, Canada. She teaches graduate courses on research methods, second language acquisition and socialization and classroom research, and teacher-education courses on second language teaching methods. Her publications on these topics have appeared in the *Journal of Multilingual and Multicultural Development, Studies in Second Language Acquisition, TESOL Quarterly, The Modern Language Journal*, numerous edited volumes, and a forthcoming book on case study research (Mahwah, NJ: Lawrence Erlbaum Associates). She has taught English as a second language and applied linguistics and conducted research in various parts of North America, Asia, and Europe, with learners from a range of first language backgrounds and in many different institutional contexts (high school to adult). Her current research examines language use in mainstream high school social studies courses with large numbers of Asian students (funded by the Social Sciences and Humanities Research Council of Canada and the National Academy of Education/Spencer Foundation).

Maaike Hajer studied Applied Linguistics and Dutch Language Arts at the Catholic University of Nijmegen and Lunds University in Sweden. From 1982 to 1993 she was senior curriculum advisor at the National Institute for Curriculum Development SLO, working in the field of second language and minority language teaching. Since 1993 she has been affiliated with the Centre for Second Language and School Development of the Utrecht University for Professional Education (Hogeschool van Utrecht) where she directs projects, in-service training, and advisory work for content-area teachers in multilingual classrooms. In 1996 she defended her PhD thesis at Tilburg University, "Learning Through a Second Language." She is currently at Groningen University as a researcher with the project "Interaction in a Multicultural Classroom: Processes of Inclusion and Exclusion." She has written a number of publications on the issues of academic language development and content-based language teaching and has conducted workshops on these themes in international contexts (e.g., the Council of Europe and Stockholm's Summer University).

Joan Kelly Hall is Associate Professor of Language Education and faculty member of the Interdisciplinary Linguistics Program at the University of Georgia, where she teaches courses in sociolinguistics, classroom discourse, and first and second language learning. She also works with foreign and second language teacher preparation programs. Her research interests include classroom-based language development, language use and identity, and intercultural communication. Her work appears in such journals as *Applied Linguistics, Foreign Language Annals, The Journal of Linguistic Anthropology, Linguistics and Education, The Modern Language Journal*, and *Research on Language and Social Interaction*. Together with William Eggington, she has published an edited textbook entitled *The Sociopolitics of English Language Teaching* (Clevedon, UK: Multilingual Matters). She is currently working on a methods text entitled *Building Communities of Learners in Foreign Language Classrooms* (Upper Saddle River, NJ: Prentice-Hall).

Celeste Kinginger is Associate Professor of French and Foreign Language Acquisition at the Pennsylvania State University, where she supervises language instruction and teaches courses in applied linguistics and language education. Her research interests include classroom discourse analysis, language teacher training, and site-independent language learning. Her publications have appeared in several edited volumes as well as the *French Review, The Modern Language Journal,* and the *Canadian Modern Language Review.*

Valerie Miller Maloof received her PhD from the Department of Language Education at the University of Georgia in the Teaching Additional Languages program. Her dissertation was on the role of a Vietnamese ethnic language school in the cross-cultural adaptation process. She has taught language arts at the middle school level, English to speakers of other languages (ESOL) at the elementary and middle school level, and has also taught ESOL on a volunteer basis at all levels.

Dawn E. McCormick is an administrator at the English Language Institute in the Department of Linguistics at the University of Pittsburgh. She has a PhD and an MEd in Foreign Language Education from the School of Education with a TESOL Certificate from the Department of Linguistics at the University of Pittsburgh, and a BA in French from Grove City College. Her English as a second and foreign language experiences include teaching English in the Katz School of Business at the University of Pittsburgh, The Heinz School at Carnegie-Mellon University, and Bar-Ilan University in Israel. In addition, for 2 years she was the director of the Nacel Summer English Program in Pittsburgh for high school students from France and Spain. She has taught foreign language methods courses at the University of Pittsburgh in the Department of Instruction and Learning and at Carnegie-Mellon University in the Department of Modern Languages. Her publications deal with sociocultural perspectives on classroom language learning, student–teacher portfolios, and classroom discourse analysis.

Yoko Morimoto holds a BA in Japanese Literature from the Tezukayama-Gakuin University in Japan and an MA in Education from the University of Pittsburgh. She has taught Japanese for more than 20 years to both children and adults in Japan, England, and the United States. She is presently a teacher of Japanese at the Falk Laboratory School at the University of Pittsburgh. She has been engaged in the development of a K–6 Japanese curriculum, and as part of this ongoing effort has been researching the development of second language skills of very young children. At the same time she has been teaching Japanese intensive courses at the university level and the Pennsylvania Governor's School for 6 years. She has co-authored papers and given presentations on teaching material development, teacher–student discourse analysis, and general information on Foreign Language in the Elementary School (FLES) programs.

Amy Snyder Ohta is an Assistant Professor in the Department of Asian Languages and Literatures at the University of Washington in Seattle, where she teaches Japanese applied linguistics and Japanese sociolinguistics. She graduated from the University of California, Los Angeles in 1993 with a PhD in Applied Linguistics. Her research specialization is in second language acquisition (SLA) with publications in the fields of Japanese sociolinguistics and Japanese SLA, particularly in the area of classroom language learning. Her recent work has been published in the *Journal of Pragmatics* and in edited volumes. She is near completion of a longitudinal study of the classroom interaction of seven classroom learners of Japanese. This research investigates acquisition of interactional style in Japanese, the role of private speech in language learning, corrective feedback, assisted performance in interactive language learning tasks, and the role of learners' use of English in the classroom learning of Japanese.

Patricia N. Sullivan has a PhD from the University of California, Berkeley, and was the Director of the MATEFL Program at Bilkent University, Ankara, Turkey from 1997 to 1999. At the University of California, Santa Cruz, she has taught various courses that focus on teacher education, second language acquisition, and world cultures. Her research interests are in the use of discourse analysis as a means of analyzing the social context of English-language teaching. Recent publications include "Language Play and Communicative Language Teaching in a Vietnamese Classroom" in J. Lantolf (Ed.), *Socio-Cultural Theory: An Approach to Second Language Acquisition* (forthcoming, Oxford, UK: Oxford University Press); "Appropriate Pedagogy," co-authored with C. Kramsch, *ELT Journal* (Vol. 50, No. 3, 1996); and "Sociocultural Influences on Classroom Interactional Styles," *TESOL Journal* (Vol. 6, No. 1, 1996). She has done research on classroom language teaching and has taught in China, Vietnam, Taiwan, Afghanistan, and Turkey, as well as California.

Etsuko Takahashi is Senior Lecturer in Japanese in the Department of Modern Languages at Carnegie-Mellon University in Pittsburgh. She is currently working on her dissertation in Foreign Language Education in the Department of Instruction and Learning at the University of Pittsburgh. Her research interests are twofold: the social aspects of language learning and second language reading. Her interests in the classroom interaction of young learners of Japanese evolved through observing a Japanese as a foreign language (JFL) class at a local FLES program. She has been influenced by work on sociocultural aspects of second language acquisition. Within the broad domain of reading, she is particularly interested in word recognition processes. She has explored how internal structures of words are perceived by second language learners (i.e., internal structures of English words perceived by English as a second language learners, and internal components of Kanji [Chinese characters] perceived by JFL learners). Her dissertation focuses on early-stage JFL learners' phonological coding strategies in reading Kanji.

Lorrie Stoops Verplaetse is Assistant Professor in the Department of Foreign Languages and coordinator of the MS Program in Bilingual, Multicultural Education/TESOL at Southern Connecticut State University in New Haven, where she teaches courses in second language acquisition, English as a second language (ESL) methodology, and principles of linguistics. Her current research interests focus on the role of interaction in second language development, particularly in interactions between native speakers and non-native speakers, both in the classroom and in other natural speech. You can read about her work in her 1998 article in *TESOL Journal*, "How Content Teachers Interact With English Language Learners." Verplaetse has trained ESL and English as a foreign language (EFL) teachers for the past 10 years and has taught ESL in adult education, industry, and precollege programs for 25 years. As a Fulbright scholar in 1995, she lived and trained EFL teachers in Plzen, Czech Republic, at the University of West Bohemia.

Author Index

A

Adair-Hauck, B., 150, *157*
Agar, M., 143, *157*
Allen, P., 245, *262, 263*
Allen, R. 6, *16*
Allwright, D., 92, 93, 101, *106*, 114, *136*
Almasi, J., 163, 166, 167, *180, 181*
Amon, E., 30, *45*
Andersen, R., 109, *136*
Anton, M., 115, *136,* 184, 185, *198*
Antonek, J., 145, *157*
Appel, G., 6, *18,* 142, *157*
Arthur, B., 3, *16*
Austin, T., 139, *292*
Avery, P., 268, *284*

B

Bailey, K. M., 92, 93, *106*, 114, *136*
Baker, C., 9, *17*
Baker, N., 50, *68, 70*
Ballenger, C., 224, *240*
Banbrook, L., 100, *106*
Barnes, D., 164, *180,* 183, *198*
Bauman, R., 73, 74, *89*
Bean, M., 116, *136*
Bell, A., 56, *68*
Bennett, A. T., 5, *19*
Bennett-Kastor, T., 112, *136*
Bent, B., 245, *264*
Bereiter, C., 155, *157*

Berenz, N., 174, *181*
Berman, R., 6, *17*
Berhhardt, E., 282, *285*
Bivens, J., 9, *20*
Bley-Vroman, R., 110, *136*
Block, D., 6, *17*
Blok, K., 248, *262*
Bloome, D., 165, *180*
Bonvillian, J., 50, *70*
Bowers, C. A., 9, *17*
Boxer, D., 203, 204, *218*, 265, 267, *284, 285*
Boyd, M., 163, 168, *180,* 288, 291
Braidi, S., 5, *17*
Branaman, L. E., 139, *157*
Breen, M. P., 42, 44, *45,* 93, *106*
Brière, J. -F., 31, 32, *46*
Brinton, D., 203, 204, *218,* 265, 267, *284, 285*
Britton, J., 163, 166, 167, 177, 178, *180*
Bronfenbrenner, U., 7, *17*
Brooks, F., 155, *157*, 163, 164, *181*, 197, *198, 200*
Broome, S., 50, *71*
Brown, H. D., 76, *89*, 109, *136*
Brown, P., 24, *45*
Brown, R., 26, *45*, 223, *240*
Bruner, J., 165, 166, 177, 178, 179, *180,* 184, *201*
Buck, K., *157*
Bullock, D., 7, *17*
Burt, S. M., 26, *45*

307

Subject Index